"The Heart of Coaching Super and Self-Care is an invaluable text that does what the title notice of and listen to our inner resources in service of others.

This text is indispensable for supervision practice because of its 'completeness' about 'self'. Each chapter brings you a different perspective on supervision illustrating the author's philosophy and approach to practice. Case studies reveal the extraordinary power of reflection for both the supervisor and the supervisee and the achievements of this combined wisdom.

What you'll experience through the eyes of the authors, who willingly share their own vulnerabilities, is validation of us as human beings. We're inspired to accept who and what we are with compassion that urges us to offer that same compassion to others; knowing we share a common humanity.

The eclectic contributions of authors exemplifying the kaleidoscope of humanity engages us with alternative and complementary approaches to supervision. You'll read about topics you've possibly never experienced, or struggled to manage, or simply another perspective on a familiar theme.

Case studies visit working with refugees to everyday corporate scenarios that draw on emotions; sometimes the stories will make you laugh and maybe sometimes you'll cry. Ultimately, you'll learn from the practices of professional supervisors about the human condition unfolding and how the power of supervision ripples beyond the immediate conversation to benefit society as a whole." – **Dr Lise Lewis, EMCC International Special Ambassador Promoting Supervision Worldwide**

"In our pursuit of coaching excellence and mastery, to enhance the fulfilment, growth and performance of others and in business, we are constantly learning the 'pillars' of what truly makes a difference for a professional coach, to be at their best. . . . Like an athlete, one of these is the need for reflective practice, and for a coach to work alongside a trusted partner to help them in this space.

This is where this wonderful, diverse book, *The Heart of Coaching Supervision* is timely, and is an important piece of work for our emerging profession. In the spirit of collaboration and valuing different perspectives, it's a necessary read for any serious coach who wants to best serve their clients. Thank you, to all the authors, for their contribution. I would highly recommend!" – **Katherine Tulpa, Global CEO and Co-founder, Association for Coaching**

"*The Heart of Coaching Supervision* is an outstanding contribution to the literature. The editors have drawn together leading names in the field including Tatiana Bachkirova, Peter Hawkins and Linda Aspey to provide a kaleidoscope of chapters which will help those interested in understanding supervision practice to deepen their knowledge and enhance their practice through new insights and techniques which are at the forefront of thinking within coaching supervision." – **Professor Jonathan Passmore, University of Evora, Portugal, and Henley Business School, UK**

"Being a coach supervisor is a great privilege — coaches bring to supervision their most interesting and challenging issues, making it a rich and eclectic form of learning for the supervisor as well as the supervisee. *The Heart of Coaching Supervision: Working with Reflection and Self-Care* captures the essence of supervision – less an intellectual process or activity, more a way of being and being with. The impressive cast of contributors each provides a different insight into how supervision nurtures coaches' efficacy and well-being, enabling them in turn to nurture their clients.

The word 'heart' implies many things, but particularly compassion and courage – two qualities central to great leadership, great coaches and, as these pages illustrate, to great supervision. It takes both compassion and courage to truly listen; and deep listening to truly understand. The essays and case studies in this book explore what it means to value and to use self; how the differences between us can, through reflection, enhance the connectedness between us; and the importance of attention to well-being in all aspects of the client-coach-supervisor system.

If coaching is a stimulus to reflective conversation, and supervision is reflection on coaching, then this excellent book adds another valuable layer – reflections on how we reflect." – **Professor David Clutterbuck, visiting professor, Henley Business School and Sheffield Hallam and Oxford Brookes Universities, UK; co-founder, European Mentoring and Coaching Council**

"Context is essential to fully appreciate the power of a professional declaration. The practice of coaching is 30-35 years young, only formally organized for 22 years, and practitioners have enjoyed the benefit of coaching supervision for far less than that. In the context of a professional vocation, this time period is minuscule and reminds us to be in beginner's mind, open and willing to be disturbed by ideas to invite disruption and innovation. Challenge to assumptions and bias requires leadership and maturity that perceives for a greater collective purpose than the self. The authors convened in this book embody this quality and bring both clear articulation and commitment to direct experience learning alive on each page. Each chapter opens the aperture of our camera lens so that we receive and absorb more of the reality in front of us as well as the abundant resources that life presents, even without us asking. Pursuit of excellence is a hallmark of being a professional and the practice of coaching supervision is an empowering and accelerating contribution. Choosing to engage it, learn it, provide it and courageously reflect and share our perspectives through this book, truly makes the whole of our profession greater than the sum of the parts." – **Janet M. Harvey, ACS, MCC, CMC, Past President, Global ICF Board and ICF Foundation**

"Supervision is coming! While fairly unknown in the US and many other parts of the coaching world, supervision has been a vital mainstay of the profession in the UK and Europe. This book organizes the latest thinking from some of the masters of our field into one volume. You don't want to miss this critical and vital development trend for the coaching profession." – **Dr. Brian O. Underhill, Founder and CEO, CoachSource, LLC and author of *Executive Coaching for Results: The Definitive Guide to Developing Organizational Leaders***

The Heart of Coaching Supervision

The Heart of Coaching Supervision takes us on a journey that starts with understanding who we are, and why we do what we do the way we do it, so that we can help those we work with understand themselves and their practice. The journey includes our background and personal and professional influences and considers the need for self-resourcing to resource others. It examines our being alongside our doing, to ensure we can provide the best possible service to all those we work with.

The book's highly experienced contributors provide a unique perspective on supervision's benefits. The chapters cover themes that support self-discovery and resourcing including the three Ps of supervision and coaching, diversity and inclusion, re-sourcing, working with intense emotions and the self as instrument. Nancy Kline's Thinking Environment© is explored in a supervision context alongside creative forms of reflective and expressive writing and resourcing through a peer supervision chain. *The Heart of Coaching Supervision* also includes ten engaging, international case studies, considering the role of supervision in depth.

A key contribution to the field, the book is essential reading for all coaches and mentors, coaching supervisors and psychologists, managers in a coaching role and anyone in a helping profession or leadership position wanting to better understand the wide benefits of supervision.

Eve Turner is a Visiting Fellow at Henley Business School, UK. She works extensively as a coach, supervisor and facilitator and is the 2018 recipient of the Coaching at Work Award for Contributions to Coaching Supervision and the 2015 holder of the EMCC European Coach of the Year Award

Stephen Palmer is Professor of Practice at the Wales Institute of Work Based Learning and Adjunct Professor of Coaching Psychology at Aalborg University. He is Founder Director of the Centre for Coaching, London and Honorary President of the International Society for Coaching Psychology.

Essential Coaching Skills and Knowledge
Series Editors: Stephen Palmer,
Averil Leimon & Gladeana McMahon

The **Essential Coaching Skills and Knowledge** series provides an accessible and lively introduction to key areas in the developing field of coaching. Each title in the series is written by leading coaches with extensive experience and has a strong practical emphasis, including illustrative vignettes, summary boxes, exercises and activities. Assuming no prior knowledge, these books will appeal to professionals in business, management, human resources, psychology, counselling and psychotherapy, as well as students and tutors of coaching and coaching psychology.

www.routledge.com/series/ECS

Titles in the series:

Creating a Coaching Culture for Managers in Your Organisation
Edited by Dawn Forman, Mary Joyce and Gladeana McMahon

Essential Career Transition Coaching Skills
Caroline Talbott

Group and Team Coaching: The Secret Life of Groups, Second Edition
Christine Thornton

Coaching in Three Dimensions: Meeting the Challenges of a Complex World
Paul Lawrence and Allen Moore

The Heart of Coaching Supervision: Working with Reflection and Self-Care
Edited by Eve Turner and Stephen Palmer

The Heart of Coaching Supervision

Working with Reflection and Self-Care

Edited by Eve Turner and Stephen Palmer

Routledge
Taylor & Francis Group

LONDON AND NEW YORK

First published 2019
by Routledge
2 Park Square, Milton Park, Abingdon, Oxon OX14 4RN

and by Routledge
711 Third Avenue, New York, NY 10017

Routledge is an imprint of the Taylor & Francis Group, an informa business

British Library Cataloguing in Publication Data
A catalogue record for this book is available from the British Library

Library of Congress Cataloging in Publication Data
Names: Turner, Eve, editor. | Palmer, Stephen, 1955- editor.
Title: The heart of coaching supervision : working with reflection and self-care / [edited by] Eve Turner and Stephen Palmer.
Description: Abingdon, Oxon ; New York, NY : Routledge, 2018. Series: Essential coaching skills and knowledge | Includes bibliographical references and index.
Identifiers: LCCN 2018027459 (print) | LCCN 2018029412 (ebook) | ISBN 9781351746694 (Abode Reader) | ISBN 9781351746687 (ePub) | ISBN 9781351746670 (Mobipocket) | ISBN 9781315189635 (Master Ebook) | ISBN 9781138729759 (hardback) | ISBN 9781138729773 (pbk.)
Subjects: LCSH: Counselors—Supervision of. | Personal coaching. | Executive coaching. | Employees—Coaching of.
Classification: LCC BF636.65 (ebook) | LCC BF636.65 .H43 2018 (print) | DDC 158.3—dc23
LC record available at https://lccn.loc.gov/2018027459

ISBN: 978-1-138-72975-9 (hbk)
ISBN: 978-1-138-72977-3 (pbk)
ISBN: 978-1-315-18963-5 (ebk)

Typeset in New Century Schoolbook
by Swales & Willis Ltd, Exeter, Devon, UK

MIX
Paper from
responsible sources
FSC
www.fsc.org   FSC® C013056

Printed and bound in Great Britain by
TJ International Ltd, Padstow, Cornwall

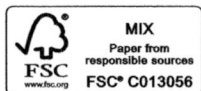

Dedication

To Peter: your wonderful gifts of endless support, belief, love, compassion and understanding, make everything possible; to our son Dom for continually adding to my learning edge. I am also infinitely grateful for the endless learning and laughter with the people I have been lucky enough to work with, and to those engaged in making the world a more compassionate place. (ET)

To Kate and Tom; to my supervisees who have taught me so much about supervision.

To Dave Ellis, for his support and humour over many decades. You will be missed by family, friends and colleagues. (SP)

Acknowledgements

"East Coker" from *Four Quartets* by T.S. Eliot. Copyright © 1943 by T.S. Eliot. Copyright renewed 1971 by Esme Valerie Eliot. Reprinted by permission of Houghton Mifflin Harcourt Publishing Company and Faber and Faber Ltd. All rights reserved.

Contents

Notes on the editors and contributors

Editors

Eve Turner

Eve Turner researches and writes on a range of subjects including supervision, ethics and contracting in coaching and is a Visiting Fellow at Henley Business School and the University of Southampton. She has written over 30 articles on a variety of subjects in coaching and supervision, from the use of imagery to ethical decision-making, and co-authored book chapters; this is her first edited book. Eve works extensively with public and private organisations as a coach, supervisor, supervisor of supervisors and facilitator, from team-leader level to the Board. She has been coaching since 2004 and has delivered several thousand hours of coaching and supervision to a range of organisations, large and small.

In 2016 Eve set up, and now leads and finances, the Global Supervisors' Network, a unique, free-of-charge, participative network for supervisors worldwide working in coaching, mentoring and consultancy. Members provide each other with, and receive, Continuing Personal and Professional Development virtually every month with the aim of supporting best practice: http://www.eve-turner.com/global-supervisors-network. Eve's work in the field was recognised in the 2018 Coaching at Work Awards as the winner of the Contributions to Coaching Supervision Award. Eve is the 2015 holder of the EMCC European Coach of the Year Award, and of the Special Group in Coaching Psychology's

2008 award for a distinguished research project in coaching psychology. She has Master Executive Coach and/or Supervision accreditation from three professional bodies, APECS, the AC and the EMCC, and actively volunteers for some of the coaching professional bodies. Eve is a supervisor for CoachActivism (see Chapter 1) a pro-bono coaching initiative to support volunteers and front-line workers involved in the global refugee crisis.

Eve's background includes working in music (she has a Diploma in classical guitar) and senior leadership in the BBC where she began her coaching career internally. Her qualifications include an MBA, MSc and MMus and her interests range from watching football, walking, going to the gym, music and reading to cooking (occasionally!).

Stephen Palmer

Professor Stephen Palmer PhD is the Founder Director of the Centre for Coaching, London. He is Professor of Practice at the Wales Institute for Work Based Learning and Adjunct Professor of Coaching Psychology in the Coaching Psychology Unit, Aalborg University, Denmark. He is Honorary Consultant Director of the Coaching Psychology Unit at the Federal University of Rio de Janeiro, Brazil and Co-ordinating Director of the ISCP International Centre for Coaching Psychology Research. He is an Association for Professional Executive Coaches and Supervisors (APECS) Accredited Executive Coach and APECS Accredited Executive Coach Supervisor, an International Society for Coaching Psychology (ISCP) Accredited Coaching Psychologist and Supervisor. He qualified as an Approved Albert Ellis Institute, Supervisor in 1995. He is President and Fellow of the ISCP and is former President and now Fellow of the Association for Coaching. He was the first Chair of the British Psychological Society Special Group in Coaching Psychology. Stephen has authored over 225 articles and written or edited over 50 books including the *Handbook of Coaching Psychology* (with Whybrow, Routledge, 2007), *The Coaching Relationship: Putting People First* (with McDowall, 2010), *Developmental Coaching: Life Transitions & Generational*

Perspectives (with Panchal, 2011) and *Cognitive Behavioural Coaching: An Evidence Based Approach* (with Neenan, 2012), *Psychological Stress, Vols 1,2,3* (with Gyllensten, Sage, 2015), and *Psychological Resilience and Wellbeing Vols 1,2,3* (with Gyllensten, Sage, 2015). He is co-editor of three journals, including the *European Journal of Applied Positive Psychology*. In 2000, he received the Annual Counselling Psychology Award from the British Psychological Society (BPS), Division of Counselling Psychology, for his "outstanding professional and scientific contribution to counselling psychology in Britain". In 2008, he received a Distinguished Award for his outstanding and continued contribution to coaching psychology by the BPS Special Group in Coaching Psychology.

Stephen sees himself as a pracademic being active in both research and practice. He has run his own group of companies for over 40 years and he is the publisher at *Coaching at Work* magazine. His interests include jazz, art and coastal walking and in his spare time he is a producer of a jazz internet radio station.

Chapter authors

Jane Adshead-Grant, MCC

Jane has worked in people-centred roles within the corporate environment for 30 years. She began coaching in 2002 and became a Time to Think Consultant in 2017, studying predominately with Nancy Kline. Jane's mission is to support individuals and organisations develop more conscious leadership and human-centred cultures nurturing independent thinking, personal growth and high performance. She is the author of 'Are you Listening or Just Waiting to Speak?'

Dr Eunice Aquilina, D.Prof, MSc

Eunice is the founder of eaconsult, a leadership and organisation development consultancy. She works with leaders, executive teams and organisations to unlock their capacity to navigate change, clarify their purpose, cultivate leadership presence and learn skilful ways to connect with others. Eunice studied somatics for over a decade and is an accredited master coach and coach supervisor. She is the author of *Embodying Authenticity: A Somatic Path to Transforming Self, Team and Organisation*.

Linda Aspey, FBACP

Linda had been a coach, therapist, supervisor and OD consultant for many years when she began training with Nancy Kline in 2008. Inspired by the significant results her clients were achieving with the Thinking Environment, she continued to train with Nancy, becoming Time to Think Global Faculty in 2014. Now, alongside her consultancy and coaching, she teaches, supervises and qualifies others in helping their own clients and colleagues to also create inspiring and sustainable Thinking Environments.

Professor Tatiana Bachkirova, PhD

Tatiana believes in the power of knowledge when it becomes part of the practitioner's self and is skilfully applied in the immediacy of coaching or supervisory relationships. She looks for different opportunities to contribute to knowledge in her various roles and enjoys supporting others in developing knowledge. Nature and philosophy are some of Tatiana's passions that complement her professional mini-selves as Professor of Coaching Psychology at Oxford Brookes University and as a coaching supervisor.

Sarah Gilbert

Sarah brings broad expertise in people development to help her clients tackle the complexities of individual and organisational change. Her career roles span HR consulting, executive assessment, career transition, coaching, mentoring and counselling. Highly trained and experienced, Sarah has been supervising since 2003. Based in the UK, she works globally in corporate, professional services, academic and voluntary settings, supporting leaders, supervisors, coaches and mentors. She encourages collaborative learning, creativity, fresh insight and personal growth.

Dr Damian Goldvarg, PhD

Damian provides services in executive assessment and coaching, leadership development, talent management and facilitation in over 50 countries. He is a Master Certified Coach and received his PhD in Organizational Psychology from Alliant University in California. He is also an Accredited Coach Supervisor (ESIA) and facilitates certifications in Professional Coaching, Mentor Coaching, and Coaching Supervision. He was the 2013–2014 ICF Global President. Damian has published three books on coaching and several book chapters and articles.

Anne Hathaway, MA, MBA, MAC

Anne became a founder member of the Time to Think Faculty in 2009 when she was asked to take on the supervision and assessment of Nancy Kline's own students. Formerly a senior leader, Anne first trained with Nancy in 1993 and has spent the last 20-plus years practising as a coach, supervisor, consultant and teacher, bringing the Thinking Environment to a diverse range of organisations and individuals throughout Europe. Anne is a member of the Global Supervisors' Network, and the recipient of the 2018 Coaching at Work External Coaching/Mentoring Champion award, for her work with Time to Think.

Professor Peter Hawkins, PhD

Having spent many years as a business entrepreneur, academic, organisational consultant, coach, team coach, psychotherapist, spiritual student and teacher, writer, gardener, farmer and woodlander, Peter now tries to integrate these both in himself, the organisations he consults to and the many coaches, systemic team coaches and consultants he trains. He is the author of many bestselling and internationally

xviii   EDITORS AND CONTRIBUTORS

translated books including: *Leadership Team Coaching in Practice* (Kogan Page, 2nd ed, 2018); *Leadership Team Coaching* (Kogan Page, 3rd ed, 2017); *Coaching, Mentoring and Organizational Consultancy: Supervision, Skills and Development* (with Nick Smith, McGraw-Hill/Open University Press, 2nd ed, 2013); *Creating a Coaching Culture* (McGraw-Hill, 2012).

Jackee Holder, MA

Jackee is a Londoner by birth and enjoys the urban landscapes and green spaces of the city. She appreciates the restorative nature of walking and has a passion particularly for the forest of trees that line the streets of London showing the diversity in the city through its tree heritage. Jackee enjoys reading for pleasure and reading related to her work as a coach, facilitator and interfaith minister. She is a long-time journal writer and committed reflective practitioner who enjoys spreading the message about the therapeutic benefits of reflective and expressive writing. She is the author of four non-fiction books.

Dr Peter Jackson, PhD

Peter is interested in complexity and in integrating ideas from different disciplines and different points of view. His teaching, research and professional practice reflect this and draw on different influences from his work history: languages, travel, IT, HR, academia, as well as coaching and supervision. In 2016 he completed a PhD on physicality in the coaching relationship. Alongside his own practice, he has taught on postgraduate programmes in Coaching and Mentoring Practice at Oxford Brookes University since 2004.

Lesley Matile

In her working life, Lesley has a passion for learning and development. She specialises in facilitating others to find the motivation and determination to harness their best personal attributes and skills to achieve the success and fulfilment they seek. She feels privileged to have worked with such a diverse range of clients. In her leisure, Lesley is a massive sports fan. In summer, she is often found pottering around her garden.

Keri Phillips

Keri has enjoyed exploring and writing about organisational dynamics and relationships for several decades. Recently he has had a particular interest in the rapidly evolving roles of the coach and coaching supervisor as agents of organisational change. As part of this he has examined feelings such as betrayal, anger, vulnerability and envy. His early background in training as a transactional analyst proved invaluable.

Dr Judy Ryde, PhD

Judy has been a psychotherapist for more than 40 years and a supervisor almost as long. Much of her career has involved training both psychotherapists and supervisors (including coach supervisors) and she has developed integrative theory in both disciplines. For at least 25 of those years, the lack of diversity in these professions has been a preoccupation and led to doctoral research into whiteness within a racialised society. Her book 'Being White in the Helping Professions' was published in 2009 and another 'White Privilege Unmasked: How to be part of the solution', will be published in February 2019. She is the founder and Director of the charity Trauma Foundation South West, which provides counselling and psychotherapy for refugees and asylum seekers.

Lily Seto

Lily lives in Victoria BC Canada and is grateful for the diversity of her practice of coaching and supervising across the globe. Her passions include travelling, reading, being in community, and her two precious and joyful grandchildren, who keep her grounded. She teaches the virtual "Intercultural Competence and Global Coaching" graduate studies course in the Advanced Coaching Program at Royal Roads University.

xx EDITORS AND CONTRIBUTORS

Case study authors (Chapter 10)

Dr Christina Baird, PhD

Christina Baird nurtures creative wisdom through coaching, supervision, blogging and training. She has a PhD in social psychology, a graduate diploma in theology and a postgraduate certificate in professional supervision. She has worked in Christian ministry for over 12 years and is an associate member of the International Society for Coaching Psychology.

Leona deVinne, PCC

Leona is a Professional Certified Coach who works with business leaders and teams. Leona is a tenacious, intuitive business gal who owns three companies: one passively to make money while she sleeps; one purposefully and her absolute Joy Spot, Accendo Consulting, where she coaches entrepreneurs/business leaders, and develops and delivers custom workshops and coach training programs; AND, just for fun, she runs a non-profit – www.joysocks.ca – to donate colourful socks to people in hospitals, shelters, and charities who could use a smile.

Sam Farmer

Sam is Director of Enhance Facilitation Limited and an Associate Fellow of the International Society for Coaching Psychology. A registered psychologist (Aotearoa/New Zealand), he has learnt his supervision skills through workshops, other ongoing professional development and continuous application over 15 years.

Laurie Hillis, MA Leadership, PCC

Laurie is a passionate and courageous lifelong learner, who is honoured to be a Facilitator and Consultant of The Daring Way™ based on the work of Dr Brené Brown. As well as running her own leadership/coaching/supervision practice Megatrain, since 1992, she is a senior faculty member at Executive Education at the University of Alberta's School of Business (Alberta, Canada) where she gets to practise magic in the classroom all the time.

Sarah Jaggers

Sarah Jaggers is a Leadership and Executive Coach. She has coached hundreds of directors, and executives over the last 15 years. Sarah graduated in 1984 with BSc (Hons) Psychology. Following 18 years in senior management in technology in the financial services and supply-chain industries she moved into organisational development consulting and coaching. Sarah has an MBA and MSc in Occupational Psychology and runs a coaching business, Managing Change, in Cambridge, UK.

Katerina Kanelidou, MA, PCC

Katerina has over 20 years' experience as a coach, trainer, mentor, educator and therapist. Based in Athens, she works with leaders globally, supporting them to overcome their challenges and thrive even in the most adverse environments. She is founder of SixStepsAhead, global faculty member of the International Coach Academy and steering committee member of the CoachActivism programme, a pro-bono coaching initiative in response to the global refugee crisis.

James Marshall

James is a Leadership and Executive coach and owner of Talking Ape, an L&D Consultancy. James has over 30 years' experience as a Chartered Surveyor and as a BBC radio and TV producer. Talking Ape provide Leadership and Coaching to some of the world's largest organisations using the latest psychology and neuroscience research to help people change mindset, habits and results.

Dr Michel Moral, PhD (Psychology), MSc

Michel began as a manager and executive in Eastern Europe, the Middle-East and Africa. After leaving IBM he created a coaching and supervision practice. He trains supervisors (ESQA school) and coaches in several French universities and around Europe. He leads the EMCC's individual supervision accreditation (ESIA) workgroup and actively researches on supervision. Michel has published ten books on management, coaching and supervision.

Edna Murdoch

Edna is an experienced supervisor working with coaches, supervisors and leaders. She is Director of the Coaching Supervision Academy – a global leader in supervision training for coaches and leaders.

Dr Alanna O'Broin, PhD

Dr Alanna O'Broin is a Chartered Psychologist, and a practising Coaching Psychologist. She has authored several book chapters and peer-reviewed articles on the coaching relationship and related topics, was Co-Editor of *Coaching: An International Journal of Theory, Research and Practice* between 2013 and 2016, and is a Consulting Editor of *The Coaching Psychologist*.

Dr Siobhain O'Riordan, PhD

Siobhain is a Chartered Psychologist and Associate Director of the Centre for Coaching and Centre for Positive Transitions. She is Chair and a Fellow of the International Society for Coaching Psychology. Her professional interests are within the arenas of executive health, well-being and developmental coaching psychology.

Karen Pratt, PCC

Karen Pratt TSTA (E) PCC is a learning and development specialist working with people through coaching, training facilitation and supervision. She uses transactional analysis as the lens through which she understands herself and her clients. Karen's passion is lifelong learning and enabling people to reconnect with their authenticity and essence.

Ram Ramanathan, MCC

Ram is a coach with the ICF MCC credential, trainer accredited by ICF, EMCC and CCE, as well as a mentor and supervisor to coaches. Ram works in the leadership coaching space using his past experience as a corporate leader. His passion is blending Western psychological interventions with Eastern spiritual ones in what he practises as a Mindless approach.

Alex van Oostveen, CRS, CCP, ACC

Alex uses various disciplines to bring about change in business and people's personal lives, the focus being on creating effective relationships and healthy communication. As supervisor he holds a special appreciation for transactional analysis' ability to cut to the core of inter- and intra-personal dynamics. Prior to this vocation, Alex was a senior flight instructor in the South African Air Force where he was both a wingman and leader of the Silver Falcons formation aerobatic team.

Dr Qing Wang, PhD

Qing is a Chartered Psychologist and Associate Professor in the School of Psychology and Cognitive Science at East China Normal University, Shanghai. Her interest is in coaching psychology for knowledge construction, learning and growth in various educational contexts. Qing has ten years' experience in counselling and coaching. She is (probably) the first scholar who officially introduced coaching psychology to the Mainland of China.

Illustrations

Figures

Tables

Foreword

Liz Hall

As Buddhist monk Thich Nhat Hanh writes (Hanh, 2014), "The best thing we can offer another person is our true presence."

Coming into presence requires mindfulness, being able to switch easily to being mode and to pay close attention to what is unfolding within and without. It requires us to be compassionate, in touch with our vulnerability and with our common humanity. It requires profound self-awareness. And one of the greatest outcomes that can arise from us being truly present for another is that they feel more able to be truly themselves.

One of the many things I welcome about *The Heart of Coaching Supervision: Working with Reflection and Self-Care* is that it embraces such territory, going far beyond a narrow focus on tools and techniques, although the reader will find plenty of practical pointers to hone their craft. It is about understanding who we are, and what our beliefs are, so we can better understand what, why and how we do what we do in supervision (or coaching). It's about getting to grips with our philosophy, purpose and process (PPP), which is explored as a framework in detail in Chapter 2 by Peter Jackson and Tatiana Bachkirova, and which serves as a framework for the book.

The Heart of Coaching Supervision is timely in its turn towards what, as Peter Hawkins points out, has been an under-explored aspect of supervision: that of resourcing, particularly pressing in these challenging times. After all, how can we grow and support others fully if we do not first take care of ourselves? One of the book's editors, Eve Turner, quotes in Chapter 11 her supervisor, who finds the following question useful with clients: "What do you need to do for time to be your friend, not your enemy?" In the 24/7 highly electronically connected modern-day culture, time has become the enemy for so many of us. We genuinely don't feel we have time for any "extras" – ten minutes before a session to "tune in" to our bodies, to breathe, to tune into the client we are about to meet; quietly reflecting in our journals; practising mindfulness; practising self-care. This book urges us to make time for what are not actually extras, but the foundations for best and meaningful coach supervision practice. Chapter 6 by Eunice Aquilina, on using self as instrument, Chapter 7 by Jackee Holder on reflective practice, the pioneering Chapter 8 by Jane Adshead-Grant, Anne Hathaway, Linda Aspey and Eve Turner on using the Thinking Environment in supervision and Chapter 9 by Lesley Matile, Sarah Gilbert and Eve Turner on peer supervision are among those that explore ways we can resource ourselves and thus be more effective.

Being in touch with our vulnerability, as research professor Brené Brown has so eloquently expressed, is a profound strength. "[Vulnerability] is about the willingness to show up and be seen when you can't control the outcome. It's our greatest measure of courage," says Brown (Brown, 2015). This book is made all the richer through the inclusion of stories in which vulnerabilities are shared, and in which our common humanity is highlighted, such as in Katerina Kanelidou's moving "I am enough" story in the Introduction. It doesn't shy away from exploring working with the shadow; for example, Keri Phillips' Chapter 5 looks at working with intense emotions.

This collection has been skillfully curated by the editors Eve Turner and Stephen Palmer, and is ambitious both in its reach and in its representation, with rich diversity in contributions including in terms of experience as authors, gender, geography and race, and the exploration of diversity and inclusion in supervision in Chapter 3 by Judy Ryde, Lily Seto and Damian Goldvarg.

Of course, as in coaching, at times good supervision will lead the coach to question whether they should even be coaching at all. I loved the intriguingly named case study "Air Mattresses, Gardens and Supervision", which shares how supervision led the client to set up a company making joyful socks, seeing her shift from "super serious leadership coach to a true self, a goofy, wise, smart and a wee bit sassy self".

Ultimately, isn't that what's at the heart of coaching, and coaching supervision? Helping us and thus helping others be our true selves? Essentially, this book is a journey during which we explore who we are as supervisors, clients, human beings, and what is made possible when we support and dance with others from that space – for ourselves, others and the world at large.

Liz Hall
Editor of *Coaching at Work*

References

Brown, B. (2017). *Rising Strong: How the Ability to Reset Transforms the Way We Live, Love, Parent, and Lead*. New York: Random House.

Thich Nhat Hanh. (2014). *No Mud, No Lotus: The Art of Transforming Suffering*. Berkeley, CA: Parallax Press.

Preface

Why "The Heart of Coaching Supervision"? There are an increasing number of books on supervision now, but in this one we believed it was important to get to the heart both of what coaching supervision is, and of understanding who we are as supervisors (coaches, leaders and so on). This increases our reflectiveness on, and supports our exploration of, how we ourselves might impact the supervision process. To achieve our aims, we sought chapter and case study contributions from a range of supervisors who had different and complementary ways of ensuring they resourced themselves and others.

Each of us may, at times, have wondered about the perennial question: "Who am I?" – most likely without a clear answer. We can, though, attempt to understand what motivates us, presses our hot buttons; we may even, at times, judge ourselves harshly. Yet, how easy is it for us to accept ourselves with all our vulnerabilities, to understand ourselves, our cultural and other influences, supporting ourselves as well as supporting others, ensuring self-care? This need for reflection and self-care was underpinned at a masterclass on "The Future of Coaching", when Sir John Whitmore (2007) said: "If you only have time for one piece of development, do it on yourself."

The nascence of this book is linked to one of the co-editor's (Eve) training as a supervisor with Tatiana Bachkirova and being required to consider PPP (Philosophy, Purpose and Process, see Chapter 2). Questions Carl Rogers (1951: 20) asks are very relevant:

How do we look upon others? Do we see each person as having worth and dignity in his or her own right? If we do hold this point of view at the verbal level, to what extent is it operationally evident at the behavioural level? Do we tend to treat individuals as persons of worth, or do we subtly devaluate them by our attitudes and behaviour? Is our philosophy one in which respect for the individual is uppermost?

After reading 78 publications, including books, Eve was considering giving up the supervision course, seeing only difference, when, luckily, it fell into place and she began to see coherence and similarity. For each of us, congruence is the key, understanding who we are and therefore what we consider as our purpose in coaching and supervision. It links to a theme of our book, what Yalom described as "being fully seen and fully understood" (Yalom, 2002: 18) and, we might add, "accepted". It can also help us where there is a disconnect between the Ps of PPP for ourselves and others.

We thank all those who assisted with *The Heart of Coaching Supervision*, including our publishers for their continuous support and encouragement, the contributors for their insightful chapters and the case study authors for such a range of diverse cases. We would like to acknowledge the support of Michel Moral in the introductory chapter. We are also grateful to others who have helped, not just our family members for putting up with us disappearing into our offices and closing the door, but also the generosity of our supervisees, coachees and colleagues for the learning they have brought us through their support, challenge and endless good humour.

References

Rogers, C. (1951). *Client-Centered Therapy*. London: Constable.

Whitmore, J. (2007). The future of coaching. Association for Coaching masterclass. Held in London, 22 May.

Yalom, I. (2002). *The Gift of Therapy*. London: Piatkus.

Introduction to *The Heart of Coaching Supervision*[1]

Eve Turner and Stephen Palmer

Introduction

The stance of this book is that supervision can be a positive benefit and an activity that is re-sourcing and profoundly beneficial for coaches, mentors and more widely for anyone in a helping profession or leadership position. Its impact extends beyond those receiving it to others in the wider system(s) – all our clients, both individual and organisational, for others within organisational systems such as our peers and direct reports, for other systems such as our families and friends, for our sectors, our profession and for the world at large. This wide-ranging claim is not, as yet, backed up by substantial research, although this is slowly changing (Hawkins and Turner, 2017; de Haan, 2017; Palmer, 2017; Sheppard, 2017).

In writing this book we are starting with the need for self-awareness for ourselves as supervising practitioners, the need to provide ourselves with space and opportunities for reflection and learning. In Chapter 8 (p161) Kline says she learned from her first employer, a Quaker head teacher, Thornton Brown, that "students are learning you" (Kline, 1999: 68–69). We are the role models, and if we are dealing with one of our own "hot buttons", for example, how do we manage this and retain our ability to be the compassionate observer, to hold what Hawkins describes as wide-angled empathy and compassion (Chapter 4, p74)? This is combined with an understanding of the complexity that supervisors, coaches, mentors and leaders face, day to day, the challenges that brings, the intense emotions that may be surfaced (see case study). The authors wish we had been given a pound, Euro or dollar (we are not fussy!) for every time someone has mentioned a lack of time as a factor for not being able to do something; that also applies to reflection and self-care. In this book, alongside a depth and breadth of reflective practice, there are also practical ways to support ourselves that need only take one minute, many of which we can do alone. There are also approaches we can choose to do alone and with others, and also those that will encourage us to work with others collaboratively in partnership (Chapters 8 and 9).

This book sets out to explore who we are as supervisors, but the exploration and the exercises associated with it, are equally suitable for coaches, mentors, leaders; in fact, anyone could benefit from the content. The emphasis is on growing our self-awareness, developing our understanding of how we are in relation to ourselves and others, and then building our relationships with others and wider systems. When we do this, as entertainer and mental health advocate Ruby Wax (2016: 232) concludes having studied and practised mindfulness: "I still have the same hot emotional triggers – I don't think they ever go – but they're fainter; I can watch them coming down the pipeline and remember that they're just triggers, not facts."

What is supervision?

There are many definitions of supervision. What they have in common suggests that supervision:

1. Provides fresh perspectives.
2. Attends to the quality of what we do and ensures safe practice.
3. Attends to how we develop ourselves personally and professionally.

4. Requires us to grow high levels of self-awareness and to work on ourselves, as we are "the tool".
5. Has many stakeholders and is about interconnecting relationships, involving systemic work; it is not only about what is created between the coach and supervisor.
6. Is a place to re-source the coach, mentor, leader and supervisor.

In point 1. (providing fresh perspectives), we are not limiting this to the idea of review (of sessions, recordings, conversations, agreements etc.). Hawkins (2017) argues that supervision can be dominated by the car rear-view window, looking back at what has happened, and he asks: "How do we rebalance reflection with preflection, building our capacity for the challenges of the future world?" We cannot predict the future, and indeed trying to do so could be both time-consuming and frustrating. It is also widely accepted that the strength of the supervision room and of coaching is in our ability to be present in the moment, in the here and now. But without being alert to the future we may miss opportunities and challenges and the chance to grow our ability to deal with them.

Some quotes from writers in the field describing supervision illustrate the six common themes. Hawkins and Schwenk (2006: 4) talk of

[a] structured formal process for coaches, with the help of a coaching supervisor, to attend to improving the quality of their coaching, grow their coaching capacity and support themselves and their practice. Supervision should also be a source of organisational learning.

Hay (2007: 4–5) says:

I think of it as two words – super and vision – as in supervision. To me, it is the process of helping you to step back, metaphorically, from your work so that you can take a meta-perspective, or broader view, of your practice.

Carroll and Shaw (2013: 255) see

> One of the key tasks of supervision is in helping individuals and groups look at their work from new and different perspectives. It is a process that involves looking at what we do and how with super-vision, new eyes, new perceptions, new visions we can see things differently.

They talk of looking beyond our comfort zones, taking many stances "beyond, beside, beneath, above, below, against for" and ask: "what would happen if I looked at myself, my client, our relationship, the organisation in another way?" (Carroll and Shaw, 2013: 255).

Murdoch believes (2013: xxvii) that

> who you are is how you coach . . . and supervise. My experience is that operating alongside all of our professional trainings, our thinking, tools and models, is the personhood of the practitioner – our humanity matters, as does our maturity, our open-heartedness and our generosity of spirit.

Over the years, as supervision has developed across the helping professions, from social work (Kadushin) to counselling (Proctor) and then coaching (Hawkins and Smith) three main functions have been identified but described variously, illustrated in Table 1.1.

At the start of Chapter 4 Hawkins describes his reason for describing the third leg as resourcing rather than restorative or supportive. He argues that each of us needs to find ongoing ways of being and staying "topped up", of

Table 1.1   The three functions of supervision

Kadushin (1976)	Proctor (2008)	Hawkins and Smith (2013)
Administrative/ Managerial	Normative	Qualitative
Educational	Formative	Developmental
Supportive	Restorative	Resourcing

(adapted from Hawkins and Smith, 2013: 173)

being re-sourced constantly. This will ensure we do not get depleted and rely, in the worst extreme, on supervisor input to be "whole" again, to be restored.

As one factor in achieving this, Hawkins (2017) tells a story of a colleague, a Sufi teacher who encourages us to "focus on life as a generous teacher, developing capacity around us, through us and within us". In this, Hawkins advocates a move from dialogue to generative trialogue where "life" in all its forms, including the more than human world, provides us with learning that we bring to supervision, to coaching and beyond. Within the book there are many places where we can take stock and allow this to happen.

What does research tell us?

Corrie with Lane and Watts (2016: 7) sum up the current situation when it comes to evidencing the impact of supervision: "enthusiasm for supervision currently outstrips the evidence base, including the evidence that attests to its impact on practice." Corrie and associates also talk of the relatively little attention that has been paid to the development of supervisors, as opposed to supervisees. In a review of coaching supervision Tkach and DiGirolamo (2017: 56) note that there are currently "no universally accepted guidelines or best practices". They advocate the "development and agreement amongst researchers of standardised measures" to move the industry forward in its understanding of what takes place in coaching supervision (2017: 59).

We do know that the growth in coaching supervision has been relatively rapid since 2006, at least among those coaches who are able to be reached, for example through membership of professional bodies and forums. In 2006 "only 44% of UK coaches received continuous and regular supervision" (Hawkins and Schwenk, 2006: 4). This compared to 88% of organisers of coaching and 86% of coaches believing they should have it. By 2014, in a survey carried out by Hawkins and Turner, with 428 coaches completing the supervision section responding via professional bodies (in particular the AC, EMCC and ICF) and with *Coaching at Work* magazine, there had been a "massive increase in coaches having coaching supervision, a rise from 44% to 93.3% in the UK, and 83.2% globally. North America is significantly lagging behind other regions; however, it is roughly where the UK was in 2006" (Hawkins and Turner, 2017: 106).

The motivation for supervision was described positively. For the vast majority, 92.6%, their motivation was as "part of my commitment to good practice" (2017: 107). For 51.6% it was considered as part of their CPD. When it came to having supervision "as a requirement", the figures were relatively low: 33.9% for membership of a professional body, 25.6% for accreditation by a professional body, 19.2% to work in an organisation as an external coach and the lowest, 14.7%, to work as an internal coach. Where coaches didn't receive supervision, fewer cited difficulties in finding a supervisor, the main reason in 2006. Instead it was because coaches chose to access peer networks or use their own reflective practice or their own coach (2017: 107).

The variety in practice is clear from the research that does exist. In Grant's 2012 study of Australian coaches "50% of those who provided formal supervision had received some training in supervision" and a "major issue raised by many participants was the difficulty of finding training in coach supervision and being assured of the quality of any such training" (Grant, 2012: 28). While 82.7% of coaches were having some form of supervision, 30% reported having had a negative experience (2012: 17). Research published soon after, with 33 executive coaches from Australia/New Zealand, and 29 purchasing clients, found that

> though coaches cited supervision as the intervention they would be most likely to deploy if they felt the need for emotional support, few coaches said they often felt the need for such support. The predominant function of coaching supervision for coaches was developmental. For purchasing clients, on the other hand, the primary purpose of supervision was quality control, though only 21% of purchasing clients insist on supervision as part of a quality assurance process.
> (Lawrence and Whyte, 2014: 39)

While the majority said they would use supervision if stuck,

About 36% mentioned supervision as a component of their ongoing learning plan, 27% said they used supervision to ensure they were practising ethically and just 6% mentioned supervision as part of their strategy for ensuring they successfully navigated the needs of both client and coachee.

(Lawrence and Whyte, 2014: 43)

The French organisation, the Professional Supervisors Federation (2014), had 269 respondents to a survey looking at the state of supervision in France of which 148 were coaches and 89 described themselves as supervisors. The supervisors were highly experienced, and the vast majority, 94%, themselves had supervision. However, 80% had not been trained as supervisors, and only 36% of those not trained, planned to do so (2014: 22–25). When it came to the dangers of supervision the main fears expressed were of dependence and amateurism for both supervisors and coaches and the benefits were mainly seen as sharing methods and standing back (2014: 35). Interestingly, 40% of respondents did not know if their supervisors were supervised themselves. This mirrors a finding with coachees where almost half, 48.3%, did not know if their coaches were supervised (Turner and Hawkins, 2016: 34).

DeFilippo (2015: 12) did a qualitative project with "nine supervisory dyads which includes coaches and coach supervisors" and found results that included "increased confidence and objectivity for coaches, as well as satisfaction and learning for coach supervisors". In a unique study, to date, Moral (2015: 126) examines whether there is a "specific personality profile of supervisors, or of coaches who want to become supervisors". In looking at whether they have a specific defensive style, he concludes that little difference has been noted between coaches and supervisors and the general population but believes that "a better understanding of the defence profiles of coaches and supervisors will help to design new supervision techniques" (Moral, 2015: 131).

Lamy and Moral (2013: 218) have developed the work of Buber and Schultz on inclusion, having noticed a link between the tool used at the start of group supervision sessions and the "level of authenticity and openness" achieved during the session. In their study they noted that "putting words related to identity and professional identity strengthens the consciousness of the participants and has positive developmental effects" (2013: 229). Moral and Lamy (2016: 168) have also begun to explore what group supervision process would "best serve the system formed by the group, the supervisor, the supervisees and the context of the client", as they assess there are currently around 100 processes in use. Their research objective is to open new areas of investigation that could be studied, and as yet have not tested a hypothesis.

Hodge, in a small-scale UK-based doctoral, qualitative study emphasises the importance of supervision in providing a restorative space. She also found that through the "discipline of writing up their supervision sessions, the research participants became more appreciative of their experience of being in supervision. They acknowledged that they were reflecting on their development more deeply" (Hodge, 2016: 95). This links to Holder's chapter in this book. Hodge concludes that

> as indicated by the participants, professional executive coaches need to consider the volume of coaching and number of client assignments they are engaged in at any one time as well as other personal or professional demands that affect how they show up with their coachees. Together with their supervisors, they calibrate and monitor how they are taking care of themselves, so they are able to engage effectively and consistently with their clients thus avoiding '"burnout" or "compassion fatigue" (e.g. Stamm, 2010).
>
> (Hodge, 2016: 98)

In 2017 there were a number of publications relating to supervision and, in particular, the relationship between supervisor and supervisee. De Haan (2017) conducted a substantial survey into trust and safety in supervision, which had 518 coach respondents from 32 countries and concludes that levels of trust are high. The research shows that the majority, 85%, had "explored the most concerning, worrying and/or shameful episode in the coach's practice over the last few years" in supervision and had found supervision helpful (2017: 42). Of the remaining 15%, 5% had found supervision unhelpful, 7% answered that they could have brought the episode to supervision but didn't for some reason, 2% choose not to because they "did not trust their supervisor" and 1% didn't because "it was too shameful" (2017: 42–44).

Sheppard (2017) gathered empirical evidence about how supervisees – and the research participants included supervisors, given they also had supervision – can help and hinder their own supervision. Her aim was to ensure that supervisees at all stages of professional development can get more from their coaching supervision, and this provides useful information for supervisors particularly when contracting with their supervisees. She researched what inhibited and enabled supervision and identified four distinct themes on how supervisees get in their own way during supervision: "anxiety, fear of judgment and shame, I'm blocking myself, lack of agency and not seeing myself as an equal partner" (2017: 115). Sheppard also found supervisees articulated how "they have learnt to enhance their coaching supervision over time and these activities fell into four themes – adopting a positive mindset, co-creating the relationship, participating actively in the process and undertaking supervisor training." (2017: 117)

Palmer (2017) used an online survey to investigate the supervisor–supervisee relationship. He had 112 respondents whose coaching practice was based in a total of 22 countries. There were 80 completed responses to the 22 questions. The participants were members of a range of national and international professional coaching and psychology bodies. Sixty-seven per cent had been in practice for six or more years. Ninety per cent rated "trust" within a coaching supervision relationship as "very important" and 88% reported that their current supervisor was "'very trustworthy". Supervision Enhancing Thoughts (SETs), attitudes or beliefs held by respondents included:

- It's challenging but required for growth personally and professionally.
- This is a space where I can be vulnerable and feel safe and supported.
- Supervision is a quality guarantee for my clients, and a protection for myself.

In contrast, Supervision Interfering Thoughts (SITs), attitudes or beliefs included:

- I may be judged as a coach.
- Imposter syndrome is my main interfering thought.
- I would hate my supervisor to think I was a rubbish coach!

Respondents also reported that supervision enhanced coaching performance and their well-being, the latter being an under-researched area of the benefits of supervision.

Overview of the book

Supervisor, supervisee and client well-being is core to this book. We have asked writers to consider different approaches to how we understand and resource ourselves. The common theme is about how we bring ourselves to supervision – our use of self and how we work with and resource ourselves continuously to achieve that. When we talk of the "heart" of coaching supervision, we are considering two perspectives: it is about using more than the head, and also examining what is at the core of supervision. What can we put in place to support ourselves as supervisors, coaches and mentors, to be the best we can be in service of our clients and beyond? It is not meant as a book of tools in the conventional sense, but rather aims to show what we can do to put self at the core.

So, in Chapter 2 the book starts with us considering who we are through our philosophy on life, as that influences how we choose to practise, what we see as the purpose of supervision, and the choices we make about how we carry it out. This will, of course, also influence how we work as coaches, mentors or leaders and influence areas such as power dynamics. By understanding something about our-selves and our views about the world, we may begin to understand why it is we behave in a particular way, react to a client in a certain manner, perhaps when their values are different. Peter Jackson and Tatiana Bachkirova talk of this as PPP – Philosophy, Purpose and Process.

The book continues in Chapter 3 by Judy Ryde, Lily Seto and Damian Goldvarg looking at who we are through reflect-ing on our diversity, and how our history may influence how we supervise. Each individual is uniquely influenced by a combination of geographical, cultural and other back-grounds, which combine in our role as supervisor, coach, mentor or leader. Do we understand their significance and how we then include others? These dimensions mean each of us has a different response, and without awareness we may not be present to those influences and the underlying power issues that may play out. This may encompass our race, gen-der, religion, sexual orientation, age, socio-economic status, physical and mental abilities. The American Psychological Association has developed guidelines that are also a helpful reference (APA, 2017).

We then turn our attention to self-resourcing, looking at the role our emotions play in our work, and compas-sion. While a lot has been written about two of the planks of supervision practice – the managerial-administrative/ normative/qualitative and educational/formative/develop-mental (using Kadushin, Proctor and Hawkins and Smith's terms respectively, see Table 1.1, p4") – less attention has been paid to the supportive, restorative or, in coaching/men-toring, the resourcing aspect. In Chapter 4 Peter Hawkins seeks to remedy what he considers an omission, believing that only through paying attention to our own well-being can we hope to support and challenge others. This is par-ticularly true when dealing with intense emotions, whether viewed as positive or negative, so considering areas such as pain, grief and suffering as well as joy, love and hope, which Keri Phillips covers in Chapter 5. The focus on positive psy-chology has had many positive benefits for clients. But in this chapter, we also examine how we can deal resourcefully with emotions that may be more challenging for us as practitioners and leaders, while also having their own positive benefits. Phillips argues we need to connect with self to connect with others.

The following chapters continue to develop this theme of self and connection. We look at ways to be present for our clients (supervisees, leaders) and to have strategies to support ourselves as practitioners and stay the best we can be. Eunice Aquilina highlights the use of self as instrument in supervision in Chapter 6, and how this is embodied in our presence and impacts on those around us, and of course ourselves. She considers how we can cultivate this and learn practices to develop somatic sensibility, working with all our resources through sensations, emotions and narrative. In Chapter 7 Jackee Holder then draws on a body of evidence and practical applications to share with us ways to use reflective, therapeutic and expressive writing and journaling as a way we can resource ourselves and others. Through the many innovative and creative approaches, she explains, we see how we can connect better with self, and others.

Next, we include two approaches where we can provide additional support to ourselves and others. The first is Time to Think, Chapter 8, which is primarily a philosophy towards supervision, coaching and life more generally, rather than a technique. Jane Adshead-Grant, Anne Hathaway, Linda Aspey and Eve Turner believe that attention and listening are at the core of supervision, allowing us to be open to our own and others' feelings and emotions. The notion is of supervision as a partnership underpinned by the spirit of co-creation and co-enquiry as its essence; here the supervisor intervenes only when requested, and we may reflect on how that links to our PPP from Jackson and Bachkirova's earlier chapter. Remen (2006: 219–220) captured this when she wrote that

> [w]hen we listen, we offer with our attention an opportunity for wholeness. Our listening creates sanctuary for the homeless parts within the other person. That which

has been denied, unloved, devalued by themselves and by others. That which is hidden. In this culture the soul and the heart too often go homeless. Listening creates a holy silence. When you listen generously to people, they can hear the truth in themselves, often for the first time. And in the silence of listening, you can know yourself in everyone.

We then look at the use of peer supervision as a way to support ourselves in Chapter 9. This is an additional resource and Lesley Matile, Sarah Gilbert and Eve Turner consider how we can make peer supervision as effective as possible so that we can use it to support ourselves as practitioners. In doing so they are drawing on what is a case study based on years of experience working in a peer supervision chain called Evolve.

The penultimate chapter provides a rich range of case studies from around the world. Chapter 10 draws on the experiences of supervisors and supervisees from a range of backgrounds and disciplines. Our final chapter, Chapter 11, attends to some of the other elements that will impact on how we look after ourselves and touches on ethics, contracting, continuous development and supervision of supervision, and draws together self-care.

Case study

Katerina Kanelidou is a coach, trainer, mentor-coach and mentor-trainer based in Greece. Since 2016 she has been a member of the steering committee of CoachActivism, a pro-bono coaching initiative responding to the needs of volunteers and front-line workers involved in the global refugee crisis. Katerina's story recalls for me (ET) Bronnie Ware's book describing the top five regrets of the dying from her time working in palliative care. She wrote: "The mind knows no answers. The heart no questions. It is the heart that guides you to joy, not the mind." (2011: 213). The gifts we give may be the simplest, but we may underestimate the joy they can bring.

"I am enough" – Katerina Kanelidou's story

"The year 2017 was my second as part of the CoachActivism programme. We coach mainly volunteers and front-line workers with refugees either in camps, shelters, homeless or relocation sites, mainly in Europe.

"One of the critical elements of the programme is supervision: all the coaches are required to attend monthly sessions. And to be honest: it is supervision that helps us balance the programme's many challenges, one of which is about boundaries. While having topics like the drama triangle and boundary management in our initial training is one step, the nature of our assignments, our work and the work of our coachees, demands more than that.

"I met my coachee one summer evening. Our first meeting was in Athens, and nothing was ordinary about that session: it was a Sunday at an almost empty hotel roof garden. He was there with a small group of refugees, two young men and a 72-year-old woman. We sat at another table and before we started I learned that the woman was living in a basement, alone with no help. He had just found a new place for her to live and for the first time, for a long time, she was going out for the day.

"When we finished the session the coachee introduced us. The lady didn't speak English or Greek, I didn't speak Arabic, but we 'talked' for a few minutes. She asked to take a photo with me; she was smiling and hugging me. Half an hour later, we saw the photos, we smiled and hugged again, and I left. I felt guilty. I hadn't done anything to deserve this hug, nor to be in the photo. The coachee had located her, taken her for a day out from her basement and found her a new home.

"I had my next supervision session with Eve shortly afterwards and shared the story, without knowing exactly why. I don't remember much of what and how, I just remember that all the emotions came to the surface, that I only felt like crying. I think I was crying. I had seen the conditions of the refugees in the port of Piraeus and other sites, had witnessed the superhuman efforts of the volunteers, had heard some of their stories and felt despair and anger. I was often struggling with the thought that I wasn't doing enough, that I should be doing more than just supporting the volunteers. So, when the old lady hugged me, I felt ashamed and unworthy of that hug. I felt that I hadn't done anything to deserve it. And I felt deep sadness, despair for the human suffering.

"It was then our supervisor shared with us a story, the story of 'I am enough', as I like to remember it. In supervision we are not focused on performance. The space of supervision gave me an opportunity to be in touch with, and let out, all my emotions, to articulate and express them. There is acceptance, and the compassion allowed me to openly share how I felt without judgment. At the same time the 'I am enough' (Remen, 2006, see Chapter 11, p224) story shifted my perspective of that encounter.

"It may only have been a brief interaction and given me a feeling of not doing enough ('what should be'). But that brief interaction was very significant for another human being; a simple chat, a hug, the human contact that lady had been deprived of for some time and made her smile so generously. The transparency of my supervisor in showing her emotions at the story, gave me an important lesson for my own presence as a coach. While we do not want to overwhelm clients with our emotions and the context is always important, we share a common humanity and it is ok to be seen in our vulnerability.

"Working in this project has challenged boundaries and emotions in many different levels. It is thanks to supervision that I have been able to become aware of them, be supported and hopefully manage them effectively."

Conclusion

Supervision has the potential to enhance well-being – of the supervisor, supervisee, the coachee and of wider society and systems. Through reflection and self-care, through sharing and being heard, we can learn to accept ourselves, to be vulnerable and to put ourselves in the best position possible to support others. Through the authors in this book who often share their own journeys, including their vulnerabilities, as readers we can gain further insights, opportunities, ideas, and space to reflect and develop our self-understanding and our understanding of others.

Practice points

- Discuss with supervisees their understanding of supervision, and how it has changed over time; include an open conversation about their attitude to supervision – is it an "ought" or is it something that is their contribution to learning and so on.
- Explore with supervisees whether they feel the three "functions" of supervision – qualitative, developmental and resourcing (Hawkins and Smith, 2013) – are being attended to and whether they feel the balance is appropriate for their needs and those of their clients.
- Ask supervisees to consider both what supports their supervision and what gets in the way.
- Support supervisees in attending to competing needs and demands in supervision, for example between the client, the different stakeholders and systems in operation.
- Reflect on which processes are most appropriate for different supervisees; how do you know and how might you check?
- Encourage supervisees to reflection on, and write up learning from, their supervision sessions and facilitate a discussion with your supervisees about how they can get the most out of supervision and apply their learning in practice.

Discussion points

- Who are you? What is it that makes up your heart, your essence, and is this congruent between your different roles?
- What evidence do you rely on and use to demonstrate that supervision has a beneficial effect for you, and for your supervisees and coachees? And how do you apply that

learning in service of your individual and organisational clients, supervisees and wider systems?

- How do you deal with "hot, emotional triggers"; what strategies do you have in place? And how do you balance knowing "I am enough" with wanting to do more?
- In what ways do you ensure trust and safety for yourself, and your supervisees and clients?

Note

1. With thanks to Katerina Kanelidou for the case study for this chapter.

Suggested reading

Hall, L. (2013). *Mindful Coaching*. London: Kogan Page.
Hawkins, P. and Smith, N. (2013). *Coaching, Mentoring and Organizational Consultancy: Supervision, Skills & Development.* Maidenhead: Open University Press.
Murdoch, E. and Arnold, J. (2013). *Full Spectrum Supervision.* St Albans: Panoma Press.
Remen, R. N. (2006). *Kitchen Table Wisdom*. New York: Penguin.

References

American Psychological Association. (2017). Multicultural guidelines: An ecological approach to context, identity, and inter-sectionality. Washington, DC: APA. Retrieved 1 August 2018 from: www.apa.org/about/policy/multicultural-guidelines.pdf
Carroll, M. and Shaw, E. (2013). *Ethical Maturity in the Helping Professions: Making Difficult Life and Work Decisions.* London: Jessica Kingsley.
Corrie, S. with Lane, D. A. and Watts, M. H. (2016). The role of supervision in contemporary psychological practice: an intro-duction and orientation. In D. Lane, M. Watts and S. Corrie (Eds), *Supervision in the Psychological Professions.* London: Open University Press.
DeFilippo, D. (2015). Coach, keep it professional. *Chief Learning Officer,* 14 (6), 12.
de Haan, E. (2017). Large-scale survey of trust and safety in coaching supervision: Some evidence that we are doing it right. *International Coaching Psychology Review,* 12 (1), 37–48.

Grant, A. (2012). Australian coaches' views on coaching supervision: A study with implications for Australian coach education, training and practice. *International Journal of Evidence Based Coaching and Mentoring*, 10 (2), 17–33.

Hawkins, P. (2017). Resourcing – the neglected third leg of supervision. A webinar for the Global Supervisors' Network, 14 and 15 December 2017.

Hawkins, P. and Schwenk, G. (2006). Coaching supervision – a paper prepared for the CIPD coaching conference. London: Chartered Institute of Personnel and Development.

Hawkins, P. and Smith, N. (2013). *Coaching, Mentoring and Organizational Consultancy: Supervision, Skills & Development*. Maidenhead: Open University Press.

Hawkins, P. and Turner, E. (2017). The rise of coaching supervision 2006–2014. *Coaching: An International Journal of Theory, Research and Practice*, 10: 2, 102–114.

Hay, J. (2007). *Reflective Practice and Supervision for Coaches*. Maidenhead: Open University Press.

Hodge, A. (2016). The value of coaching supervision as a development process: Contribution to continued professional and personal wellbeing for executive coaches. *International Journal of Evidence Based Coaching and Mentoring*, 14 (2), 87–105.

Kadushin, A. (1976). *Supervision in Social Work*. New York: Columbia University Press.

Kline, N. (1999). *Time to Think: Listening to Ignite the Human Mind*. London: Cassell.

Lamy, F. and Moral, M. (2013). Symbolism and inclusion in supervision. Developing professional identity and reinforcing the group dynamic. *EMCC Mentoring and Coaching Conference 2013*. Dublin: EMCC: 216–233.

Lawrence, P. and Whyte, A. (2014). What is coaching supervision and is it important? *Coaching: An International Journal of Theory, Research and Practice*, 7 (1), 39–55.

Moral, M. (2015). Who is the supervisor? In Z. Csigás and P. Lindvall (Eds) *5th Mentoring and Coaching Research Conference*. Poland: EMCC: 125–132.

Moral, M. and Lamy, F. (2016). Selecting a supervision process in collective supervision. In Z. Csigás and I. Sobolewska (Eds), *6th Mentoring and Research Conference*. Hungary: EMCC: 168–179.

Murdoch, E. (2013). Introduction – Overview of coaching supervision. In E. Murdoch and J. Arnold (Eds) *Full Spectrum Supervision*. St Albans: Panoma Press.

Palmer, S. (2017). Beyond the coaching and therapeutic relationship: the supervisee-supervisor relationship. Keynote given on 15 September at the 7th International Congress of Coaching Psychology, 2017, Aalborg University, Aalborg, Denmark.

Proctor, B. (2008). *Group Supervision*. 2nd ed. London: Sage.

Professional Supervisors Federation (2014). 2014 Grand survey on supervision in France. Paris: Professional Supervisors Federation.

Remen, R. N. (2006). *Kitchen Table Wisdom*. New York: Penguin.

Sheppard, L. (2017). How coaching supervisees help and hinder their supervision. *International Journal of Evidence Based Coaching and Mentoring* Special, Issue No. 11, 111–122.

Stamm, B. H. (2010). *The Concise ProQOL Manual, 2nd Ed.* Pocatello, ID: ProQOL.org.

Tkach, J. T and DiGirolamo, J. A. (2017). The state and future of coaching supervision. *International Coaching Psychology Review*, 12 (1), 49–63.

Turner, E. and Hawkins, P. (2016). Coming of age: The development of coaching supervision 2006–2014. *Coaching at Work*, 11 (2), 30–35. Available from: www.coaching-at-work.com/2016/03/08/coming-of-age-the-development-of-coaching-supervision-2006–2014/

Ware, B. (2011). *The Top Five Regrets of the Dying*. Bloomington, IN: Balboa Press.

Wax, R. (2016). *A Mindfulness Guide for the Frazzled*. London: Penguin.

2

The 3 Ps of supervision and coaching

Philosophy, Purpose and Process

Peter Jackson and Tatiana Bachkirova

Introduction

In this chapter we outline an approach to developing practice in coaching and supervision aimed at achieving a
practice that is congruent with the self of the practitioner.
The PPP framework is inspired by an original idea of
David Lane's (Lane, 2006), but has been developed further
to reflect our particular philosophy of professional development. In the introductory sections that follow, we outline
what the PPP framework is, and describe the educational
philosophy and logic that sits behind it. In the central section of the chapter, we expand on the three elements of the
framework: *philosophy, purpose* and *process*. We reflect on
the hurdles practitioners experience in developing their
practice model using the framework and report first-hand
experiences of those who have used it in our supervisor
professional development programmes. Finally, recommendations are given for further reading and reflection.

The logic of the model's development: the concept of practising 'from who we are'

In our educational and academic work in relation to coaching over the last 15 years, we have consistently emphasised
practitioners' priority to develop a practice of coaching *from*

who we are or to put it another way, that the coach is the main *instrument* of coaching (Bachkirova, 2016). Our explanation for such a proposition comes from the way we see the coaching engagement. However important the knowledge of coaching theories, methodologies and techniques may be, we cannot say that coaching is simply a direct application of this knowledge. Because of the extent of uncertainty, complexity and instability inherent in our work, coaching cannot just rely on rational models of practice, however persuasive they are. Such practice is also not value-neutral – it is a very personal experience for our clients and therefore cannot be done mechanically. Recognition of the personal connection at the heart of coaching also implies the importance of the trustworthiness of the coach: their ability to resonate with clients' concerns. Even the use of explicit theoretical models is value-laden in practice, as the coach's choices are so intertwined with their personal values that it is not possible to say which interventions come from theories and which from personal beliefs. Indeed, one can argue that all "interventions are the expression of the coach's life experiences, current worldview, and the stage of his or her personal learning journey" (Bachkirova, 2016: 144).

Following the principle that the coach is the main instrument of coaching, our programmes are designed with the main purpose of developing the coach. Education in this case becomes twofold. On the one hand it is an opportunity for the developing coach to become familiar with the knowledge of the trade, not only to assimilate it but also to evaluate it, to be discerning about it. On the other hand, coaches need to grow in terms of personal reflexivity: to understand themselves, to find out their values and principles of change and development in order to build an approach to practice that is congruent with who they are.

In our role as educators for coaches, then, we see professional education being achieved through a programme of developing reflexivity and critical appreciation of the body of knowledge that informs the discipline. In our role as practice supervisors we see this principle from two slightly different perspectives. On the one hand, we see the opportunity to bring that constructive and developmental process into the wider supervisory landscape of normative, formative/ developmental and restorative functions (Proctor, 1994; Hawkins and Shohet, 2012). That is to say, to provide the opportunity for the coach to develop themself through the reflective learning process in supervision. On the other hand, we also see our own obligation to supervise *from who we are*. The same logic of personal professional development applies to ourselves as it does to our supervisees, as it does to delegates on our professional and academic practitioner programmes. So this principle of developing a personally congruent practice (a practice *from who we are*) applies equally to the coach, the supervisor and the supervisor's developmental work with the coach.

Before going on to explain in this chapter the background, history, structure, logic and the application of the '3 Ps of supervision and coaching', we should provide a short description of what it actually is. It is not a method or model of supervision (or coaching) practice in itself, but rather a method or model of modelling practice. More specifically, it is a process of enquiring into and articulating the kind of practice congruent to the self of the practitioner as described above. The 3 Ps suggest three different strands of how the practitioner identifies the way that they practise and can develop their practice. The 3 Ps apply equally to coaching and to supervision. We have been formally supporting both coaches and supervisors in exploring their practice in this way for over a decade (and sometimes the same practitioner has ended up looking at both practices at different times). For the purpose of this chapter, however, we discuss how it relates to supervisors.

The 3 Ps represent the following perspectives:

- Philosophy: What is your philosophy of change and support? This may include values, beliefs, theoretical perspectives, main assumptions about human nature, change and influence.
- Purpose: What purpose does your supervision serve? This may include intention, outputs, results of your supervision.

- Process: What process is appropriate to that purpose and philosophy? This may include a description of what you do (what happens) when you supervise.

Models and frameworks help focus attention on a wider range of "parts" of any system. A good example is the way that the seven-eyed model (Hawkins and Schwenk, 2011) helps supervisors take notice of aspects of the supervision process and relationship that they might otherwise overlook. By exploring practice from the three perspectives of the 3 Ps we aim to bring to light the practitioner's espoused theories, their theories in use, their underpinning assumptions, their preferences and thereby crucially their blind spots, their neglected backwaters and their inconsistencies. The aim of this process is not necessarily to get the practice 'right' (not least because we struggle with such a concept – see, Bachkirova and Lawton Smith, 2015) and it is most certainly not to show that the practice is 'wrong'. What we have found is that it allows the practitioner to develop a coherence to their practice, both in terms of its internal consistency, and in terms of its alignment to the *self* of the practitioner.

This framework was originally influenced by the work of David Lane presented at the British Psychological Society's Special Group in Coaching Psychology (SGCP) Conference in 2006 (Lane, 2006 and more extensively developed along its original lines by Lane, Watts and Corrie, 2016). At first, we experimented with Lane's original formulation of the framework, which argued that supervisors needed to have a clear *purpose*, a framework of underlying *perspectives* and a respectful *process* of working. However, we felt constrained by the central logic of Lane's structure and developed a different formulation of the framework: *philosophy, purpose* and *process*. In Lane's approach, the leading role was given to the purpose, with an apparent assumption of the subservient role of the philosophy in the way practitioners conceptualise their practice. This approach could imply that the only role of philosophy was to justify the aims. Working this way around, the discussion of philosophy could become little more than post-hoc rationalisation. We believe, however, that it is the system of beliefs and assumptions that define what the aims of practice are going to be and what process is to follow. This revised structure of the framework was consequently adapted for the assessment task in our postgraduate programme in Coaching Supervision, and later for our professional development programme, which was derived from it. Reflecting the fact that this structure of the PPP is fully consistent with our educational positions on the role of self in the development of coaching practice, it also became part of the requirement for award-bearing programmes in Coaching and Mentoring Practice.

Structure of the model

In this section we describe in more detail the discussions that might take place when viewing practice from the three perspectives represented by the 3 Ps. We have presented the 3 Ps in the sequence that seems most logical in order to understand the process: building from the more foundational to the more visible. Thinking about one's own practice model, however, can move in both directions. We can equally ask, "What does my preference for this technique or approach tell me about my values?" as we can ask, "What kinds of approaches follow logically from my underpinning beliefs?" It is also worth noting that it is articulating the "process" part that comes most immediately to most practitioners: we have found working with students that people tend to have preferences even if they have not really investigated the rationale for those preferences. So there is no single or correct direction to follow your thinking. Indeed, as a developmental framework, there is some logic, as well as a practical attraction, in working from the process backwards: the intuitive choices practitioners make in the immediacy of their practice offer both a more concrete starting point and one which we believe is likely to reflect the practitioner's values and beliefs with less rational filtering.

Philosophy

The very mention of the word "philosophy" can cause students of coaching and supervision to feel paralysed. It would be useful briefly to demystify the idea of philosophy and to clarify our use of the term here.

Simon Blackburn does a good job of summarising briefly the point of thinking about philosophy:

> . . . our ideas and concepts can be compared with the lenses through which we see the world. In philosophy the lens is itself the topic of study. Success will be a matter not of how much you know at the end, but of what you can do when the going gets tough: when the seas of argument rise, and confusion breaks out.
>
> (Blackburn, 1999: 5)

Studying philosophy provides a vocabulary for exploring the nature of ideas, but we do not need to go so far as to actually *study* philosophy in this chapter. Here we need only to reflect on those "lenses through which we see the world" (Blackburn, 1999: 5). Using another metaphor, philosophy, in Blackburn's description, can be imagined as the keel of a boat. "Our philosophy" is therefore that thing that tells us what we should do when we don't know what to do: that keeps us more or less moving in a particular direction. So the task in relation to understanding why we practise the way we practise, is to understand something about that keel and those lenses: where the keel points us, and what the lenses allow us to see, or even where they allow us look in the first place.

We may actually experience this sense of direction, and how we look, as our values or sometimes as our theories. Grady McGonagill describes his own process of uncovering what drove his practice when, as he describes it, "All too often I had found myself winging it – while of course pretending that I knew exactly what I was doing" (2002: 59). He recounts turning to reflection – a term Blackburn uses extensively in his introduction – and reflective practice. He chooses as a specific and vital focus for that reflection, his own "frames for understanding human behaviour" (2002: 62).

So the aim here is to discover through reflection what values and assumptions our practice is informed by (or what values we wish it to be informed by if we are designing our model bottom-up), and how that might be expressed through our preferences for ways of working (or "theories-in-use" – Argyris and Schön, 1974) Following on from that examination, we might then identify contradictions or difficulties between competing priorities.

We can start this process by thinking about values. As practising coaches, supervisors may well have their own favourite values exercises that they use with coaching clients. We tend to favour open-ended processes rather than approaches that involve selecting from lists, as the former seem to encourage more spontaneous and personally meaningful responses. The important thing here is to identify what is *really* important to you; what values would take priority over all else. If we take a different context we can illustrate how these values affect practice. Imagine junior school teachers. Some might feel a strong sense that we have obligations to our society and that it is therefore incredibly important to impress on children the value of hard work as a route to fully realising their potential to contribute. Others might feel that every child is entirely individual, and that their autonomy and self-expression are to be respected. We can imagine that these different values might suggest different ways of practising in the teaching context.

One way of testing this for your own practice is to ask yourself what actions or behaviours in others you have a strong reaction to. The things that make us angry, and even more so, the things that make us irrationally angry, may well point to some value or other that has been transgressed. The potential trap here is to fall into describing how we would ideally like other people to see us. Not many people would espouse values of unfairness, ignorance and brutality, so claiming to set great store by fairness, wisdom and kindness might not be telling us that much about our characteristic view of the world. There are social and professional norms that we all work within, but what makes you *you*?

The next question is what assumptions we make about people and how they act in the world. We put this question to a research participant once, whose answer was, "I don't make assumptions about people . . . because everyone is different". So we can see from that exchange that the question is not an easy one to answer. To put the question another way, then, what do you assume to be common to all people? What values? What behaviours? Our research participant, if we had asked a better question, might have been able to say that he deeply respected the individuality and autonomy of every individual (his own values), that people expected that individuality and autonomy to be respected (a theory or assumption about the values of others) and that therefore he and, in fact, everyone should avoid judging the actions of others. This is hypothetical – we did not ask a better question at the time, unfortunately – but is intended to illustrate the difference between our values and our assumptions.

Finally, we might ask what theories of practice work best for us. By theories of practice we mean the kind of theories that encompass the values and assumptions described above, such as person-centred, existential, solutions-focused or Gestalt. You might be exposed to these theories through conference presentations, workshops and events arranged by professional bodies, or through your own reading. With these perspectives you can ask yourself the following questions:

- Who has inspired you?
- What would you like to know more about?

Often the logic and background of these theories are more fully explained in coaching handbooks (e.g. Cox, Bachkirova and Clutterbuck, 2014) and in supervision handbooks (e.g. Bachkirova, Jackson and Clutterbuck, 2011). So these sources can be used with questions in mind such as:

- Which theories most influence your practice?
- Which theories can you relate to?
- Which theories present a rationale for the practices you use?
- Which theories are built on values that are similar to yours?

Equally, a sense of these preferences may emerge in less explicit or abstract ways:

- What books are you drawn to?
- Whose writing do you return to repeatedly?
- What films resonate for you?
- Which painters attract you?
- What music?

By looking at your values, assumptions and main theoretical influences it is possible to build a strong sense of what keeps your practice on track, to discover what might be added to that practice and what might not fit as well as it used to.

Purpose

The articulation of purpose in this framework is about what one as a supervisor aims to achieve with and for the client, the client system, or wider stakeholders. Different supervisors will have different commitments to all these different parties and systems. So not only is it important to do this to establish an explicit concept of what we want to achieve in order to evaluate whether we have done a good job or not, but it is an important aspect of individualising – perhaps the right word would be "personalising" – our practice and its principles. Of course, one might say that the coach one is supervising can be the final judge of how satisfied they are, but relying on this criterion alone is insufficient. Coaches may feel satisfied for various reasons, which might include not being disturbed too much, or feeling comfortable rather than learning. Clarifying your own image of what constitutes a good job, as well as what you believe your supervision should look like and feel like, allows you to scrutinise your practice and continue challenging yourself even when the feedback from the coaches is positive.

However, to identify the purpose of supervision (as well as of coaching) is not that easy. The first challenge we could consider comes from the statement by Kegan (1982: 295) who argued that, "amongst the many things from which a practitioner's clients need protection is the practitioner's hopes for the client's future, however benign and sympathetic these hopes may be". How can we define an aim of supervision that does not include hopes for the client's future – a vision of what is good for him/her? And without such a vision we are left with the aim that is defined only by the client and thus we become completely dependent on their feedback.

Another challenge comes from the potential confusion between the ends and means when we aim to define the purpose of our work. For example, if your purpose of practice is to provide a reflective space for the coach it may sound reasonable, but this purpose is more about the process rather than the outcome that you wish to achieve. In order to extract a purpose from this process you may benefit from asking yourself: "What is this reflective space for?" The answer will be more about what you are trying to achieve as an end of providing reflective space. Although some may argue that ends and means are inseparable, in the exercise of creating your framework it is important not to stop the inquiry prematurely but to continue to drill down to a better understanding of what you are hoping to achieve.

At the same time, it is important to recognise that the ultimate purpose of your professional practice, however you articulate it, should not completely overshadow the real coach in front of you in the supervision session. If, for example, you have a personal commitment to serving the profession or humanity as a whole, this ultimate purpose has to be translated into something more concrete that allows you and the coach you work with to have reasonably clear expectations of what the progress or lack of it would look like.

Here are some specific questions that you may want to consider when thinking about the second P of your framework:

- When contracting with a coach, how would you know that you could add value to their practice?
- What would tell you that your supervision session was a good one?

- What would tell you that your long-term supervision of a coach has been successful or at least worthwhile?
- On what basis would you say that a session was a waste of time?
- On what basis would you stop supervising someone?
- What sort of feedback from the coach would make you change your model of supervision?

Process

Thinking about the "process" element of the 3 Ps probably requires the least explanation. Models of the process of sessions such as GROW (Whitmore, 2002) and CLEAR (Hawkins and Smith, 2013) are often our very first guide to practice as coaches. We become familiar with these models, use them on a day-to-day basis, and we have found that most practitioners we have worked with on developing their own practice model find it easier to think about this level of their model than the deeper, less explicit influences we have discussed in the previous two sections. The challenge here may be less about the abstract thinking involved and more about finding a way of looking at our practices with fresh eyes.

In a small-scale research project, we found that the coaches we interviewed tended to adopt practices according to preferences that are predicted by Bandura's "self-efficacy theory" (Bandura, 1977). That is to say coaches seemed to adopt processes most readily, using Bandura's terms, in the following order of priority: as a consequence of "performance accomplishments" (i.e. they had experienced success using the technique); "vicarious experience" (they had witnessed the technique working); and, finally, "verbal persuasion" (someone with credibility had told them to use it or that it works). These findings certainly appear to have face validity and interestingly it also reflects how trainers might structure a learning event.

Importantly for the current discussion, this suggests that we may have built up practices based on quite immediate experiences *at a particular time in our development*. These practices may not thereafter come under a great deal of overt scrutiny. The pattern for most people is more likely to be that our initial experience has a very strong impact, and then we gradually evolve our practices in ways that are comfortable for us. They may no longer reflect the practice we wish to build.

We therefore need to ask ourselves the following questions about the practices we adopt:

- What appeals to me about this approach/method/tool?
- Where does it work well, who for?
- How do we know it works?
- Where has it not worked well?
- When we think of it working well, to what *purpose* does it contribute?
- In what ways does it fit our *philosophy*?
- What does using this method tell our clients about our philosophy and purpose?

The process is not just about pruning out dead wood, though. We also have the opportunity both to understand our own practice more clearly and to grow our own toolkit in ways that are appropriate to that understanding. Consequently, there are two further questions to ask:

- What approaches do I feel antipathy towards and why?
- What new methods would embody my understanding of my philosophy and purpose now?

Integrating the model

Unsurprisingly, carrying through the whole process of investigating one's own model may be more difficult in practice than it might appear on paper. As we have the same assumptions, beliefs and perceptual lenses when practising as we do when reviewing our practice, it is easy to miss things. Some of the struggles we have witnessed include the following.

An over-concentration on the process element: as a natural consequence of our coaching practice being an applied discipline there is a tendency to think only in practical terms. Some practitioners' training may further have focused on the "how" more than the "why". Whether this is the case for an individual or not, it is much easier to think in those terms about practice and we have a ready vocabulary for doing so.

It is sometimes difficult to align different elements: in thinking about the 3 Ps, we are shifting perspectives and thinking about an issue from many angles at once. This is not a familiar exercise for everyone, and it is quite natural to try to resolve problems *within* each frame. Looking *across* frames is like comparing apples and oranges. We need to consider carefully how elements at each level of the resulting model connect to those at different levels of the model. Where there are mismatches there may be unresolved incongruences within the practitioner's own belief system, which could ultimately result in conflicts in practice.

The use of eclecticism as a rationale in itself: various writers on coaching argue persuasively for strongly practically oriented criteria of "fitness for purpose" that is manifested in the use of multiple theories, instruments and styles of practice (Clutterbuck and Megginson, 2009; Cox, 2013). However, it is easy for such eclecticism, as it is often termed, and its legitimate pragmatic foundations, to be used carelessly as a surrogate for proper investigation. While a practitioner may well fruitfully draw influences from many traditions, the principle of practice reflecting the *self* demands some form of integration. The PPP framework is attempting to make that integration explicit and reflexive.

There are therefore some useful questions about alignment. It may be easier to explore these with a "critical friend" (perhaps even a coach or supervisor):

- In what way are your Ps aligned?
- Are there any elements of practice that don't have a rationale in your philosophy?
- Are there any principles in your philosophy that have not materialised in action?

Case studies: personal experiences of using the PPP model

In this section we would like the process, as far as possible to "speak for itself". Here we present two accounts from coaching supervisors with whom we have worked through the Advanced Professional Certificate in Coaching Supervision.

James

Dr James Pritchard came to the process as, he says, after "coaching for 25 years . . . it was time to learn more". In part wanting to formalise and integrate his extensive experience in both coaching and supervision, he also wanted a process that would push his learning. The following is reproduced with permission.

> Clearing space to think and write is always a struggle for me, so many activities are more seductive than a blank page! But in this case, I was fortunate to be able to borrow an apartment in the Swiss Alps for a few days and this proved a wonderful opportunity. Armed with a laptop, internet connection and a couple of indispensable books, I established a routine of working for a few hours and then walking in the mountains until hunger got the better of me. It was between seasons, so everything was shut for maintenance, adding to the air of tranquillity.
>
> The brief was to develop and explore a model based on the three components of Philosophy, Purpose and Process. We were also offered a list of areas to be assessed, giving a welcome structure to what would have been a self-indulgent ramble. The exercise encouraged me to link a strand of thinking, coming from mindfulness practices in yoga and Buddhism to what I actually do as a coach or supervisor. All too often we may express a particular belief, but not ask the question; "If I really believed that, how would it change what I do?" My starting point was how different elements of an individual human being

interact to generate and articulate an issue for coaching. This is loosely drawn from the idea of sheaths underlying much of yoga and Ayurveda. The complexity increases when, as supervisors, we include the coach as part of the system and the supervisor him/herself. As well as passing the external validation, I was keen to meet my own "so what?" test. I wanted a model to support the supervisee towards a next step, rather than simply provide a way of organising what he/she already knows. So, this model needed an algorithmic property.

In my own practice, I use this model in four different ways:

1.   This philosophy has become embedded in how I work, so in one sense I can't not apply the thinking, but it is largely unconscious and just pops up occasionally as a conscious connection.
2.   Less commonly, I base my enquiry quite deliberately on the model, without sharing the model itself with the client, much in the way a coach might use GROW to inform their questions.
3.   Occasionally, I discuss the model with the coach/client and engage in a shared enquiry of how it might shed light on the case and how we could proceed.
4.   In some cases, where there is explicit permission, I have been able to act out the model, through physical yoga practice, linking back to the model elements.

Both the model itself and application in practice are work in progress, but provide a helpful focus for reflection on how to intervene fruitfully in the coach/client system. Without the discipline of researching and writing, I may continue doing what I have always done and miss out on what I already know.
(James Pritchard, personal communication, 14 June, 2017)

James' account describes an interesting balance of discipline and patience to allow a full understanding to emerge.

James has described the ways in which the PPP process encouraged him to connect his supervision practice with other practices and beliefs that already constituted his professional world. He has also emphasised a personal pragmatism in the process of making his philosophy meaningful. We may not all have the opportunity to create such a reflective space as James was able to in his mountain retreat, but it demonstrates the necessity of time and space.

Natalia

In a second account, Natalia de Estevan-Ubeda illustrates a very different way of interacting with the model.

> What does it take to develop a supervision model and what happens in the process?
>
> After the training week was completed, I had a sense that "things" were falling into place in as much as I had had the theoretical input, the practice "runs" and the supervision feedback on my supervision during a very enriching week, full of experiential learning. I was faced with the challenge of making it all my own, and by this I mean, understanding how my values, my background, my own experiences, were shaping "me" as a supervisor in the making.
>
> The process of understanding who I am in the context of my learning was invaluable, and not easy. It took months of reflection and introspection, endless trips from a micro-level where I would go through detail, to a meta-perspective taking me where bigger themes came together. For instance, that was when I put together how values and beliefs are linked to my model, which in turn is underpinned by theory, congruent with who I am and how I practise.
>
> Once I had the building blocks, it was a matter of testing that my model was indeed "showing up" in my practice. This was another invaluable part of the process because it helped me to examine my practice from another dimension, one which allowed me to reconcile what I thought my model was all about and the evidence that was coming back through analysing my practice, which was telling me there

were aspects I hadn't noticed before. Examining one's practice through recordings and feedback is perhaps something we have all gone through to some extent, however, what has been fundamentally different this time is what, in my view, gives this process of accreditation the value-add as a true transformational learning process. And the difference has been that I have had to evaluate my own practice, decide what was a good session and a session which I wouldn't be too happy with and be able to put my arguments forward and check them against my model in the first instance.

I have had to articulate my model and discuss my practice with the Faculty, through an extremely helpful process of enquiry which was, without a doubt, one of the richest moments of learning I have experienced. This process has allowed me to become more aware of my habits when supervising, my comfort areas, my tendency to default to certain functions of supervision and the most valuable learning of all for me at the time, and still to this day, "meeting my client where my client is".

Thinking about my practice in this way is different from what I have done before because it has given me the opportunity to take the time to consolidate my learning and revisit my supervision model through a period of time. This has not been a process of dreaming up a plausible model and putting it aside; instead, this has truly given me the opportunity to capture my model at a point in time, test it, revisit it, evolve it, find its core and its edges. It has made my model alive. The impact of my practice is such that I am now much more able to stay with the client and not be drawn towards displaying all the competences, because even when you do, it can still fall short of being a good session. The most challenging part of the process for me has been the part that relates to time. A supervision model is not born out of a training course, it is borne out of a process of reflection, enquiry, dialogue, and time . . . time to practice.

(Natalia de Estevan-Ubeda, personal communication, 30 June 2017)

Natalia gives a flavour of how she moved from the conceptual side of building a model, to practice, and back again. She talks about the process of "developing, testing and evolving my supervision model". Although her problem-solving style, as it emerges in the way she addresses the exercise, is very different from James' approach, she similarly highlights how the model challenges her to integrate her practice with her sense of self, even extending to re-evaluating previously held assumptions.

These cases illustrate not just a process of explaining a pre-existing practice, but developing that practice, and particularly developing its integration with the practitioner's sense of self, through the process of an analytical and reflexive articulation.

Conclusion

In this chapter we have explained the derivation of our PPP framework from David Lane's earlier work, the rationale for adapting that framework to one that orients more clearly to the development of a personally congruent model of practice, and how we have put the framework into effect with coaches and supervisors. While thinking about the philosophy, purpose and process of one's practice model may take some effort (and time and space) to achieve, we fervently believe that it takes practitioners' ethics, performance and professionalism beyond what can be specified through a skills or competency approach. The accounts generously provided by James and Natalia illustrate all this and, further, the personal satisfaction derived from the process.

We hope that, in the course of our explanations, we have also given enough practical guidance to create sufficient opportunity for readers to explore this framework for thinking about their own practice model. Supervision, coaching, group work and whatever facilitates your own thinking are of enormous assistance here.

Practice points

1. You can start from where you are comfortable; the process is cyclical and iterative, so as long as you stay open to change it doesn't matter where you take the first step.

2. When you reflect on process, include a prompt to connect your reflections to *purpose* and *philosophy*.
3. Notice when your work feels congruent.
4. Engage with new ideas, especially those that you might normally dismiss. When you look from an appreciative stance, what now works for you (or still doesn't)?
5. Use values exercises.
6. Reflect on PPP in supervision.

Discussion points

1. In what situations or with which clients are you least comfortable working? Explore where these situations present challenges for the different aspects of your model.
2. Take no more than five minutes to bullet point what you know about your own *Philosophy, Purpose* and *Process.* Now expand just one of them.
3. Whose practice excites your curiosity? Explore why.
4. Explore what gives you strength and energy when you are practising.

Suggested reading

Bachkirova, T., Jackson, P. and Clutterbuck, D. (2011). *Coaching and Mentoring Supervision.* Maidenhead: Open University Press.

Lennard, D. (2010). *Coaching Models: A Cultural Perspective: A Guide to Model Development for Practitioners and Students of Coaching.* London: Routledge.

McGonagill, G. (2002). The coach as reflective practitioner: Notes from a journey without end. In C. and J. G. Berger (Eds), *Executive Coaching: Practices and Perspectives,* Palo Alto, CA: Davies Black.

Rowan, J. and Jacobs, M. (2002). *The Therapist's Use of Self,* Buckingham: Open University Press.

References

Argyris, C. and Schön, D. A. (1974). *Theory in Practice: Increasing Professional Effectiveness.* San Francisco, CA: Jossey-Bass.

Bachkirova, T. (2016). The self of the coach: Conceptualization, issues, and opportunities for practitioner development. *Consulting Psychology Journal: Practice and Research*, 68(2), 143–156.

Bachkirova, T., Jackson, P. and Clutterbuck, D. (2011). *Coaching and Mentoring Supervision*. Maidenhead: Open University Press.

Bachkirova, T. and Lawton Smith, C. (2015). From competencies to capabilities in the assessment and accreditation of coaches. *International Journal of Evidence Based Coaching & Mentoring*, 13(2), 123–140.

Bandura, A. (1977). Self-efficacy: toward a unifying theory of behavioral change. *Psychological review*, 84(2), 191.

Blackburn, S. (1999). *Think: A Compelling Introduction to Philosophy*. Oxford: Oxford University Press.

Clutterbuck, D. and Megginson, D. (2009). *Further Techniques for Coaching and Mentoring*. Oxford: Butterworth-Heinemann.

Cox, E. (2013) *Coaching Understood: A Pragmatic Enquiry into the Coaching Process*. London: SAGE.

Cox, E., Bachkirova, T. and Clutterbuck, D. (Eds). (2014). *The Complete Handbook of Coaching*. 2nd ed. London: Sage.

Hawkins, P. and Shohet, R. (2012). *Supervision in the Helping Professions*. 4th ed. Maidenhead: McGraw-Hill Education (UK).

Hawkins, P. and Schwenk, G. (2011). The seven-eyed model of coaching supervision. In T. Bachkirova, P. Jackson and D. Clutterbuck (Eds), *Coaching ing Supervision: Theory and practice*. Maidenhead: Open University Press.

Hawkins, P. and Smith, N. (2013). *Coaching, Mentoring and Organizational Consultancy: Supervision, Skills and Development*. 2nd edition. Maidenhead: Open University Press.

Kegan, R. (1982). *The Evolving Self: Problem and Process in Human Development*. London: Harvard University Press.

Lane, D. (2006). The emergence of supervision models. *Presentation at the Annual Conference of the Special Group in Coaching Psychology of the BPS*, (unpublished).

Lane, D., Watts, M. and Corrie, S. (2016). *Supervision in the Psychological Professions: Building Your Own Personalized Model*. London: Open University Press.

McGonagill, G. (2002). The coach as reflective practitioner: Notes from a journey without end. In C. Fitzgerald and J. G. Berger,

Executive coaching: Practices and Perspectives. Palo Alto, CA: Davies-Black, 59–88.

Proctor, B. (1994). Supervision-competence, confidence, accountability. *British Journal of Guidance and Counselling*, 22(3), 309–319.

Whitmore, J. (2002). *Coaching for Performance: GROWing Human Potential and Performance*. 3rd ed. London: Nicholas Brealey.

3

Diversity and inclusion in supervision

Judy Ryde, Lily Seto and Damian Goldvarg

Introduction

Open and reflective supervision is essential for understanding and working with the way that diversity and culture enter into the work of the coach as well as into the work of the supervision itself. Basic to working effectively in a diverse world is the understanding that we, as supervisors, are participants in the three-cornered meeting that is supervision. We bring our own culture and its assumptions with us as do the other two participants, the coach and the coachee. To fully understand this, we need to discover and acknowledge the particular norms, prejudices and assumptions that we can fall into. We cannot exclude ourselves from the field of inquiry and neither can our supervisee. This exploration includes the power dynamics between us, and between our supervisee and their coachee, both those given to us by our role and by our culture. So, understanding ourselves, our supervisees and their coachees within a diverse world is truly at the heart of all supervision, not on the margins as it sometimes seems to be but ever-present, whether or not it is acknowledged.

Relating across difference in culture, used in its widest sense to include gender, sexual identity, sexual orientation, age, heritage and disability, is not something that is in a different "box" to the normal relating in supervision or with coachees. It is almost always present. This chapter explores these considerations using an approach that understands relationship to be at the core of the work and will help supervisors learn how to approach diversity and cultural difference in a sensitive and inquiring way rather than make sweeping readymade assumptions.

The development of this relational approach to supervision

Our simple definition of culture is that it is a human grouping that provides a holding milieu of accepted ways of being that are implicit in groups (Ryde, 2009). Culture can be narrowly understood as concerning nationality or race but in this chapter, we are including all types of culture. These include: *geographical* cultures such as countries and regions; *social* cultures such as race, class, sexual orientation, sexual identity and gender; and *organisational* cultures including different sectors such as private, public and third sectors. We explore how culture is present within coaching and supervision and how understanding its influence can lead us to work more effectively as supervisors.

Three of us wrote this chapter. There are cultural differences between us which have been helpful in providing some breadth to our writing. Judy Ryde is a white English woman who trains coach supervisors in working across cultures and with diversity. Lily Seto is an experienced coach, mentor and coaching supervisor, of Chinese heritage, and teaches on an intercultural coaching programme in Canada, and Damian is from Argentina, working in the USA and is a Master Certified Coach.

Addressing diversity and cultural difference in supervision has been somewhat ignored for many years though has been flagged as an issue, for instance by Brown and Bourne (Brown and Bourne, 1996: 32). Hawkins and Shohet included a chapter in the third edition of *Supervision in the Helping Professions* (2007). It has become, over the years, more and more evident that the reflective space offered by supervision can help the manager or professional to better understand the complexity of the work, including intercultural aspects, and ensure that a blindness to their own issues does not get in the way of effective work.

An understanding of the geographical, social and organisational cultural contexts of our supervisees and their coachees and client organisations should always be part of this learning as well as of ourselves as supervisors. It would be tempting to think that working across difference of culture was just tricky but interesting, if it were not for power differences between the different cultures. These can include, for example, differences between men and women, black and white, differences in gender and sexuality and class differences. Power of this sort is not always easy to recognise or challenge and plays into historical uses and abuses of power. In regard to race, the echoes of slavery and white domination can be heard to this day (Alcoff, 2015: 137; Eddo-Lodge, 2017: 134). This domination includes the ownership of land and property, which brings wealth and power in its wake, including access to education and political institutions. More recently discriminatory practices and institutional racism in the job market, housing, police etc are evident (Alcoff, 2015: 68; Eddo-Lodge, 2017: 420; Frankenberg, 1999: 319). The secondary place of women within a gendered society is still apparent in spite of laws banning discrimination. Deeply embedded class differences, particularly in Britain, are woven into the fabric of society (Savage: 2015:4). These factors, of course, play themselves out in the coaching and coaching supervision situation. A supervisee of Judy's seemed withdrawn and defensive in supervision. When I tentatively approached this with her, she revealed that she thought I was patronising her by explaining what I meant too simply. This led to a good exploration in which I owned my own part in this and she explored her previous experiences as a working-class woman who was very aware of this kind of subtle undermining.

It is important to remember that power differences will also include other power dimensions as well as cultural ones, particularly role power and personal power. Role power is assigned to people who have been given authority, often, but not necessarily, within a work setting; personal power is taken by people who have a natural or learnt ability to carry authority; and cultural power is held by people who

Role power

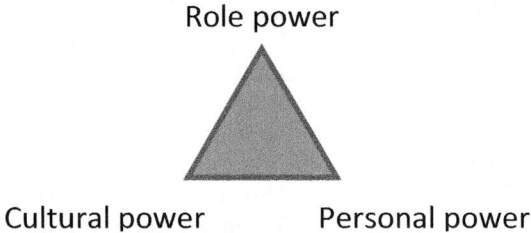

Cultural power   Personal power

Figure 3.1   Power triangle

come from cultures that are the most privileged. Figure 3.1 helps us to keep these in mind when coaching or supervising (Hawkins: 2012: 121).

Each of these will influence the other. For instance, the supervisor always has the role power within a supervision session with a coach. If the supervisor is black and the coach is white then the coach will nevertheless have a more powerful cultural place in the interaction (Brown and Bourne, 1996: 39). If, however, the coach's personal power is great then this will mitigate the effect of the role power and cultural power.

The practice of supervision across difference

So how can we get beneath, understand and recognise our own ways of thinking so that what we normally understand as "just how things are" is seen only as our own assumptions and not necessarily shared by all of humanity? Some things seem so obvious that we don't even notice that they exist. As the Chinese proverb goes, "the last one to know about the sea is the fish".

The Indian philosopher, Krishnamurti, said: "You might think you are thinking your own thoughts but you are not, you are thinking your culture's thoughts" (Mang and Haggard, 2016: 208). He is pointing out that we have the impression that we have complete agency over our own thoughts but that, in fact, we are limited to ideas and ways of thinking that are endemic within our cultures and therefore see the world through that lens. He says:

So your mind is not apart from society, it is not distinct from your culture, from your religion, from your various class divisions, from the ambitions and conflicts of the many. All this is society, and you are part of it. There is no "you" separate from society.

(Krishnamurti, 1989: 32)

He also says: "But if you don't know how your mind works you cannot actually understand what society is, because your mind is part of society; it is society."

If we accept this idea, it has a profound effect on how we understand ourselves within our cultural context.

When training supervisors we have a way of helping them to discover these allusive assumptions. We ask them to say what immediately comes into their mind when they finish certain sentences like these (the reader may also like to try this):

Assumptions exercise

I assume that:

People are ....

I feel ashamed when ....

The most important thing in life is ....

Time is ....

Money is ....

When in trouble I always ....

Black people are ....

White people are ....

Disabled people are ....

Homosexuality is ....

Heterosexuality is ....

Remembering the past is ....

In this way, we can quickly see what we hold to be truths, even those that are not conscious or are semi-conscious. It can reveal things we would rather not own but also things we think are self-evidently true. Discussing this with others who hold different assumptions can show us that they are not shared universally.

The assumptions revealed by this exercise may expose our ways of thinking that arise from the different cultures in which we are embedded, including membership of small cultural groups like our family or profession. For instance, in one group where this exercise was carried out, finishing the sentence that begins "Money is . . ." revealed cultural differences between coaches and other helping professionals. Helping professionals tended to avoid talking about money, which, on reflection in the group, revealed a denial of its importance. Coaches, who often come from business backgrounds or work within companies, were not so shy of being clear that money could be a motivating factor for them in the choice of becoming a supervisor. The challenge to cultural norms and the subsequent dialogue about it was useful and productive on both sides.

There are also assumptions that arise in much broader cultural groups. Psychological and coaching professions arise, in the main, from western culture and, in many ways, share the underlying assumptions of the western world where assumptions based on the primacy of the individual are important. On the other hand, people from many other parts of the world come from cultures that have collectivist assumptions (Laungani, 2004; Tulpa and Bresser, 2009). This chart (Table 3.1), which Judy developed for her teaching, shows some of these assumptions and how they differ between the two types of culture. These two are not as hard and fast as this chart might imply, particularly as many people from collectivist cultures are influenced by the West. However, there is a tendency in these directions and, in our experience, it is useful and productive to recognise them.

Table 3.1 shows the ways in which very different ways of thinking seem natural, self-evident truths to members of each type of culture. These differences can lead to massive misunderstanding. Catching these misunderstandings in supervision can help your supervisee to find empathy for people they found hard to comprehend and to whom they feel quite alien.

Table 3.1 Values and assumptions of individualistic and collectivist cultures

Values and assumptions	Individualistic cultures	Collectivist cultures
The unit of society is	The individual.	The family or community.
Individuals	Should develop themselves as far as they can – in Maslow's terms "self-actualise" (Maslow: 1972: 40).	Should work towards the good of their family or community.
The self	Is something that "belongs" to an individual.	Cannot be extricated from a group identity.
Authenticity is	Important as we have a "true" self and it is important to be true to it.	About honouring the collective context and your role within it.
Membership of community	Is there to support individual well-being.	Is there to support the wellbeing of the family and community.
Coaching, psychotherapy, counselling and healing	Help people to know themselves more deeply and resolve personal difficulties and conflicts.	Stresses the connections within relationship and can be in the context of ancestors. Sometimes within a religious or spiritual context.
Supervision	Help individuals to reflect on their work with other individuals.	Help individuals or small groups reflect on how their work impacts on the groups they live and work with.

Here is an example given by Lily:

I was raised straddling two cultures (Canadian and Chinese) and I have, over time, learned to shift back and forth between the two modes. For example, my Chinese background has taught me to be collectivistic. When I first started coaching, and then became a supervisor, I would, at times overcompensate by becoming individualistic (especially when working with people from Western backgrounds). To take a more balanced approach I have found it helpful to explore these differences by using Rosinksi's Cultural Orientation Framework (Rosinski: 2013), as a simplified model to initiate a conversation about these differences. Rosinski's framework assesses seven dimensions/orientations of culture, which are based on the work of anthropologists and leaders in the communications and cross-cultural fields. They include the following dimensions: sense of power and responsibility, time management approaches, definitions of identity and purpose, organisational arrangements, notions of territory and boundaries, communication patterns and modes of thinking. Rosinski asserts that the optimum way to work across cultures is to leverage the polar dimensions.

In working this way, we are trying to dialogue across difference so that even though our own perspective can be very different from the person we are communicating with, their point of view is held as just as valid. We may even find some aspects of the perspective of the other person sheds light on our own experience of life.

Here is another example from Lily:

As a woman and a member of a visible minority, I am aware that there is a possibility of being seen as in a lesser personal or cultural power position. I tend to feel that I need to have even better qualifications than others to prove my worth. I recognize that I am always striving to learn more in order to be of value and service. This speaks to the research that shows many people of the non-dominant culture can feel under-confident with the same amount of training as someone from the dominant race. The first time I worked with a white male supervisee, I noticed that I was less effective than I wanted to be. I took my dilemma to my supervisor and realised that I had a learned cultural deference threshold (Hawkins and Smith, 2006: 293) to white males and that I needed to acknowledge this and work through it so that I could become more effective as a coaching supervisor (and coach). I know that my role power mitigates some of this, as well as my personal power, and was able to let this impediment go.

Intersubjective systems theory

Intersubjective systems theory (IST) is a psychotherapeutic theory based on phenomenology (Atwood and Stolorow, 2014), which helps us to understand this perspective. It is a perspective that rejects the notion that individuals have a "separate mind". It asserts that we exist within an intersubjective context or "field" and that we are constantly changing in relation to that field as different influences arise. The meeting between the coach and the coachee and between the supervisor and supervisee are therefore co-created. What happens between us does not "belong" to either of us. It is often thought that one of the jobs of the coach or the supervisor is to try to decide if what we are experiencing or feeling "belongs" to us or to our coachee or supervisee. This idea looks different when seen intersubjectively. If we co-create our experience then it belongs to both of us and, in fact to the wider world we inhabit.

Here is an example from Judy's practice, which illustrates working in this "space between".

> I worked in a threesome of myself, an interpreter and an Arabic client. There is a connection between the interpreter and the client. They belong to the same national culture so share many of the same basic assumptions and ways of approaching life. They are both Muslim and deeply religious and they both have had to flee their country, so share something of what that means to them. The interpreter and I are both professional women and work within a Primary Care Trust together. The threads of professionalism and care and respect for clients join us within a professional cultural norm. The client and I are both women in late middle age who have married and had children and know the depth of feeling and contact that that brings us. There is a web that joins us in this profound knowledge. We are all joined by our human experience and cultural knowledge though this web may be thicker in some places than others.

Intersubjective Systems Theory helps us when it comes to understanding difference in culture, as these differences exist within the space created in the meeting. It provides a third perspective that has elements of both individualistic and collectivist cultures and aids those of us who come from individualistic cultures to understand those who are immersed in a collectivist one. It helps us to understand all life as interconnected and co-created so that we do not exist within separate units but live within "nested systems" (Hawkins, 2017: 224) that are mutually influencing. This can be seen when a third column is added for IST in Table 3.1.

We see here that many of the precepts of collectivist cultures are similar to ones from Intersubjective Systems Theory but the sense of all being within a web of relating goes beyond cultural boundaries and includes all of creation including the "more-than-human world" (Abram, 1996: 256). We find that this philosophical basis helps us not only to understand collectivist cultures but to make relating across difference

Table 3.2   Values and assumptions using intersubjective systems theory

Values and assumptions	Intersubjective systems theory
The unit of society is	Indivisible.
Individuals	Do not exist except within relationships or within systemic contexts.
The self	The self is fluid and only exists as organising principles within relationship.
Authenticity is	Co-created through relationships.
Membership of community	Is the medium in which the individual forms and changes.
Coaching, psychotherapy, counselling and healing	Is undertaken within the awareness of the context of a web of relating.
Supervision	Helps individuals within their context to reflect on their work within the space opened up by the connection between themselves, their clients and the supervisor.

more natural. Within this framework, what happens in any meeting, including between coach and coachee and (Argyris, 1978) supervisor and supervisee, arises between us and this emergent reality is what we can reflect on in supervision, both by encouraging our supervisee to look at what has arisen between themselves and their coachee and between themselves and their supervisor. Here is a third example from Lily's work:

> I was raised partly in the Western culture and partly in the traditional Chinese culture. This can show up in my coaching supervision as: "women are to be demure and non-confrontational" and that it is important not to make eye contact with the dominant culture. These messages were embedded in my culture and I have had to acknowledge them and release them in order to be an effective supervisor in this Western world. While I am aware of these scripts, I also acknowledge that they are a part of who I am, and so, I am often quieter and non-confrontational. I have had to learn to be more challenging.

This example is taken from Judy's work with a refugee:

> I noticed that a particular client of one of my supervisees had not been brought to supervision for several sessions and I could see from my notes that he was about to be reunited with his wife. My supervisee immediately said she felt that she should have brought him for supervision and seemed to feel ashamed of not having done so. This client was a refugee who had gained British Citizenship and his wife was going to join him after several years' separation. My supervisee told me that he had been looking forward to this event but when it occurred they found that it was hard to re-find their connection and had had so many rows that she had moved away from him. It had taken several weeks for him to tell my supervisee that this had occurred and several weeks before my supervisee told me. We thought that there may be shame and anger in the intersubjective field which led to this being hidden. When the supervisee went back to the client, she helped the client to stay with feelings about the way his wife left him, and he began to express

his resentment both about women and about British culture which had, from his point of view, driven a wedge between him and his wife. This helped him to process very difficult feelings that he was experiencing.

A notion that is particularly helpful in understanding how culture influences our ways of thinking, is that of "organising principles" put forward by Stolorow and Atwood (1992), who are intersubjective systems theorists. These principles are imbued in us as children in both overt messages from important figures such as parents and teachers but also, more covertly and unconsciously, from our culture as the "way things are". These messages will be a mixture of communications from family and community as well as from the wider culture. For instance, a message received overtly might be "Charity begins at home, so we look after our own first" and covertly the message may be "We don't really trust people who are not just like us so we don't make friends with them or invite them into our house". The covert message is usually very powerful in its effect on our thoughts and behaviour so that, even as an adult, if we are persuaded that it is important not to be racist, the underlying message wins out in our behaviour, if not in our espoused point of view.

So how is this a useful idea in supervision and how can we work with it? First, it is good to remember that what has been learnt covertly or unconsciously is more powerful and harder to shift than conscious messages. It is harder to recognise unconscious material and bring it into consciousness where it can be reflected upon. It is also harder to access these underlying assumptions as a supervisor, so we need to find ways of contacting this material. One way is to be alive to and reflect on one's own spontaneous responses. If we take on board that we are all interconnected we can see that, although the coachee and the coachee's client are not present in the room, they are, in fact, present through the interconnection with the coach. The supervisor may well find themself having certain feelings or emotional responses or experiencing certain images when hearing about the coaching and these may well have a bearing on the coaching and be a clue to what is arising unconsciously.

None of us is immune from "thinking our culture's thoughts" as Krishnamurti said (Mang and Haggard, 2016: 208) and therefore from seeing experience through the eyes of our culture. The supervisor and coach are just as subject to this as are all the other people in the "field", such as the coachee and their clients. It is not really possible to learn to be culture-free but rather to be aware that we do see the world through those spectacles and take that into account.

For instance, Judy has a Chinese supervisee who works in Singapore where many of the population, including most of his coachees, are ethnic Chinese. Having trained in supervision with Judy he has tried to be less directive in his stance to his coaches and more exploratory, putting thoughts out to be considered rather than providing his coachees with directives to be acted upon. He said in the course of supervision: "They have to learn that I am not God and they can think things out for themselves." This led to an interesting discussion about cultural differences where Western culture encourages individual autonomy and Chinese culture gives greater value to respecting those who are older and more experienced. From our point of view there is not a definitive answer to whether or not he should act from within his culture or take on board a more Western approach. Ironically, I take this stance from within my culture, as it does not give him a definitive answer to the dilemma! It does, however, bring the issues to the surface to be considered.

This shows how an individual's way of responding may arise from their culture but can look pathological from the viewpoint of another culture. In the case of the Chinese coaches above, we could have viewed the desire to be shown what to do as evidence of being over-dependent as individuals rather than understanding them to be acting appropriately within the cultural context. Another example of this is the meaning given to eye contact. In Western cultures, an ability to hold eye contact is seen as evidence of confidence and trustworthiness. In many other cultures, including, as we saw above, the Chinese culture in which Lily was raised, it is considered rude for those of lower status to hold eye contact with those of higher status. Those of lower status might include young people or women, for example.

Case study from Lily Seto's work

Jennifer is a very experienced executive coach. We contract for six supervision sessions, and before starting our engagement, I see that she is highly educated and an experienced German coach and works internationally within a large global organisation. I am different from her in that I am a visible minority, born in Canada to Chinese immigrants. I too am experienced but only speak English. My international work is within English-speaking countries and is usually within the public and not-for-profit sectors.

As I go into my first session I wondered if I would be good enough for this highly skilled German coach. Will we understand each other, and do I need to prepare to ensure I do not offend her? I find it surprising that this white person would choose me, from a visible minority, and I feel my deference threshold (Hawkins and Smith, 2006: 293) show up. I have learnt over the years that we all have an equal voice, but this old familiar script does sometimes reappear.

To help myself, and to ensure deference does not intrude on our work, I can see that Jennifer holds the cultural power in this relationship, being from the dominant culture. I hold the role power, as a trained supervisor. When I think of personal power, I see us as equals. We are both strong, independent women working in the male-dominated business world. In this awareness, I become curious as to why she chose to work with me. I remind myself that I need to contract about how we will work together and keep re-contracting to ensure that her needs, the needs of her organisation and mine, are being met. It is important that I am willing to be a true partner by bringing my thoughts and intuition to the session. I feel a huge release of tension in my shoulders.

Our first session feels stilted. We speak about the contract; how we will work together and what she wants from me and the sessions. I ask her why she chose me to work with. She openly shares that she is drawn to how I use energy in supervision (she witnessed this in a demonstration session). She herself has a quality of energy that is inviting and open and curious. We have a couple of laughs together. We start the work and I feel into where we are going. At the end of the first session, I reflect on how we were able to hold space, that there was some good learning happening and that I am feeling good about this partnership. I learn about myself too; that I am almost putting too much emphasis on diversity. I remind myself that I have over 500 hours of supervision (both individual and group), and that my role power will serve me well. What if I held that each person is an individual within their own particular culture and context and that the key is to make no assumptions? Rather, hold the space and contract well and keep checking in on where the contract needs to potentially shift. And, more importantly, check in with myself to notice any biases. I am aware that I can never eliminate these but can bring them into my awareness.

The first time I check in on our contract is during our fifth session. I notice that there is a parallel process about contracting with her coachees and how we have been contracting. I ask what she needs more of or less of. She is very open and lets me know that this session was the best yet for her. She requests that I bring more of myself, as she found it very useful during this session. I realise that while I may share my emotional responses (Hawkins and Shohet, 2007), I don't normally share stories and examples of myself. I make a note to myself that this supervisee appreciates more stories and experiences related to her case; perhaps to normalise what is happening and her feelings.

What I have learned, as a visible minority working in a dominantly white profession, is that it is important to

- always be myself
- work on the diversity that shows up in the work
- have faith that my energy work is always valuable and remain at the service of my coachee and their client.

Case study from Damian Goldvarg's work

A colleague referred Ana for supervision with Damian because, even though she has been an executive coach for many years, she had never worked with a supervisor and wanted help with a particular client, Pat. Pat was a lesbian and had personal challenges about "coming out" at work and being able to share her personal life with colleagues. Pat was afraid of being discriminated against and was insecure about disclosing personal information but was also aware that she was not bringing the whole of herself to her work. Ana had not experienced a similar situation in the past and wanted somebody to reflect with her on her personal reactions as she thought they might impact negatively on her work with this client. She was referred by a mutual colleague who thought that Damian could be a good match for Ana and provide useful insights into her gay coachee: both he and Ana were immigrants to the US from Argentina and Damian and Pat were gay. Even though Ana was originally from the same country as Damian, there were many cultural differences, including their gender, age, sexual orientation and religion (Ana was Catholic, Damian Jewish). They had some cultural codes in common that helped them to build trust but many personal differences, even in their different professional trainings: Damian is a Master Certified Coach and Ana had never received formal training but had many years of experience as an executive in corporations, which Damian did not have. All of these similarities and differences operated in the background and played a role in the dynamics of their relationship. Ana committed to learning how to support a gay client who wanted to "come out" but risked being discriminated against.

At the beginning, it was easy for Ana to share her concerns and feelings about not being effective with a client with whom there were so many differences. However, she baulked at the suggestion that she confront and explore her own homophobic unconscious reactions and the internalised homophobia (Davies, 1996: 54) of her client. Damian considered the possibility that his cultural and role power could be affecting the relationship and decided to share his own internalised homophobia which he regards as inevitable in those who grow up gay in a heterosexual world.

He decided to ask Ana if he and Pat reminded her of people in her personal or work life. She was now more willing to be vulnerable and recognised that Damian reminded her of a white, gay boss who was younger than her. He made her feel awkward and undervalued. Pat reminded her of her daughter who doesn't like to be confronted and challenged in her thinking. Damian invited her to use this awareness and insight to express her needs with her coachee as well as with himself.

By exploring some of these diversity issues, Ana was able to open up, be more vulnerable and willing to provide and receive feedback. Ana brought some of her learning from supervision to the work with her coachee and was now able to move on constructively.

Conclusion

Working across difference in culture is not something that is bolted on to supervision or that only happens when there is an obvious difference in culture present; it is a factor that always needs to be discovered and worked with. Furthermore, we as supervisors need to understand that all the parties involved, ourselves, the coach and their coachee, each bring our own cultures into the supervision space, and it is our reflection on what arises in the space that is the work of supervision.

An attempt on our part, as supervisors, to understand others' culture whilst not owning and understanding our own will often lead to stereotyping and we will miss nuances that arise which may be key to a deeper grasp of the issues that lead to systemic shifts (Hawkins, 2012: 153). Each individual carries several cultures (including, for example, their nationality, race, class, sexuality, family and work) into meetings with others. This is made more complex by the history behind those cultures – an obvious example being slavery for African and West Indian people – which then mix and intermingle. This produces, within the alchemical vessel of the coaching supervision space, something that is a bit like a chemical reaction out of which something new arises. This, as in chemistry, is a creative, productive and exciting process, which, on the one hand, can be quite volatile if carelessly dealt with but is very constructive if it is given a benign, boundaried space in which to interact safely.

Practice points

1. How does your own cultural background as supervisor affect how your approach supervision?
2. Ask your supervisee to consider their own cultural background and the biases that might arise from that.
3. Consider with your supervisee the diversity that is within the triad of supervisor, coach and coachee.
4. Listen, with your supervisee, to what arises in the space between you all in your diversity.
5. How do differences of power affect what arises in the coaching and supervision? Consider the power triangle in helping you to do this.
6. Map each coachee you supervise in terms of cultural difference.

Discussion points

1. Think, together with your supervisee, about what constitutes diversity in culture.
2. How could individualistic or collectivist culture affect the work you are doing in supervision/coaching?
3. Is it possible to be uninfluenced by cultural difference?
4. What is the best way of improving your practice where cultural diversity is involved?

Suggested reading

Hawkins, P and Smith, N. (2013). *Coaching, Mentoring and Organizational Consultancy: Supervision and Development*. 2nd ed. Maidenhead: Open University Press.

Rosinski, P. (2003). *Coaching Across Cultures: New Tools for Leveraging National, Corporate and Professional Differences*. London: Nicholas Brealey.

Ryde, J. (2009). *Being White in the Helping Professions: Developing Effective Inter-Cultural Awareness*. London: Jessica Kingsley.

Ryde, J. (2011). Culturally sensitive supervision. In C. Lago (Ed), *The Handbook of Transcultural Counselling and Psychotherapy*. Maidenhead: Open University Press.

References

Abram, D. (1996). *The Spell of the Sensuous*. New York: Vintage.

Alcoff, L. M. (2015). *The Future of Whiteness*. Cambridge: Polity Press.

Argyris, S. (1978). *Organisational Learning*. Reading, MA: Addison Wesley.

Atwood, G. E. and Stolorow, R. D. (2014). *Structures of Subjectivity: Explorations in Psychoanalytic Phenomenology*. 2nd ed. New Jersey: The Analytic Press.

Brown, A. and Bourne, L. (1996). *The Social Work Supervisor*. London: Heinemann.

Davies, D. (1996). Homophobia and heterosexism. In D. Davies and C. Neal (Eds), *Pink Therapy*. Buckingham: Open University Press.

Eddo-Lodge, R. (2017). *Why I Am No Longer Talking to White People about Race*. London: Bloomsbury.

Frankenberg, R. (1999). *Displacing Whiteness*. Durham and London: Duke University Press.

Hawkins, P. (2012). *Creating a Coaching Culture*. Maidenhead: Open University Press.

Hawkins, P. A. (2017). *Leadership Team Coaching in Practice*. 3rd ed. London: Kogan Page.

Hawkins, P. A. and Shohet, R. (2007). *Supervision in the Helping Professions*. 3rd ed. London: Open University Press.

Hawkins, P. A. and Smith, N. (2006). *Coaching, Mentoring and Organisational Consultancy: Supervison, Skills & Development*. London: McGraw Hill.

Krishnamurti, J. (1989). *Think on These Things*. San Francisco, CA: HarperOne.

Laungani, P. (2004). *Asian Perspectives in Counselling and Psychotherapy*. Hove: Brunner-Routledge.

Mang, P. and Haggard, B. (2016). *Regenerative Development and Design: A Framework for Evolving Sustainability*. Hoboken, NJ: John Wiley.

Maslow, A. H. (1972). *The Farther Reaches of Human Nature*. London: Penguin.

Rosinski, P. (2013). *Coaching Across Cultures: New tools for Leveraging National, Corporate & Professional Differences.* London: Nicholas Brealey Publishing.

Ryde, J. (2009). *Being White in the Helping Professions: Developing Effective Intercultural Awareness.* London: Jessica Kingsley.

Savage, M. (2015). *Social Class in the 21st Century.* London: Pelican.

Stolorow, R. D. and Atwood, G. E. (1992). *Contexts of Being.* Hillsdale, NJ: The Analytic Press.

Tulpa, K. and Bresser, F. (2009). Coaching in Europe. In J. Passmore (Ed), *Diversity in Coaching.* London: Kogan Page.

4

Resourcing

The neglected third leg of supervision

Peter Hawkins

Introduction

In a recent supervision, my supervisee told me that she was so pleased that we were having supervision now, because she felt totally depleted and knew that when she came to supervision she always left feeling recharged. In the past, I would have felt flattered and worked hard to best resource her. However, on this occasion I paused and then said: "I think we might need to review how we are doing supervision together, so we can discover how supervision can stop being a petrol station where you go to be refuelled and instead becomes a place that helps you create a solar panel on your heart, so you constantly tap into renewable energy in the midst of the work. Our supervision gradually changed from being a resource she tapped into, to a place that helped her re-source herself.

I write this chapter, looking back on 40 years of being a supervisor, writing about supervision and reflective practice and teaching supervisors in a wide variety of people professions, in many parts of the world. In that time, along with many co-writers, I have written about what I have described as the three legs of the supervision stool. These are the qualitative, developmental and resourcing. In Hawkins and Smith (2006 and 2013: 173–174), we defined these as following:

The *qualitative* function provides the quality control function in work with people. It is not only lack of training or experience that necessitates the need in us, as professionals, to have someone look with us at our work, but also our inevitable human failings, blind spots, areas of vulnerability from our own wounds and our own prejudices as well as the successful aspects of our practice

The *developmental* function is about developing the skills, understanding and capacities of the supervisees.

The *resourcing* function is a way of responding to how those engaged in the intensity of work with clients are necessarily allowing themselves to be affected by the distress, pain and fragmentation of the client, how they need time to become aware of the way this has affected them and to deal with any reactions.

Over the years much has been written about the qualitative and developmental functions, but much less about the third aspect, that of resourcing. I now recognise that this is a significant oversight and gap in the literature and therefore was delighted to contribute to a book on the heart of supervision, for I now believe that resourcing is both at the heart of supervision and the core spiritual practice that underpins other important elements of supervision practice.

Development of resourcing in supervision

Supervision is constantly in service of growing our personal and collective capacities to resource ourselves to be resilient, stay mindful and compassionate and non-reactive in the face of daily distress, disturbance and dis-ease, which interact with general stresses of life that do not necessarily involve practice-based issues, but *do* impact upon them (Hawkins and Shohet, 2012: 217–218).

Resourcing is about helping the supervisee, and oneself as supervisor, work from source rather than from effort and skill. In this chapter, I am not using the word resourcing to mean the supervisee being given new resources by their supervisor in the form of insights, theories, models, tools, books, etc., although sometimes these offerings can usefully contribute. In the story above when the supervisee explained how she often arrived exhausted physically, emotionally and mentally from her work and left energised from our supervision, I had to learn how to stop trying to be her resource and focus on how I could support her in re-sourcing herself in the work. My intervention opened up an ongoing inquiry process for us both and our working relationship that has continued over many supervision sessions and informed this chapter.

Lao Tzu, the great Taoist poet who lived 2,500 years ago is believed to have written:

> (If there is to be peace in the world,
> There must be peace in the nations.
> If there is to be peace in the nations,
> There must be peace in the cities.
> If there is to be peace in the cities,
> There must be peace between neighbours.
> If there is to be peace between neighbours,
> There must be peace in the home.
> If there is to be peace in the home,
> There must be peace in the heart.
> (Lao Tzu, 6th century BCE (unconfirmed))

We live in a fractured world and maybe an updated version of Lao Tzu's words could be thus:

> If the Universe is fractured it will show up in Earth's Biosphere.
> If Gaia earth is fractured, it will show up in local environmental niches,
> There will be fractures in place, culture and tradition.
> When there are fractures in place culture and tradition there will conflict in our communities.
> When there is conflict in the community, there will be conflict in the organisation

> When there is conflict in the organisation, there will be conflict in the team
> When there is conflict in the team, there will be conflict in the individual.

Our individual fractures create internal conflict, which we project out into the world as we become reactive to others, to events, and cling to our own constructs and needs. The fractures become recycled up and down the systemic levels.

Today it is too easy to experience conflict at all these levels, from the world news, national political infighting, family conflict and personal discontent.

We are like indigenous orphans, migrants on the road, separated from our sense of place and belonging. We have lost not only our sense of rootedness in a landscape, but the feeling of being held in time by the rhythm of seasonal celebrations, rituals of the year, and life transitions ceremonies. A holding tradition. Our habits traditionally come from our habitat, the living human culture of our local tribe, and how this human culture co-evolves in relation to our ecological niche in the natural or "more-than-human world" (Abrams, 1996).

The psychoanalyst and philosopher Wilfred Bion (1962) wrote about how each individual baby develops through the relationship of container and contained, our experiences being mediated, and only digestible into thinking, through the holding relationship with the mother, or other holding adult. Without such holding, our infantile experiences remain fragmented and frightening and can become "nameless dread" (Bion, 1962: 96) that continues to haunt us in later life.

Our later childhood and adolescent development is also mediated by a container/contained relationship. In this developmental stage, this is with our family, peer group, local culture, tradition sand place. But many of these in modern western and urbanised societies have become fractured. When I was young, I would be asked: "Where do you come from? What is your religion? What do your parents do?" as ways of ascertaining the container in which I had developed, or the marinade that I had been steeped in. Many today could not answer those questions. Their place has been one of wandering, their religion has become undefined, or based on changing interests or desires, and their parents may have had many occupations and roles, but not necessarily a craft or profession or an occupational container.

Our peer groups today may be mediated through Facebook, LinkedIn, or other networking sites and be ever-changing and globally dispersed. Our family and friends spread around the world. The stable narratives that gave our particular experiences greater meaning, have, for many, been deconstructed in the postmodern world of dissolving meta-narratives.

What holds us when our containers have become fleeting and dispersed? With what holding structures do we co-evolve our stories and our sense of meaning and purpose? Where is the source that resources us, the holding presence that sustains us and provides meaning to our work, our lives and our existence?

We cannot heal the world just one person at a time, for the fracturing will overcome the best intent of a whole army of coaches, therapists, counsellors, mediators and healers, even if they were all well supervised! We need to build holding containers at all levels of the systemic interconnected world. To work effectively, our own work needs to be held by good reflective practice and supervision and belonging to a community of practice. Organisations need to think of themselves as human holding systems, where all those that are part of them are developing and growing, organisations that also attend to their own healing and wholeness. At the collective level, we need new holding stories (Mead, 2011; Reason and Newman, 2013; Parlett, 2015) and meaning-making and new rituals of seasonality, life transitions and ways of being with each other. Homo sapiens has been an extraordinarily successful species at adapting and evolving within a great variety of different localised ecological niches, from tropical forest to arctic tundra, and from mountains to deserts, but now, for better or worse, we have created one hyper-connected globalised niche, and homo sapiens as a species has little idea how to flourish in and with this ecosystem.

Our times call for a new mythos, a new creation story (Swimme and Berry, 1992), a new collective sense of purpose that can hold our collaboration in service of a greater whole, and our individual fragmentation and disorientation within collective sense making. If the last 30 years of coaching has been about developing greater E.Q. (emotional quotient) alongside our I.Q., the next thirty years will be about moving from "I.Q." to "We Q" – the developing of collaborative intelligence, recognising that today's challenges mostly lie in the connections between individuals, between teams and between organisations, and that these challenges cannot be resolved by heroic individuals.

Coaching supervision becomes an important processing container for not only creating new meaning and understanding but also for growing each of our capacities to re-source ourselves.

My coaching supervision practice includes supervising:

- those who coach people working with traumatised refugees (see Chapter 3 in this book);
- people who coach small businesses going through a transitional crisis from charismatic founders to second generation leaders;
- people who coach multi-national leadership teams drawn from different national and professional cultures who need to find ways of taking collective and collaborative leadership;
- those who coach CEOs who are at breaking point trying to meet the conflicting needs of complex stakeholders, while helping their company innovate for a volatile, uncertain, complex and ambiguous (VUCA – Stiehm and Townsend, 2002) emerging future.

Through the privilege of supervising across many different countries and sectors I meet people from hundreds of different organisations every year. They may be very different in size, sector, country, culture, but all of them share the challenge of what I refer to as "the unholy trinity" of: the demands to do more; at higher quality; with less resource. Many think they are alone in this pressure, or that it is a temporary phenomenon, and that all will be well "when austerity ends and we get back to normal". I try and wake them up to the fact that so-called "normal" has been abolished and that the global context we have collectively created dictates that this unholy trinity will be with us for generations to come. In a world that:

- has three times more people living in it than there were when I was born;
- where we are all hyper-connected in a way that the rest want what they see the richest already have;
- and when we are depleting the world's natural resources.

the human species is needing to evolve new capacities at an accelerating rate.

To respond to such a world requires better trained, better resourced coaches with greater capacity to respond with "whole intelligence" (Parlett, 2015). Many of the team and individual coaches I supervise have been well trained in being empathic, particularly with the people who are present with them in the room. However, they have often been less trained in how to build their resilience to be able to stay open to high levels of anxiety, conflict and distress without falling into their own vicarious trauma, or becoming reactive, or closing down their feelings and thus becoming less empathetic to others in the field.

Supervision has an important role in enabling coaches to increase their resilience, which can be defined as: "the capacity of a system (or a person) to absorb disturbance and still retain its basic function and structure" (Boyatzis and McKee, 2005: 76). The same authors go on to say that: "In complex environments, resilience often spells success" (2005: 76).

Nassim Taleb (2012) captures a similar concept with the term "anti-fragile systems". Fragile systems, he argues, are those that are damaged by shocks; robust systems weather shocks; and anti-fragile systems, like immune systems, can benefit from shocks. So, we need to explore how supervisors can best develop the resilience and anti-fragile capacity of their supervisees as well as their own, while still working with an open heart and open mind.

The practice of re-sourcing in supervision.

So how can a supervisor help to build up a supervisee's capacity to re-source themselves? Here are ten practices I have gradually developed that help me re-source both myself and my supervisees.

1. Contracting and initial session

For many years I would start supervision contracting by asking the supervisee what they wanted from supervision. It took me several years to realise that this implied that the supervisee was the customer of supervision and I as the supervisor was the supplier. Now I start from a different assumption, namely, that supervision is a joint endeavour where both supervisor and supervisee are working in partnership to focus on what the work requires.

I start a supervision relationship by asking the person to tell me about themselves, their life, their work, their purpose and their strengths and weaknesses as they see them. I want to meet the whole person and their context, not just the professional and their problems. In doing this I will listen carefully to their story. I listen, not just with my ears and my neo-cortex sense making, but with my whole body, so I have a full embodied experience of their world. I am also listening to how they construct their narrative, the frames and mind-sets through which they make sense of their life and their world.

2. Intent

I prepare for every supervision in three ways:

a) First I need to clear myself of what I have been doing before the session. This may be writing up notes on a previous session and closing the file, or maybe closing down my computer and putting the phones outside the room. I want to create a clear receptive space both inside me and around me to welcome them into. Regular journaling and reflective writing are also helpful approaches (Chapter 7).

b) Then I need to centre myself and tap into the elemental resources. To do this: I relax my body; ground my feet on the floor to connect with the resource of the earth; watch my breathing, thus ensuring that I am fully connecting to the resourcing of the air; drink some water, the life-giving resource of water; and feel the fire of focus in my belly and in a clear mind.

c) Then, in order to clarify and deepen my intent, I may use a short invocation, such as: *"May this supervision be in service of the supervisee, their current and future clients, the organisations they and their clients work for, the whole human family and the more-than-human world."*

3. Appreciative inquiry

It is important that I discover when and how the supervisee is most resourced in the work and start from an appreciative rather than from a deficit model. To do this I may inquire:

"Tell me about when you are working at your best . . . when you are most in flow with the work."

"Tell me about when you are working from source, rather than from effort or skill. How do you access this ability?"

4. Reactivity Triggers

Whatever our capacity to stay fully present with our clients, attending to them, their eco-systemic context, ourselves and the relationships between all of these (see the seven-eyed model, Hawkins and Smith, 2013: 186–207), our capacity will be punctured by events or interactions that trigger our reactivity. It is therefore important that we attend to the reactivity triggers of our supervisees and help them explore them, not with shame or judgement, but with compassionate curiosity. We need to explore what triggered the reaction, both in the coaching session and what was stirred up in the emotional patterns of the coach (mode 4 of the seven-eyed model, Hawkins and Smith, 2013). When we are emotionally triggered, it is not helpful simply to ask: "Is this the client's stuff or mine?", as in nearly all cases it is both. Often what clients find most difficult to communicate, they cannot put into words, as it is part of their "unthought known" (Bollas, 1987), what they emotionally and somatically experience but cannot articulate. What we cannot articulate we are doomed to replicate. Thus, the only way some clients can communicate their feelings is to get the coach to experience it. If the coach cannot process this unconscious communication, they will often do to the supervisor what the client has done to them; this is referred to in the literature as "parallel process" (Searles, 1955; Doehrman, 1976; Hawkins and Smith, 2013: 196–198).

Under pressure, our emotions may be triggered into a response in the part of the brain, the amygdala, that is activated when we are in danger, sometimes graphically described as an "amygdala hijack" (Goleman, 1996), where our reptilian brain takes over as it senses a threat to our identity or our safety or our survival. These are the kinds of responses that may occur when we are triggered into classic amygdala survival mode:

- "fight", anger with the client or others in their story;
- "flight", wanting to get out of the relationship;
- "freeze", feelings of being paralysed and unable to move or intervene;
- "fragment", not being able to think clearly or focus;
- "fold" or "fawn" to placate, give up power, and avoid anything that could be construed as critical or as threatening of the other's approval.

As a supervisor, I need to watch for these signs of my supervisee being triggered into reactivity of vicarious trauma by the work and gently respond to bring this into awareness. It is also important to help supervisees to raise their own capacity to catch their reactivity as it happens. I offer them a four-step process:

- Notice it.
- Catch it.
- Use it as data – of what may be going on in the client and the client's system.
- Act on it – work with the coachee or supervisee on how to move from reaction back into partnership.

5. Learning edge

I try to minimise the time spent in our supervision on the coach telling me what they already know, and my responding to them with what I already know, as one of my own supervisors put it: "burdening them with the weight of your wisdom!" Instead I focus on how quickly we can move to our collective learning edge: a challenge that life is throwing up to which neither they nor I know how to respond.

6. External resources

As part of resourcing supervision, it is important to explore the different ways a supervisee taps into external resources. I have several methods of helping supervisees increase their connection with external resources:

a) I will ask a supervisee: "Who stands behind you when you are doing your work? Who stands either side of you? Who are your supportive teachers and mentors and loving companions that you take with you into the work?"

b) I find my work is better resourced if I can invoke my connection to the one human family. Many years ago, with the help of a spiritual teacher, I realised that when I travelled to work by train or plane, I would always try and be the first off and the first in the queues for the ticket barrier, passport checks or security. I would rush down the escalators or along the travellators. I was creating inside myself a consciousness that saw other human beings as barriers who got in the way of me getting to where I wanted to get to. Not a great consciousness to start work with other human beings. For many years now, I have used the simple practice of standing still on the escalator or travellator and watching the people coming in the other direction. For each person, I say: "This is my brother, this is my sister, this is my daughter, this is my son, this is my mother or father", depending on age and gender. Within the few minutes of the ride my consciousness has changed to being supported by the oneness of the human family.

c) I will sometimes also ask supervisees: "How is your work supported by the more-than-human world – nature, birds, trees, flowers, sun and rain?" and "How do you keep your connection to this eternally renewing source through your work?" This has led some supervisees to change their travel to work, in order to be more refreshed by a walk through a park or along a river. Others have adopted putting fresh flowers, or a bowl of water, or special stones or a nature picture in their room as a constant connection to the greater whole in which we live, breathe and have our being.

7. Internal resources

With a modern western consciousness, we often look externally for resources to help us solve problems, develop, learn or be happier, rather than tap into internal resources already present to us but seemingly out of reach.

The supervisor can enable the supervisee to access these internal mental, physical or spiritual sources, by simple invitations:

- "Just breathe and see what comes."
- "Put your feet firmly on the ground/earth and become aware of how you are supported."
- "What is your inner wisdom, or internal supervisor telling you, right now?"

- "Who do you know, in life or in fiction, who would know how to deal with this situation and what would they do?"
- "If you stopped trying with such effort and just trusted the deeper source beyond yourself, what would you allow through?"

8. *Mindfulness*

Mindfulness has drawn on the great and long meditation tradition of Buddhism to develop a western psychological process of bringing one's attention to experiences occurring in the present moment with non-judgmental curiosity (see Hall, 2013).

Jon Kabat-Zinn, seen by many as the founder of modern-day psychological mindfulness, defines Mindfulness as: "paying attention in a particular way: on purpose, in the present moment, and non-judgmentally" (Kabat-Zinn, 1994: 4).

Mindfulness can be used in supervision to invite the supervisee to focus less on their rehearsed narratives of what happened in their coaching work, and instead on what is happening to them in the present as they recall their work. We can then invite them to become aware of body sensations and feelings, spontaneous thoughts and images, that occur as they start to reflect on aspects of their work and to share these as they happen. The supervisor helps them remain curious and non-judgmental about anything that occurs and just report what arises as interesting phenomena.

At the same time, the supervisor may also attend to the phenomena that emerges in them as they listen (mode 6 of the seven-eyed model) and may share anything that is unusual or may be significant.

We can also develop non-dual practices, drawn from the many rich wisdom traditions. These practices can open us beyond developing compassion for the other, to direct experience where the separation of self and other melts from consciousness. They can also take us further to where the separation of the human and the more-than-human world dissolves, and where there is only the oneness of being, where our individual self disappears, and we are just part of pure awareness (Fenner, 2002; Amidon, 2012).

9. Wide-angled empathy and compassion

Mindfulness is a great starting place, but should not become a resting place. We need to move from the foundation of an open, relaxed and alert mind, on to "Compassion Training" that takes us beyond the narrow-self or selves (Armstrong, 2011; Jinpa, 2015). For we can become fixated on seeing everything through the lenses of the three central individuals – client, coach and supervisor – and fail to attend to the wider patterns that are showing up through these players. In my work teaching Systemic Team Coaching (Hawkins, 2017, 2018) I encourage people to "focus on the dance not the dancers".

One practice I use in my own coaching and supervision is what I have termed "wide-angled empathy". In this practice the supervisor (or coach) attends to every person, system or entity mentioned in the story of the supervisee (or client) and focuses on being as empathic and compassionate to each being as you are to the supervisee or client right in front of you.

This is a tough practice, which requires much practice. It can also be practised watching the news and being empathic with every person including those you agree with and like and those who you see as wrong, bad or enemies.

A further refinement of this practice can be found in the Buddhist practice of Tonglen, whereby you visualise empathically taking in the suffering of the other person, mentioning them on your in-breathe and then breathing out with a focus on giving recognition, compassion and succour to all sentient beings.

This practice stops us taking sides and being drawn into potential drama triangles such as: "client as victim, organisation as persecutor, coach as rescuer".

10. Systemic Hope

In "East Coker", one of T. S. Eliot's *Four Quartets*, he writes: "I said to my soul, be still and wait without hope, for hope would be hope *for the wrong thing* ..." (Eliot, 1943, my emphasis).

In supervision, we can easily place our hope in any of the following: our supervisee learning and benefiting from our help as supervisor, or in the supervisee's insights creating beneficial impact in their practice and for their client, or the supervisee developing and becoming better at their craft.

Systemic hope comes from a belief that suffering, difficulty, problems, etc. are a product of our limited consciousness and ways of thinking. Systemic hope is hope placed in the knowledge that the greater system has a greater wisdom and that together we can attend to and listen to that greater wisdom. The greater system may be accessed through seeing the events in a wider time horizon, or by zooming out to see how the individuals are representing different systemic needs that have not yet found a way of being connected, or by realising that in nature there is a constant changing, healing and adaptive process. With systemic hope, we can listen to how healing is emerging in the system and be attendants to it, like a good midwife.

The relational container

Coaching supervision is fundamentally a reflective relationship attending to a series of reflective coaching relationships, which is in service of enhancing reflective practice. The essential relational quality of this craft means that we must attend to developing the capacity of the supervisory relationship to be an effective container for processing what emerges from the work. To resource the capacity of the supervisee to do the work, it is also important that we resource the relationship.

Preparing ourselves before we start the supervision, or helping the supervisee develop personal mindfulness and compassion, are important. However, more demanding is the need to resource the dialogical engagement between the supervisor and the supervisee. This can also be considered as a "trialogical" engagement, for the dialogue is essentially carried out between the supervisee, their work and the supervisor, all three elements co-creating the exploration.

In Hawkins and Smith (2013: 283) we introduced the concept of "creating the space for grace". We discussed how, for a dialogue to have grace, it needs to move between what David Bohm (1987, 1996) terms 'thoughts' and 'thinking', to create generative dialogue where new thinking emerges in the space between us, unbidden and often surprising. To create this relational space both supervisor and supervisee need to share their current thinking with each other without attachment and with an inquiry and interest into what may lie beyond this current understanding, inviting each other to challenge their implicit assumptions and propose invitations to areas beyond the currently known. When both partners enter into this space of inquiry and unknowing, new insight emerges not just within both parties but in the space between them.

Case study

I was working with a supervisee, a well-trained and very experienced coach, who had worked with many senior executives, both in commercial companies and in Government.

On this particular session, she arrived looking cramped. She sat on the chair, her legs tightly entwined and her shoulders raised.

She told me about how she had taken on coaching a new CEO, and how the H.R. Director had told her she needed to be "on her metal", as this person had already turned down two other possible coaches. The H.R. director did not want to risk a third failure from his recommendations.

The chemistry meeting had gone well, but since then, the sessions had often been rescheduled or reduced in length. The CEO, when they did meet, would often pace up and down the room and talk of the pressure he was under from his Chairman and certain very demanding Non-Executives. He would talk of how several of his "key reports" were "just not stepping up to the plate", and he was constantly having to rewrite their reports himself, before they went to the board.

"I feel exhausted after each session, particularly when he changes the date and time of our meeting. I find myself getting very angry with him, but when we do get together I feel for him. He is under such pressure and the Board are not giving him the time he needs."

She continued: "I want to help him, but I don't know I have what it takes. What do you think I should do? Do you think I am up to it?"

At this point I was very struck by the parallel process of the Board putting pressure on the CEO and then the CEO putting pressure on his executives and his coach, and perhaps she was now getting me to feel the pressure from her. I was about to comment on this, when I realised that could be received by my supervisee as another demand, for her to understand the replicating patterns, when she was already showing me the pressure she was under.

I considered reassuring her and reinforcing her self-confidence with reminders of the senior leaders she had been successful with in the past.

Then I recognised that I was swinging between rescuing her and being demanding of her, so instead I stepped sideways and invited her to just pause and breathe more and notice what she was feeling.

She closed her eyes and deepened her breathing somewhat, and after a short pause said: "My neck is hurting. It feels locked. I am not sure where or how to turn."

I asked her what her neck needed. And she paused again and said: "I need to get my shoulders moving – stop being so cramped."

I invited her to do that right now and she began to move more freely and stood up and stretched.

I stood up next to her and said: "As you continue to stretch, what is the truth you need to speak to your client."

As she continued to move she said, as if to her client: "You need to stand up to those bastards that are either demanding of you or not supporting you."

Once again, I realised I was being invited to join my coach as rescuer and invited to see the CEO as a victim of demanding Board members and unsupportive colleagues.

Internally, I held the colleagues and Board members with "wide-angled empathy" and compassion; they too were probably under a great deal of pressure from the Shareholders and other stakeholders, and much of the pressure in the system was being recycled rather than processed.

While continuing to stand alongside her, I turned to her and said:

> "I think you are inviting me to see the Board and colleagues as persecutors of your client, and I must politely decline that invitation, and instead I wonder what we can do together in this supervision to increase our space to process the ricocheting pressure?"

She half laughed, put her hand over her mouth and sat down. "You know, Peter," she began, looking straight at me.

> "I find it very difficult to hold my anger and my compassion and caring together. When I am with him I feel sorry for him and when I am away from him I feel angry. I need to find a third space within me that brings these two together."

We spent the rest of the supervision exploring that new capacity, that new source from which she could work with this client and rehearsing how she could work from that place.

Conclusion

Supervision is not just in service of better quality work with today's coachees and organisational clients, or the learning and development of coaches, it is also in service of tomorrow's client and the future coaching profession, by growing our capacity to work from a deeper source of both knowing and being. Working from this source we become energised by the work rather than depleted.

As supervisors, it is helpful to tap into this renewable energy within us and in the wider field. We need to enter the supervision space with an open mind, open heart and open will, curious about what stories will emerge as well as what new insights and ways of responding.

In doing supervision in this way we become part of a much bigger endeavour, which is contributing to the evolution of human consciousness and capacity, a necessary precondition for us being fit for the twenty-first-century world that, for better or worse, we have co-created.

Thank you for reading this and may your work be constantly renewed and resourced.

Practice points

1. It is important to attend to how you resource yourself, before you can increase your capacity to resource others. As they say on air flights – "remember to fix your own oxygen mask first".
2. Bring in "the third" that needs to be present in every supervision, for supervision is co-created by the supervisor, the supervisee and "the work" comprising the lessons and challenges that life is generously providing.
3. Rather than ask your supervisee: "What do you want from supervision?", it is more effective to ask: "What is the work we need to do today, to create the most value for you and your stakeholders?"
4. Rather than ending the supervision by asking your supervisee: "What was helpful from supervision and what could be more helpful next time?", it is more effective to ask: "If your stakeholders had been listening to the work we have done together what would they have valued and what would their challenge be to us?" This overcomes the implied conceit that the supervision has been done by the supervisor.
5. Pause frequently before the session starts, after it ends, and in the middle when a new level of engagement is called for. When pausing – relax, ground yourself, breathe more fully and be open to what emerges.

6. Practice "wide-angled empathy", in supervision, having as much compassion for everyone in the supervisee's stories as you do for yourself and the supervisee. You can also practise this watching the news!

Discussion points

1. How do you recognise when you are "working from source" rather than "working from effort"?
2. List five external and internal resources that deepen the work you do as a supervisor and coach.
3. What simple practice could you adopt that would further deepen your supervision?
4. How do you enable your supervisees to be more fully present to their clients without becoming over-identified with the client's story or reactive to it?

Suggested reading

Hawkins, P. and Smith, N. (2006 & 2013). *Coaching, Mentoring and Organizational Consultancy: Supervision & Development* (1st ed. and 2nd ed.). Maidenhead: McGraw-Hill Open University Press.

Einzig, H. (2017). The Future of Coaching: Vision, Leadership and Responsibility in a Transforming World. London: Routledge.

Hall, L. (2013). *Mindful Coaching*. London: Kogan Page.

Hawkins, P. (2018). *Leadership Team Coaching in Practice* (2nd ed.). London: Kogan Page.

References

Abrams, D. (1996). *The Spell of the Sensuous*. New York: Random House.

Amidon, E. (2012). *The Open Path: Recognizing Non-Dual Awareness*. Boulder, CO: Sentient Publications.

Armstrong, K. (2011). *Twelve Steps to a Compassionate Life*. London: The Bodley Head.

Bion, W. (1962). *Learning from Experience*. London: Heinemann.

Bohm, D. (1987). *Unfolding Meaning* (D. Factor, ed). London: Routledge & Kegan Paul.

Bohm, D. (1996). *On Dialogue* (L. Nichol, ed). London: Routledge.

Bollas, C. (1987). The Shadow of the Object: Psychoanalysis of the Unthought Known. London: Free Association Books.

Boyatzis, R. and McKee, A. (2005). Resonant Leadership: Renewing yourself and connecting with others, through mindfulness, hope and compassion. Boston, MA: Harvard Business School Press.

Doehrman, M. J. (1976). Parallel Processes in Supervision and Psychotherapy. *Bulletin of The Menninger Clinic*, 40, 1–104.

Eliot, T.S. (1943). *Four Quartets*. London: Faber and Faber.

Fenner, P. (2002). *The Edge of Certainty: Dilemmas on the Buddhist Path*. Newburyport, MA: Nicolas-Hays.

Goleman, D. (1996). *Emotional Intelligence: Why it matters more than IQ*. London: Bloomsbury.

Hall, L. (2013). *Mindful Coaching*. London: Kogan Page.

Hawkins, P. (2017). Leadership Team Coaching: Developing Collective Transformational Leadership (3rd ed.). London: Kogan Page.

Hawkins, P. (2018). *Leadership Team Coaching in Practice* (2nd ed.). London: Kogan Page.

Hawkins, P. and Shohet, R. (2012). *Supervision in the Helping Profession* (4th ed.). Maidenhead: McGraw-Hill Open University Press.

Hawkins, P. and Smith, N. (2006, 2013). *Coaching, Mentoring and Organizational Consultancy: Supervision and Development* (1st ed. and 2nd ed.). Maidenhead: McGraw-Hill Open University Press.

Jinpa, T. (2015). A Fearless Heart: Why Compassion is the Key to Greater Wellbeing. London: Piatkus.

Kabat-Zinn, J. (1994). Wherever You Go, There You Are: Mindfulness Meditation in Everyday Life. New York: Hyperion.

Mead, G. (2011). Coming Home to Story: Storytelling Beyond Happily Ever After. Bristol: Vala.

Parlett, M. (2015). Future Sense: Five Explorations of Whole Intelligence for a World that is waking up. Leicester, UK: Matador.

Reason, P. and Newman, M. (Eds). (2013). *Stories of the Great Turning*. Bristol: Vala.

Searles, H. F. (1955). The informational value of the supervisory emotional experience. *Psychiatry*, 18, 135–146.

Stiehm, J. H. and Townsend, N. W. (2002). The U.S. Army War College: Military Education in a Democracy. Philadelphia, PA: Temple University Press.

Swimme, B. and Berry, T. (1992). The Universe Story: From the Primordial Flaring-forth to the Ecozoic Era – A Celebration of the Unfolding of the Cosmos. New York: HarperCollins.

Taleb, N. N. (2012). *Antifragile: Things That Gain from Disorder*. New York: Random House.

Tzu, L. (6th century BCE). If there is to be peace in the world. Retrieved 1 August 2018 from http://paulocoelhoblog.com/2012/12/22/some-prayers/

5

Working with intense emotions

Keri Phillips

Introduction

Supervision can be a time of intense emotions such as sadness, anger, fear, joy, guilt and hope. There are the challenges and opportunities that then flow. Questions such as the following may arise: Whose feelings are they – the supervisor's, the supervisee's, others', a mixture? What might the interplay be with these emotions? Is one more significant than another? Sometimes love and joy can be as difficult to deal with as pain; love can bring an increased sense of fragility and a fear that ultimately the pain of loss is inevitable.

In this scene-setting the insights of May and Fromm are helpful. May suggested that as a result of the Enlightenment sometimes too sharp a distinction is made between the emotional and the rational. He proposed that reason works better when emotions are present (May, 1976). Such balancing is needed, just as when the "helper" – counsellor, coach, therapist or supervisor – seeks to be both a part of and apart from the world of those she or he seeks to help. Fromm (2000) wrote of loving being as much about skill as passion. Supporting others in handling intense emotions requires versatility. In exploring the broader, existential dimension one needs to be equally alert to the day-to-day and the pragmatic, and vice versa.

Through all this each supervisor needs to find his or her own way, ensuring that it accords with personal values and beliefs, makes sense, feels right and pays attention to the relevant code of ethics. There is a need consciously to step back and regularly revisit assumptions about oneself and one's world. Sometimes that which was accepted as an eternal truth needs to be reassessed and even discarded.

The development of the approach

Since the Second World War there has been a growing emphasis on research into, and exploration of, emotions at work. This has taken a wide variety of forms including T-Groups (Smith, 1969), experiential personal awareness training based on transactional analysis and gestalt (Clark et al., 1984), the development of psychometrics such as FIRO-B (Schutz, 1989) and the concept of emotional intelligence (Goleman, 1998). It has also been examined through the lens of organisational cultures (Merry and Brown, 1987) and a recognition that those involved in organisation development consultancy need to be alert to that which may be happening at a process level, that is emotionally below the surface (Phillips and Shaw, 1997).

Coaching and coaching supervision have entered this world of exploring emotions at work for a variety of reasons:

- The recognition that any type of coaching has the potential to bring emotions to the surface. The coaching of basic work skills can evoke personal challenges for the coachee, such as a lack of self-confidence or a fear of "looking stupid" in front of others (Phillips, 2004).
- Organisational coaches extending their repertoire of approaches as they engage in various interventions where intense emotions may be involved. This includes conflict management, career change, loss of motivation, redundancy and stress management (Leimon et al., 2011).
- The growth of family business coaching has meant that family relationships and feelings have needed appropriate exploration because of their potential to strengthen or undermine the venture (Shams and Lane, 2011).
- The professions of counselling and therapy have engaged with coaching in recent years, bringing a significant contribution of various philosophies and practices where working with emotions is vital:

- those with counselling and therapy backgrounds becoming coaches and bringing with them their experience and knowledge of supervision which has a longer and well-established history, rationale and code of practice (Page and Wosket, 2002)
- the importing of key ideas; for example, the notion of "parallel process", that is, "the unaware replaying within the helping relationship of a pattern of relationship brought from outside" is now well established in coaching (Phillips, 2010a). It had been a key concept in counselling for many years (Clarkson and Gilbert, 1991). Equally and more broadly, the idea of "the unconscious" (Frosh, 2002) underpins many schools of practice in the helping professions.

The rapidly evolving role of coaches, particularly as agents of organisational change (St John-Brooks, 2014) has brought a need to be sensitive to organisational cultures. Consequently, some have built on the work of people such as Schein who drew links between leadership and parenthood (Schein, 1986; Clutterbuck and Megginson, 2005). Alongside this, some leadership coaches have sought the wisdom of those who researched the intimacy and patterns of parenting, including the ability to "hold" others emotionally (Winnicott, 2005; Mountain and Davidson, 2015).

The need, indeed desire, to "work below the surface", for example as described by the Tavistock Consultancy Service (Huffington et al, 2004), has provided an opportunity to examine the less visible aspects of culture, namely the unconscious, both individual and collective. The stories, beliefs, rituals and myths of the organisation's culture may fuel the archetype, a manifestation of the collective unconscious (Jung, 1991; Storr, 1992); examples include, The Creator, The Orphan and The Warrior, each of which has particular emotions and its Shadow, that which it seeks to hide and disown (Pearson, 1991). As an illustration, Pearson refers to, "the villain, who uses Warrior skills for personal gain without thought of morality, ethics, or the good of the whole group" (Pearson, 1991: 16).

The impact of the points above has been a growing need for coaches and supervisors to be aware of their feelings, thereby reducing the chances of bringing their own "unfinished business" into the room. One incitement for such "unfinished business" may derive directly from the professional world of coach training and development. As research into this world carried out by Doherty indicates, there are sometimes contradictory and confusing values and behaviours; promises made are not always delivered (Doherty, 2016). The supervisor and coach may therefore sometimes have a sense of not being "held" adequately and authentically whilst nevertheless being expected to "hold" others (Winnicott, 2005). This may sometimes be experienced as having links back to inconsistent parenting. Mum and Dad may have each had contrasting values and behaviours regarding child-rearing. Or they did not practise what they preached (Phillips, 2005). Or they were simply unpredictable. One could not be sure what would lead to hugs or what to smacks (Bowlby, 2005). Any of this has the potential to mirror that which is currently happening in the client organisation.

A crucial part of the current background regarding coaching practice and development is acknowledging the present era of rapid and extensive change and its increasing complexity (Hamel, 2000; Boulton et al, 2015). From this perspective, people's lives can fluctuate dramatically, leading to a sharpened sense of vulnerability. At the same time there may be an ever-greater unwillingness to show such apparent frailty. This itself may lead to a greater sense of vulnerability and the need to armour oneself (Lowen, 1997).

A linked theme is an increased connectedness and a sense of potency and impotency. Sometimes there are clear opportunities to influence, but also the distinct possibility of being swept aside (Tufekci, 2017). There can be a sudden move from insider to outsider. This is sharply illustrated in the world of social media where one can be transformed from hero to villain in a moment. This may happen because of a trivial throw-away remark (Wallace, 2016).

Turbulence can also create a great desire, indeed urgency, to belong. People may want to belong even as their organisation fundamentally changes and is no longer the one they used to love. Such contortions can be painful physically, mentally and emotionally. Equally, turbulence may force to the surface that which had been long buried, together with an opportunity to undertake invaluable reassessments (Phillips, 2013). It may bring one's Shadow into stark relief, together with significant light and learning. In the words of Jung, ". . . the brighter the light, the blacker [darker] the shadow . . ." (Jung et al., 1976: 318).

So, the history and development of working with intense emotions in supervision indicates that there are likely to be many challenges, but at the same time there are traditions with rich resources constantly being enhanced. In this, the energy flowing from shared learning is vital.

Practice

Core points about emotions

As indicated, supervision can be a time when intense feelings begin to surface. Indeed, supervision may, for some, be a rare opportunity to explore what is happening at an emotional level in the coaching room and beyond.

The model below, Figure 5.1, provides a framework for an examination of this process and is linked to the various examples given later.

It is based on the idea of scripting in transactional analysis (Steiner, 1975). Scripting suggests that in the light of certain experiences in life particular feelings, such as envy, delight, indifference or optimism, will arise, which then prompt the creation of a story, that is, the script about self, others and one's position in the world. This then leads to seeking, creating and interpreting certain experiences that are likely to confirm that storyline. It will be unique for each individual and, broadly speaking, a mixture of the "helpful" and the "unhelpful". Somebody might learn in childhood that it is best to merge into the background in order to avoid provoking the envy of his elder brother. In later life "the quiet one" then needs

Experiencing:
Real and imagined threats,
challenges, opportunities,
receiving love, anger, indifference,
support, sabotage

Confirming:
Seeking, creating, interpreting
experiences and people which
back up the storyline

Feeling:
Vulnerable, excited,
threatened, clever, stupid,
adoring, furious, confused

Creating:
Developing a story of optimism,
pessimism, dreams, despair, rigidity
and fluidity

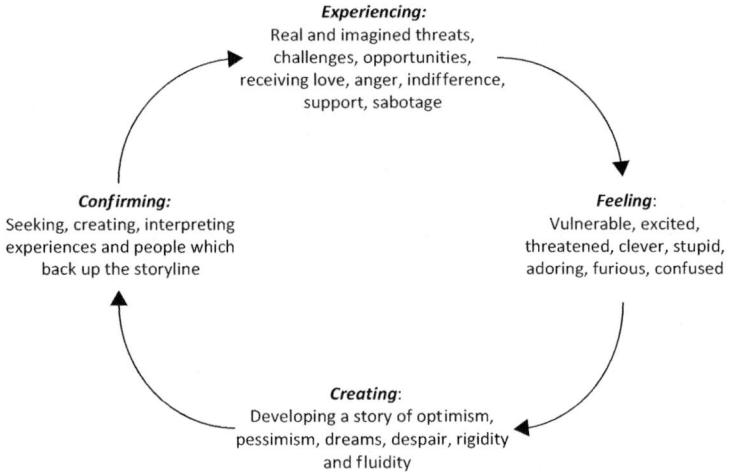

Figure 5.1   Scripting

to develop the skills of making himself much more visible in order to market his talents.

Throughout this whole process of creating and living a script, awareness can vary considerably. The supervisee may be aware of the intensity of her feelings. She comes to supervision furious about the senior leadership behaviour within the client organisation. She is outraged how some of her coachees have been treated and believes, perhaps correctly, that it would be unhelpful to discuss this with them. She also judges that it would be unwise, indeed unethical, to give even indirect and non-attributable feedback to the leadership. She is relieved to have an opportunity to "unload" with the supervisor.

Another supervisee under similar circumstances may be unaware of the intensity of his feelings, or indeed of any particular feelings at all. It is only when the supervisor comments on his frequent brief grimaces that the subsequent conversation helps him realise the depth of his fury. He had not grasped how upset he was. As well as being angry with the client organisation he is also angry with himself for becoming too financially dependent upon a client whose values are so very different from his own. He has a sense of having contorted himself, just like some of his coachees.

There are layers of feelings, a distinct combination for each person dependent upon the various experiences and histories involved (Woollams and Brown, 1978). Sometimes feelings are near the surface and readily accessed. Others are more deeply buried. Some feelings are so personal, indeed private, that one does not want to talk about them even to oneself.

Story – Layers of feelings

> One of my supervisees, "Anne", experienced herself as being sidelined despite, indeed because of, her success in carrying out her role. She had reshaped the organisation's approach to coaching and linked it to action learning sets as a way of changing the culture. She believed she was successful and said that her boss had started claiming credit for her work. As she reported it, he had sufficient allies at a senior level to undermine Anne's reputation. So, when the question of redundancies arose as a cost-cutting exercise, she was amongst the first to be removed. Initially she was distressed and sad about losing a job that had meant so much to her. She then moved into a phase where she was angry with herself for having been politically naive, as she put it. Then she became angry, indeed furious, with her boss for his seeming betrayal and plagiarism. Finally, she allowed herself to feel angry with the leadership team of the organisation since it had, in her eyes, rewarded her boss for his destructive behaviour. She saw him as a ruthless sycophant who had developed close alliances that he used to deflect attention away from his hypocrisy (Babiak and Hare, 2006; James, 2013). It takes energy to suppress the energy of emotions, so having given herself permission to be angry with others she was then better able to focus on what her next steps might be and what she really wanted. Simply acknowledging her own anger was emancipating, even though she did not express it directly to those who had been the cause of it.

Where certain feelings are "permitted" and others "forbidden", based on the script (Holloway, 1977), then a vicious circle may be generated. For example, a coachee may believe he is permitted to express anger, but not fear. Consequently, anger may be expressed as a substitute for fear (Woollams and Brown, 1978). The unexpressed fear accumulates, anger is expressed instead, quite possibly inappropriately in terms of time, place, intensity or a mixture. He comes to a coaching session eager to talk about a recent, deeply embarrassing incident. He had exploded in fury because the coffee in the staff canteen was currently only available with low-fat milk.

A culture of certain feelings being permitted or forbidden may have echoes of childhood (Jacobs, 1995). Hence somebody may have a sense of himself as somehow "not being fully grown up" in the situation. Equally, the impact and expression of intense emotions may be an indicator of past times, but not necessarily extending back to childhood.

The supervisee realises that the dramatic and extensive restructuring of the business currently taking place in the client organisation reminds her of a painful experience from her first managerial role ten years previously. There had been, in her eyes, a phoney consultation – blatant but unchallengeable. She recognises that her anger and sadness are a mixture of the past and present and that she needs to separate them sufficiently in order to behave appropriately. She acknowledges that her fury is partly the result of unfinished business from the past and that she can have most impact by reporting on her anger in the present; that is, talking about it in a cool, assertive and controlled way, with clear examples of the consequences if the changes are not handled more authentically.

A linked point is that sometimes people do not update their sense of themselves. They are living a script where a key element is outdated.

Story – Not updating self

Another of my supervisees, "Denise", had achieved a huge amount in pioneering coaching in her organisation; this included some major landmarks in her professional development. Yet she still saw herself two years later as a novice or newcomer, and was a harsh critic of herself, fearing that somehow, she "would be found out". I suggested that without putting herself under pressure she note any "random gifts from the universe" that might occur prior to our next session. By such gifts I meant an image, an overheard conversation, a chance remark, a moment in a soap opera, a suddenly rediscovered precious object – that is, anything that might somehow resonate with her, even if she was not sure why. She spent the next two weeks occasionally capturing such moments. Something that particularly struck her was travelling on a train and seeing a child, perhaps seven years old, in the seat in front of her asking her mum if she could hold the tickets. The mother simply handed them over with a smile. My supervisee said she knew for sure that her father would never have allowed her at that age to hold onto the tickets. He would not have trusted her to be careful with them. Our conversation then moved on to how she might learn to trust herself more, including an acknowledgement that clearly her colleagues trusted her. So, referring back to the scripting model, an important element in our work was about disconfirmation in order to confirm new truths.

Evidently, any of the points made above about the supervisee, coach or coachee may also apply to the supervisor. As already mentioned, with the helping role there is always the challenge of being a part of, and apart from, the world of the person one is seeking to help. Boundary flexibility is important. Emotional intensity has the potential to bring insight through introspection and the stimulus of one's own internal supervisor. Equally there can be a rigidity or excessive fluidity of the script boundaries that impedes learning through over-identifying with the person one is seeking to help or armouring oneself against the pain of the other in order to avoid engaging with one's own pain (Guggenbuhl-Craig, 1992).

Suggestions for working with intense emotions

Be alert to the wider context

As indicated, the roles of the coach, whether internal or external, and the supervisor have been rapidly evolving and consequently it becomes increasingly important for each to be aware of the wider context. Here there may be a wide variety of intense emotions at play, potentially having a direct or indirect impact on that which happens in supervision. This is illustrated below in Figure 5.2.

It outlines the wide range of emotions that may be present in the supervision room with varying degrees of intensity, awareness, ownership and history. This wider perspective may be about the explicit and that which is generally acknowledged. For example, the supervisor and coach may need to be aware of a recent merger and the combination, perhaps clash, of cultures. One may be bureaucratic and the other entrepreneurial. Certain feelings may be "permitted" in one culture, but not the other. Or, looking more widely, the business sector as a whole may be undergoing

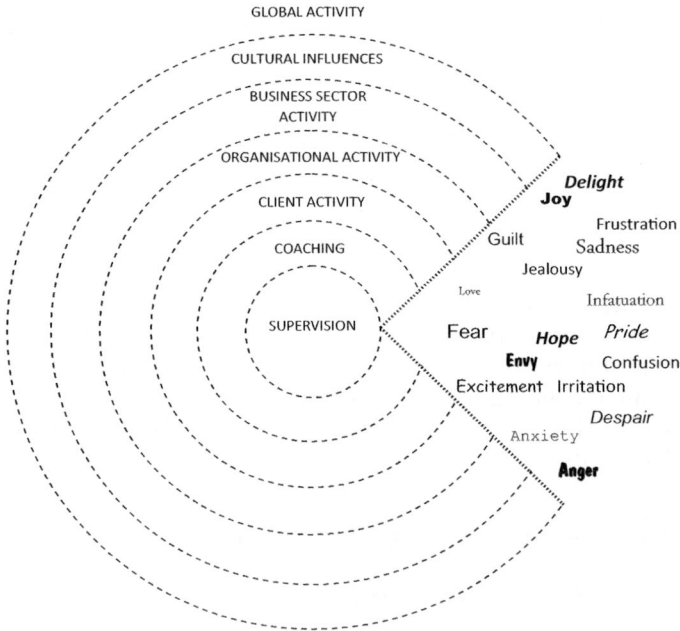

Figure 5.2 Emotions in the Context of Supervision

dramatic change with a profound impact on the expectations and emotions of those who had joined only a few years
before. Equally, there might be a growing frustration flowing from a recognition that there are racial or gender divides
restricting access to positions of influence.

In contrast there may be vital strands of the context that
are implicit and not acknowledged. There may be the unexpressed pain regarding the loss of ideals that used to be a key
source of energy and focus. Such pain may be a time when
"skilled incompetence" is most honed (Argyris, 1986: 74).
People are adept at making the very fact of "undiscussabil-
ity" itself undiscussable. This can be sensed almost as a dark
cloud in the supervision room: the noisiness of the unspoken.

At a deeper level again, there may be important
aspects of culture that are buried in the unconscious and
are more accessible through intuition and the impression-
istic (Phillips, 2006). Hoyle refers to the "sycophant" and
the "saboteur" as representing a spectrum of responses to
change (Hoyle, 2004: 93). Perhaps within a particular organisation there are dramatic switches between the sycophantic
and the sabotaging. Yet this may be accompanied by an act
of profound self-delusion amongst the leadership team that
any problems associated with the implementation of the new
strategy are solely technical. The supervisor and supervisee may both be hypnotically inducted into this world view
(Clarkson, 1995).

Being alert to the wider context is not about putting self
under pressure to understand everything that might be happening. Such a stance is ultimately self-defeating. Rather it
is about being open to possibilities and essentially going on a
journey with the supervisee to see whether particular experiences and ideas resonate sufficiently, both mentally and
emotionally, to support individual and collective learning.

Be alert to one's habits

As referred to earlier, boundaries may become rigid when
intense emotions are present. Hence a platform of presumed
good practice becomes a snare. One traps oneself into a particular way of working. This is illustrated below by a model,

Figure 5.3, inspired by Proctor (Proctor, 2000: 7). In it there are three potential roles for the supervisor (Phillips, 2013).

Teacher: educating the supervisee about the theory and practice of coaching. What more does the supervisee need to learn? What are her skills and talents on which she could build? Where and with whom could she progress further?

Guardian: maintaining the ethical and practical standards of the profession. Does she maintain appropriate ethical standards when working? Do her interventions match the remit of the contract? How does she manage the risk level?

Healer: offering personal support to help the supervisee cope with the emotional challenges of the work. In what ways does the supervisee need to be "held" at the moment? How can she develop a greater resilience?

These can be seen as archetypes, ways of thinking derived from the collective unconscious, with the potential for the shadow within each to emerge (Jung, 1991).

Story – The Archetype and the Shadow

One of my supervisees, "John", was part of a team helping a high-tech company make a culture change. They were supporting the leadership in becoming more skilled in working with others, and being less systems driven. I remember an occasion when John gave me feedback about over-using the model of transactional analysis in our work. Although

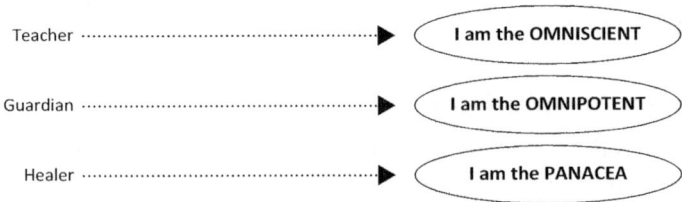

Teacher ···➤ (I am the OMNISCIENT)

Guardian ···➤ (I am the OMNIPOTENT)

Healer ···➤ (I am the PANACEA)

Figure 5.3 Archetypes In Supervision

I was not giving lengthy theory inputs, I was habitually using transactional analysis to capture what I saw as the key themes. My shadow of The Omniscient had emerged and I was unwittingly trying to make sense of everything. I had deluded myself that this was for the benefit of my supervisee, whereas in truth I was clinging to supposedly safe ground whilst other aspects of my life, particularly the personal, were turbulent. With hindsight, it may also be that I was taking an overly technical approach, thereby unwittingly working against the intended culture change.

Hold the space of uncertainty

Where there is an urge for clarity and resolution it can be productive for the supervisor to hold the space of uncertainty. There are two strands to this:

- Amorphousness. The supervisee has vague and shapeless glimmerings of unease and doubt. They are scarcely sensed, let alone open to articulation.
- Ambivalence. The supervisee feels profoundly torn, pulled in two very different directions. She may both love and hate her organisation. She may even feel ambivalent about her ambivalence – sometimes agitated and sometimes indifferent.

Such amorphousness and ambivalence are often indicators of transition. This might be moving from amorphousness to ambivalence, then to audacity or acceptance or points in between. Potentially therefore, it is a place for rich insights. However, time and space are needed for the learning to emerge. Forcing the pace is counterproductive. The supervisee might be uncomfortable with the space of uncertainty:

- The client organisation is one where reflection is shunned. It is regarded as passivity rather than an opportunity to learn. One must be seen to be busy and always be looking forward.
- The supervisee intuitively recognises that the space of uncertainty increases the possibility of having to face up

to some fundamental issues, such as the assumptions that he had been making about assumptions (Argyris and Schon, 1978). His eternal truths, central to his script, are crumbling. The issue is about identity, rather than just actions.

• The supervisee feels ambivalent about the supervisor. The space of uncertainty creates an opportunity for greater openness and intimacy but is also higher risk. Consequently, along with greater vulnerability there is both a craving for and abhorrence of an altered way of looking at self. The ambivalence is accentuated. This may be evidenced by door-handle dynamics, namely throw-away remarks by the supervisee at the end of the session when there is no time to follow-up (van Deurzen and Adams, 2011).

The supervisor needs to balance permission and protection (Crossman, 1966). Permission is needed to go exploring, and protection for setting appropriate limits. The parallels with child-rearing are apparent. Excessive permission may feel like abandonment and excessive protection may feel like engulfment.

The supervisor needs to offer herself permission and protection in order to offer it to her supervisee. She gives herself protection by contracting well even in an environment characterised by an unspoken longing for unconditional love. She gives herself permission to be uncertain; that is, to live with contradictory feelings and motivations. At any time, the consequential joy, guilt or confusion can be a gift she then holds out with an open hand to the supervisee.

Show compassion towards self

A volatile environment can mean that people are driven to make intense and rapid judgements in their hunger for solid ground. Such judgements can be stark and polarised – good, bad; wonderful, terrible; brilliant, useless. These judgements may be directed towards self, leading to excessive pride and deep shame (de Haan and Kasozi, 2014). The supervisor might be drawn into this world by being excessively self-critical. Showing oneself compassion instead can be invaluable for several reasons:

- The chances of learning are increased. Supervision and coaching are about balance – balancing the emotional and the rational, the detail in-the-moment and the bigger picture. One needs to lose balance in order to learn how to maintain it. Developing and deepening one's skills means being willing and able to take risks. However, one may regard one's mistakes as acts of betrayal, thereby on occasion colluding with the client organisation's culture (Phillips, 2010b).
- Potentially powerful role modelling takes place, even if it is not openly discussed. Supervisees often have an intuitive sense of the extent to which the supervisor practices what he preaches. A supervisor who encourages the supervisee to show compassion towards self but does not do so for himself rings untrue for the supervisee. Arguably this is an indicator of inconsistent parenting (Bowlby, 2005).
- Difficult issues are more accessible. Turbulent times can trigger a survival mentality. This may have echoes of childhood and early decisions in creating the script (Steiner, 1975). Those decisions can be about how to avoid being told off or punished. Being compassionate to oneself in the present means that the child within us is more willing to visit some of those early decisions; decisions that may have now become outdated, unhelpful or perhaps even profoundly undermining. A lack of compassion and punishing oneself for being self-sabotaging may well simply increase the urge to self-sabotage; the undermining aspect of the script is thereby confirmed (Holloway, 1977).

Story – Showing self-compassion

I recall supervising a coach to family businesses. My supervisee, "Robert", brought for discussion his handling of the coachee, the managing director of a small financial services firm. There were three other staff including "Jane", the managing director's daughter. She was a student in her early twenties studying at college but helping out in the family business at least one day a week. She updated the office records and sometimes handled basic customer queries. Robert focussed mainly on the father, helping him take a more strategic view of the business.

I regularly asked about Jane and whether her father was giving her opportunities to develop. Robert was amused, intrigued and sometimes a bit irritated. We both agreed I needed to consider this further for myself. I took the issue to my supervisor since I seemed to be making Jane more important than was necessary to support my supervisee.

My conversation with my supervisor widened to my work as coach and consultant as well as supervisor. I realised that my concern was young women not being allowed to fulfil their potential. I remembered that my mother, Freda, was 16 when her mother died. She then spent the rest of her life as a daughter, sister, wife or mother ensuring that others had the opportunity to develop their talents and travel the world. I remembered a photograph of her playing the cello. She gave this up when her mother's death meant she stepped in to support her father and elder brothers in running the family pork-butcher business in Bristol.

My focus on Jane and some of the other young women linked to my work suddenly made sense to me. I used the word hijacking when talking to my supervisor about what I had done. She suggested I be more compassionate towards myself (though she did not use the word compassionate). She asked me what I thought my mother would have wanted me to do. I said, "She would have given me a big hug and told me to get on with the rest of my life".

Be alert to the simple

Scripts are energised and manifest through a combination of the existential and the pragmatic (Klein, 1980). That is, one's day-to-day behaviours are likely to reinforce one's broader beliefs about oneself and the world. A focus in supervision on the simple, an action taken, deferred or dismissed, can be helpful. This is the basis of the following case study.

Case study

Frequently, supervisees have a multiplicity of roles, for example having a wide-ranging organisation development remit within which individual and team coaching is offered in a wide variety of forms and purposes. The supervisee consequently has contact with and responsibility for a variety of stakeholders. Additionally, there may also be personal and family pressures. The story below, told by "Julie", one of my supervisees, confirms my belief that in complex, shifting circumstances it is vital to be alert to the simple. Even when a number of emotional script issues and questions may be in the air relating to trusting oneself, owning one's wisdom or acknowledging one's talents, an apparently small but tangible action, can be invaluable.

"Intense feelings are certainly a regular, indeed frequent part of my life. I am part of the sandwich generation with elderly family members, one of whom has Alzheimer's and I have a teenage daughter with her own age-related issues. I am also responsible for looking after staff wellbeing in a large organisation. I set up and run a wide variety of services for a wide variety of individuals, groups and teams. This includes coaching, development workshops, the handling of complaints and supporting those who may be dealing with extreme anxiety, depression, trauma, despair and threatened suicide. I need to hold people until the troops (whether an external service or their own strength of character) march in. At the same time, I have to cope with a limited budget, many different management and leadership styles and multiple levels of bureaucracy.

"During a recent supervision call full of intense and very varied incidents I felt I was waffling, rambling and completely losing the plot, with no sense of direction. Somehow any solid ground was elusive as I raced from issue to issue. Many mixed feelings seemed to be in the air – some around pleasure with what I had been able to achieve so far, some around frustration with myself and others about insufficient support and guilt about my not meeting the needs of those who perhaps deserved more from me.

"Keri reminded me that I had previously been wondering whether to apply for a new senior role. I had not applied. I felt that, at one level, I would never be chosen, so why bother? I had also missed the application deadline. With Keri's challenge I realised that I truly had nothing to lose by simply expressing an interest in the role and indeed every-thing to gain. Subsequently my small step was simply for me to declare in an e-mail to my manager, 'I would like you to know I am interested in principle'. I found the process of tak-ing action – a simple, straightforward step – empowering, by stating, 'This is me!' This in itself was important regardless of whether I ultimately applied for the job. Needless to say, on reflection I was vividly aware that some of my own coachees were also faced with similar challenges about when, whether, how to step forward whilst being true to themselves".

Through all the suggestions above it is important for super-visors to have a support network that provides plenty of opportunities for skill development and the sharing of feel-ings, even in a rather incoherent way. There is also the need regularly to revisit assumptions. Close involvement with the same people can create a rather closed mind; coaches are often brought in when the client organisation recognises that it may have drifted into unhelpful habits. In the inter-est of authenticity supervisors, as well as coaches, need actively to seek fresh perspectives.

Conclusion

Coaching has been rapidly evolving in recent years, together with its dramatically changing environment. Consequently, supervision has been faced with similar challenges and opportunities regarding its purpose and its ability to make a valued contribution. Inevitably intense emotions are a crucial strand within this journey; a vital way of connect-ing with self in order to connect with others, and vice versa. Such connections are often helped by a lightness of touch, enjoying the journey of exploration and allowing oneself to be both passionate and reflective. As always, the journey might be the destination.

Practice points

- Allow yourself transition time in and out of supervision sessions. Notice the feelings with which you enter and leave the room and to whom they belong – you, the supervisee, the coachee, another key stakeholder, the wider culture, a mixture?

- Notice whether you ever have a sense of yourself changing age during the session. How might that help/hinder your work as a supervisor?
- Let your body tell you how you might be contorting yourself.
- Be alert to random gifts from the universe and how they may help you in your practice, whether generally or with a specific client.
- Look after yourself. Failure to do so means that sooner or later you will fail to look after your client or supervisee adequately.
- When you realise you have not been looking after yourself sufficiently, lovingly make adjustments. Self-punishment is an option, not an obligation.

Discussion points

- How might your script support/hinder the effectiveness of your role as supervisor?
- Is there "skilled incompetence" between you and your colleagues? If so, how and why does it happen? What actions are needed?
- How and with whom might you extend your journey in exploring the wider context of supervision?
- In reflecting on the archetypes and shadows that may be present in your supervision practice, what excites your curiosity?

Suggested Reading

Hall, L. (2015). *Coaching in Times of Crisis and Transformation*. London: Kogan Page.

Kets de Vries, M. (2003). *Leaders, Fools and Impostors: Essays on the Psychology of Leadership*. New York, NY: iUniverse Inc.

Morgan, G. (1986). *Images of Organization*. London: Sage.

Salzberger-Wittenberg, I. (2013). *Experiencing Endings and Beginnings*. London: Karnac.

References

Argyris, C. (1986). Skilled incompetence. *Harvard Business Review*, 64 (5), 74–79.

Argyris, C. and Schon, D. (1978). *Organizational Learning: A Theory of Action Perspective*. Reading, MA: Addison-Wesley.

Babiak, P. and Hare, R.D. (2006). *Snakes in Suits: When Psychopaths Go to Work*. London: Harper Business.

Boulton, J., Allen, P. and Bowman, C. (2015). *Embracing Complexity: Strategic Perspectives for an Age of Turbulence*. Oxford: Oxford University Press.

Bowlby, J. (2005). *The Making and Breaking of Affectional Bonds*. London: Routledge.

Clark, N., Phillips, K. and Barker, D. (1984). *Unfinished Business: The Theory and Practice of Personal Process Work in Training*. Aldershot: Gower.

Clarkson, P. (1995). *The Therapeutic Relationship*. London: Whurr.

Clarkson, P. and Gilbert, M. (1991). The training of counsellor trainers and supervisors. In W. Dryden and B. Thorne (Eds), *Training and Supervision for Counselling in Action*. London: Sage.

Clutterbuck, D and Megginson, D. (2005). *Making Coaching Work: Creating a Coaching Culture*. Wimbledon: CIPD.

Crossman, P. (1966). Permission and protection. *Transactional Analysis Bulletin*, 5 (19), 152–154.

van Deurzen, E. and Adams, M. (2011). *Skills in Existential Counselling and Psychotherapy*. London: Sage.

Doherty, D. (2016). *The Lived Experience of Consuming Coaching Credentials: A Survey*. Bristol: Critical Coaching Research Group.

Fromm, E. (2000). *The Art of Loving*. New York, NY: Perennial Classics.

Frosh, S. (2002). *Key Concepts in Psychoanalysis*. London: British Library.

Goleman, D. (1998). *Working with Emotional Intelligence*. London: Bantam.

Guggenbuhl-Craig, A. (1992). *Power in the Helping Professions*. Dallas, TX: Spring Publications.

de Haan, E. and Kasozi, A. (2014). *The Leadership Shadow: How to Recognise and Avoid Derailment*. London: Kogan Page.

Hamel, G. (2000). *Leading the Revolution*. Boston, MA: Harvard Business School Press.

Holloway, W. (1977). Transactional analysis: An integrative view. In G. Barnes (Ed), *Transactional Analysis After Eric Berne*. New York, NY: Harper's College Press.

Hoyle, L. (2004). From sycophant to saboteur – Responses to organisational change. In C. Huffington, D. Armstrong, W. Halton, L. Hoyle and J. Pooley, (Eds), *Working Below the Surface: The Emotional Life of Contemporary Organisations*. London: Karnac.

Huffington, C., Armstrong, D. Halton, W. Hoyle, L. and Pooley, J. (Eds) (2004). *Working Below the Surface: The Emotional Life of Contemporary Organisations*. London: Karnac.

Jacobs, M. (1995). *The Presenting Past: An Introduction to Practical Psychodynamic Counselling*. Milton Keynes: Open University Press.

James, O. (2013). *Office Politics: How to Survive a World of Lying, Backstabbing and Dirty Tricks*. London: Random House.

Jung, C., Adler, G. and Hull, R. (1976). *Collected Works of C.G. Jung. Vol 18. The Symbolic Life. Miscellaneous Writings*. Princeton, NJ: Princeton University Press.

Jung, C. (1991). *The Archetypes and the Collective Unconscious*. London: Routledge.

Klein, M. (1980). *Lives People Live: A Textbook of Transactional Analysis*. Chichester: John Wiley.

Leimon, A., Moscovici, F. and Goodier, H. (2011). *Coaching Women to Lead*. London: Routledge.

Lowen, A. (1997). *Narcissism: Denial of the True Self*. London: Touchstone.

May, R. (1976). *The Courage to Create*. London: Collins.

Merry, U. and Brown, G. I. (1987). *The Neurotic Behaviour of Organizations*. New York, NY: Gardner Press.

Mountain, A. and Davidson, C. (2015). *Working Together: Organizational Transactional Analysis and Business Performance*. Farnham: Gower.

Page, S. and Wosket, V. (2002). *Supervising the Counsellor. A Cyclical Model*. Hove: Brunner-Routledge.

Pearson, C. (1991). *Awakening the Heroes Within: Twelve Archetypes to Help Us Find Ourselves and Transform Our World*. San Francisco, CA: Harper Collins.

Phillips, K. and Shaw, P. (1997). *A Consultancy Approach for Trainers and Developers*. Aldershot: Gower.

Phillips, K. (2004). *Coaching in Organisations: Between the Lines*. Bath: Claremont.

Phillips, K. (2005). *Transactional Analysis in Organisations*. Handforth: KPA.

Phillips, K. (2006). *Intuition in Coaching*. Handforth: KPA.

Phillips, K. (2010a). *Coaching Supervision and Parallel Process*. London: Coaching Supervision Academy.

Phillips, K. (2010b). *Coaching and Betrayal*. Handforth: KPA.

Phillips, K. (2013). *The Delights and Terrors of Betrayal: Coaching Implications*. Handforth: KPA.

Proctor, B. (2000). *Group Supervision: A Guide to Creative Practice*. London: Sage.

Schein, E. H. (1986). *Organizational Culture and Leadership*. London: Jossey-Bass.

Schutz, W. (1989). *FIRO: A Three-Dimensional Theory of Interpersonal Behaviour*. Muir Beach, CA: WSA, Inc.

Shams, M. and Lane, D. A. (Eds) (2011). *Coaching in the Family Owned Business*. London: Karnac.

Smith, P. B. (1969). *Improving Skills in Working with People: The T-Group*. London: HMSO.

St. John-Brooks, K. (2014). *Internal Coaching: The Inside Story*. London: Karnac.

Steiner, C. (1975). *Scripts People Live: Transactional Analysis of Life Scripts*. New York, NY: Grove Press.

Storr, A. (1992). *The Integrity of the Personality*. Oxford: Oxford University Press.

Tufekci, Z. (2017). *Twitter and Tear Gas: The Power and Fragility of Networked Protest*. London: Yale University Press.

Wallace, P. (2016). *The Psychology of the Internet*. New York, NY: Cambridge University Press.

Winnicott, D. (2005). *Playing and Reality*. London: Routledge.

Woollams, S. and Brown, M. (1978). *Transactional Analysis*. Dexter, MI: Huron Valley Institute Press.

6

Self as Instrument

Eunice Aquilina

Introduction

In writing this chapter I invite you into the idea that cultivating the self as the instrument of our work is as important
as expanding our repertoire of tools and techniques. For
me, the heart of supervisory work is paying attention to the
"who" we are being – the self. In my years of working as a
coach supervisor I have found that the most powerful tool
we have is the self we are, and using ourselves well is critical to the interventions we make with our supervisee. Being
able to bring our whole self to our work enables more depth
in the conversation (Cheung-Judge and Holbeche, 2011).

I am writing here from the perspective of you as the
supervisor, focusing on how we can cultivate our self as the
powerful instrument of our work. I have chosen three core
elements of my own practice to share with you: focusing
inwards to access our innate wisdom; getting present with
ourselves and our supervisees to hold a deep, broad space
for them, filled with trust; and lastly, embodying grounded
compassion for our supervisees through strong container-
ship, empathy and resilience.

The development of this approach to supervision

The idea of "use of self" has its origins in ancient teachings. It has come to the fore in modern times with Frederick
Alexander who introduced the concept of "use of self" within

his work, the Alexander Technique (Alexander, 1932). It has remained in the discourse of many helping professions, becoming integral to the fields of human and organisation development through thought leaders such as Warner Burke, Tannenbaum, Cheung-Judge and others (Cheung-Judge and Holbeche, 2011). "Use of self is the conscious use of one's whole being in the intentional execution of one's role for effectiveness in whatever the current situation is presenting" (Jamieson et al., 2010: 5).

The most powerful way, I believe, to cultivate the self as instrument is by working with and through the body. Building our somatic awareness allows us to access a deeper wisdom that resides within each of us, a wisdom that has no words and yet speaks to us loudly if we choose to listen. Somatics, a term first introduced by Thomas Hanna (1970) comes from the early Greek "soma", which means the living body in its wholeness and pre-dates the Cartesian notion of the mind–body split. We can interpret the body neither as a collection of bones, muscles and tendons, nor as an image of beauty or athleticism but rather as the unified space in which we act, learn, relate, think, feel, sense and express our emotions and mood.

As humans we are historical beings, shaped by our history over time (Flores, 2012). Throughout our lives we develop strategies that support our inherent need for safety, belonging and dignity (Strozzi-Heckler, 1984). Some people keep themselves small in order to stay safe; they contract, withdraw or freeze. Others might lean forward ready to move against, to fight or challenge. We have all met the person who is painfully shy with collapsed shoulders, and eyes turned downwards – and those who appear willing to raise a topic for the sake of argument, their voice full and their jaw tight. What we embody is exemplified in our everyday actions. Therefore, our shape is a physical manifestation of our experiences over time, which predisposes us to a certain way of being, seeing, and of taking action. In this different interpretation, our body is inextricably linked to the self; so by working through the body, we can cultivate the self (Strozzi-Heckler, 2014).

There are a number of body-based disciplines, many of which trace their roots to Eastern philosophies and spiritual traditions, humanistic psychology, body psychotherapy, psychoanalysis, philosophy and body therapy (Marlock, 2015). Dr Richard Strozzi-Heckler is a key influence in the field, with whom I studied extensively. He integrated his early career as a somatic psychotherapist with his studies in the pioneering body-work of Dr Randolph Stone, Ida Rolf and Moshe Feldenkrais. His work continued to evolve through integrating the discourses of the martial art of Aikido and his long-term meditation practice. Furthermore, having spent time working with Dr Fernando Flores, he incorporated the linguistic theory of coordination and communication into his somatic learning methodology. "Self-cultivation is a cornerstone in developing wisdom, compassion, and skilful action and it is a lifelong path" (Strozzi-Heckler, 2014: 44).

Neuroscience has established a definitive link between the brain and body, through neural pathways and through neurotransmitters in our heart, gut and connective tissue (Aquilina, 2011). Candace Pert, a neuroscientist and pharmacologist, suggested that our brain extends down into our entire body through the central and autonomic nervous systems: "I can no longer make a strong distinction between the brain and body" (Pert, 1988: 12). Recently, the relatively new field of neuro-gastroenterology has demonstrated that the enteric nervous system (also known as the "second brain") functions independently of the brain inside the head and consists of around 100 million neurons, sending as many messages to the brain as it receives (Hadhazy, 2010). Our old way of seeing the brain and the body as separate entities is being challenged.

In addition to the recent developments in neuroscience, neurobiologists now tell us that we have multiple and complex classes of sensation and perception. The original five senses fit into a particular class called exteroception and determine how we pay attention to the external world. Another class of perceptions, called interoception, determines how we pay attention to the internal state of the body, and potentially aids our self-awareness (Craig, 2009), while proprioception allows us to perceive where our body is in space (Blake, 2018). Dr Alan Fogel (2009) describes this as embodied self-awareness or our ability to feel ourselves, to pay attention to our sensations, emotions, body shape and movements. It follows, then, that when we become more attuned to our internal self we are tapping into a whole other part of our perceptual ability.

From the ancient teachings through to present-day scientific development we can follow the evolution of our understanding of how, as humans, we can connect into our whole selves – this innate wisdom that resides in each of us, enabling us to show up as genuine and authentic. This is not a simple approach, or a quick fix as the Buddhist teacher Frank Ostaseski tells us:

> Authenticity requires trust in a deep inner wisdom and willingness to bring that wisdom into conscious action. Wisdom is not about age or expertise, tools or roles. I have a lot of tools that I have collected over the years, but I find that if I start pulling those tools out and setting them down between myself and my client, then one of us is sure to trip over them.
>
> (Ostaseski, 2017: 130)

Practice

Our work starts well before the supervisee walks into the session, as we prepare ourselves to be the instrument of our work. Cultivating the self invites us to wake up to our own judgement and biases from our history, which shape the way we listen and are available to the other. We often talk about "being" and "doing" but in viewing these states as separate we prevent ourselves from showing up as a whole person. As a somatic practitioner, I hold this unity as core to my work: the "who" we are being shapes the actions we take – our doing – and the actions we take are determined by the shape we are. Refining the instrument I am requires me to be in regular practices myself to continue to deepen my capacity to draw on the innate intelligence of my body. This notion of practice comes from Buddhism (Batchelor, 2011) and refers to a regular activity through which we deepen our sense of self and begin to retrain our nervous system. We are literally building a new way of being.

By cultivating an embodied presence, I can show up authentically and create a space in which my supervisees can access safety for themselves. If I am grounded and centred, I can extend my attention, deeply listening to them from the minute they walk in the room; I am present to their shape, noticing their mood and listening to what they are saying – what is spoken and what is not spoken, from a place of "what is" as opposed to what I think it should be. This creates a sense of connection and acknowledgement. I become attuned to how they are showing up in the moment and to the quality of their presence as they bring their client work into the room.

I am holding my client with "grounded compassion". As the supervision space opens up and they move more deeply into their story, it is critical that I stay present, open and connected. This allows my supervisee to feel my compassion and share an innate understanding that I am sitting in a place of non-judgement. Being wholly present, paying attention to my own sensations, moods, historical conditioning and narratives I am consciously and consistently creating a safe, trusted space for my supervisee to be open and vulnerable, to go deeper and do their own work to learn and grow. This capacity to cultivate our innate intuitive ability is what Strozzi-Heckler describes as clairsentience (Strozzi-Heckler, 2011).

Go inside

We live in a rational world that privileges thinking, so dropping into our feeling self can feel challenging for us. It takes time to build that muscle but, through practice and doing our own work, we can develop a somatic sensibility. The following three distinctions of sensation, mood and emotions, and narrative provide a useful frame to help us access this untapped intelligence. While I describe each of these separately, in reality our sensations, emotions and narrative act in a dynamic dance together.

Sensation

Our western society privileges our intellectual, cognitive, rational intelligence and over many centuries we have become detached from our physical selves and from the life of our own bodies, (Strozzi-Heckler, 2014). So where do we start our reconnection in order to access this huge supply of unused intelligence – this different kind of wisdom? We begin by attending to our own physical sensations. For example: sensations of heat or cold, pressure or openness, aliveness or numbness. These sensations are the building-blocks of life and by paying attention to them we connect to the energy moving through us that energises us, informs us and makes us feel alive. It tells us what we care about. This animating force has been part of being a human from the time we evolved: it is our inner wisdom and deeper intelligence that, over time, we have forgotten. By simply being aware of our bodily sensations we begin waking up to the wisdom of the body.

A somatic practice

Just for a moment, turn your attention inwards and notice the various physical sensations present in your body: are your shoulders tense or your teeth clenched; is your breath high and shallow, are you holding your diaphragm, perhaps creating a knot in your stomach? As you become conscious of your shape ask yourself what occurred for you as you tuned into your own sensations? As you explore this territory, invite more relaxation by letting your shoulders relax, dropping your breath to the abdomen and softening your jaw.

Bringing our attention to the life of the body, and its wisdom, and shifting our shape in the moment, allows us to feel more spacious and therefore more available for our supervisees.

Moods and emotion

During the course of his studies into human emotions, Darwin concluded that certain moods and emotions are recognisable throughout the world. If we took a photograph of someone who is in fear and showed it to people on the streets of London, Mumbai or San Francisco, they would all say that is a person in fear (Ekman and Freisen, 2003). Our moods and emotions tend to be more in the background, which means we are often less conscious of them, and yet they are our embodied orientation to life; they determine how we show up in the world and shape our response to it. Try this: frown, contract the muscles in your face, tense your shoulders tighten your stomach muscles and clench your jaw. Now say "I am happy".

What do you notice? It doesn't work, does it? Our mood and our body's sensations are not aligned, so we can't feel the "happy" we are telling ourselves to. By tuning into our bodies, we can sense our moods and emotions, making them more accessible for us.

When we become aware of our mood we can begin to identify those moods that are conducive to our work with our supervisees, for example, curiosity, wonder, patience, confidence, and those moods that may limit our capacity such as resignation, fear, frustration or impatience. If, as practitioners, we find ourselves in an unproductive or negative mood there is nothing wrong, it is merely being human (Flores, 2016). Developing our ability to recognise our mood, and building practices to shift and cultivate our mood, is vital to our work as supervisors.

Narrative

As we go inside our bodies we can also start to notice the automatic, unbidden thoughts that come into our consciousness. They are often generated from the mood we find ourselves in. For example, when we wake up on the "wrong side of the bed" we perpetuate the mood through our interpretation of the day's events. We live in our narratives; the stories and assessments we hold about ourselves, we often hold as truths about who we are. Sometimes these circular thinking patterns can be so pervasive we begin to shape ourselves around them. In this way we embody a way of being that is pre-disposed to enacting our story – which may limit us in our practice.

As we drop into our feeling self and notice our internal narrative about how the world appears to us, we can draw into our conscious minds what is unconscious and become a better observer of our internal narrative and automatic assessments. In recognising our own history, its patterns and how it has shaped us, we can also learn to re-author our experience and reduce its hold on us.

By developing our somatic awareness, we begin to see the connection between our language, mood and internal physical experience. We learn to *be* with more sensation, to develop a stronger awareness of our historical narratives and cultivate our mood. This allows us to show up authentically, aligned with who we want to be as a practitioner. As you practice dropping into your body and tuning into your inner landscape, ask yourself: how does my internal condition shape how I show up with my supervisee?

Get present

Allowing ourselves to feel and tune into the life of the body is one of the quickest and most direct ways for us to bring ourselves present. In itself, this is an incredible practice for us, as whenever we find ourselves ambushed by thoughts, emotions or old narratives, either positive or negative, we can come back into the body and back into the present moment. Presence is a function of attention.

I have described presence as "a state of being, a moment-by-moment awareness, being connected to the truth of who we are. Cultivating presence is a practice of being awake to what is unfolding in ourselves, in others and the space in-between" (Aquilina, 2016). Presence is my ground from where I am able to tune into what is occurring and intervene effectively.

As human beings, we orient around three core concerns: safety, belonging and dignity (Strozzi-Heckler, 2014) and we learn adaptive strategies or conditioned responses to navigate our world, enabling us to feel safe and connected. Over time, and with practice, we develop the capacity to move beyond our conditioning, to know and feel when we are safe or in danger, when we belong and when we can trust. Our ability to have a strong, grounded presence is critical. It enables us to hold a space for our supervisees in which they can access safety, belonging and trust for themselves. By being present in my own body, I can simultaneously tune into myself and tune into – my supervisee; this cultivates the container and builds the environment for my supervisee to be open and vulnerable.

Trust

Supervision is a vulnerable space where our supervisees should feel they can bring all of themselves, their issues and concerns as well as their strengths. This requires us to cultivate our capacity to hold a space where our supervisee feels held, where they can feel our ground and our presence through whatever is unfolding – and for all that might unfold; a space where they can truly trust and be open.

As humans, we have an innate understanding of trust (Ostaseski, 2017). When trust is lost or absent the supervisory relationship is disabled. And once trust is present, it should not be taken for granted and needs to be regenerated constantly. We develop our capacity to build and maintain trust by tuning into our bodies and bringing ourselves present in such a way that our presence can be observed and felt in the congruence between our mood, emotions, thoughts and actions. Trust lives in the body as an instinctual source of information.

Somatic practice

> Think of a time when you immediately felt trust with someone – what did you notice in your body, what emotion was present for you and what automatic assessment popped up? Now think of someone you did not immediately trust. Again, what did you notice in your body, what emotion was present and what automatic assessment popped up? Notice the different sensations in your body as you move from trust to lack of trust.

Using the body in this way we can quickly tap into a deeper understanding of how our body shapes itself when we feel there is a lack of trust with someone.

In the supervisory conversation, as we traverse difficult or challenging territory, paying attention to trust means periodically checking in with our supervisee, staying awake to their response, and noticing if what they say is congruent with how we are experiencing them in the moment. If I sense that who they are being is not aligned with what they are doing or saying then it is important that I attend to that incongruence before anything else. In my practice, tuning into the body is the starting point for sensing what is going on for my supervisee at a deep level.

Holding the space

Being fully present to another so they feel seen, held and can access safety for themselves is fundamental to our work as supervisors. There is not a set of tools or a set of techniques that we can simply pull out (Ostaseski, 2017); it comes from the relationship, the quality of our presence and the trust we build. Holding the space for someone is being present to them, to yourself and to what is unfolding in-between. It is truly being with them as a human being wherever they are in their journey, not judging them, trying to fix them or making them wrong but supporting them as they learn and grow.

By learning to drop into our body, centring and bringing ourselves present, we can extend our attention and our energy towards our supervisee. In this way we can notice whether we are extending too much energy and possibly overwhelming our supervisee, or too little energy and disconnecting from them. Both may impact the supervisee's sense of safety and trust. It's helpful just to notice how you are sitting – are you forward in your chair and animated, or sitting back, somewhat collapsed? Get curious about how the way you are showing up may be perceived by your client.

When we embody an authentic presence, we are less likely to be trapped by our ego or our attachment to what might be best for the supervisee or even our own success. When we are in control of our ego our supervisee is able to feel our presence, our ground and that we are holding them with compassion and care. This opens up the possibility for them to feel safe enough to share what they might otherwise have kept hidden.

Cultivating this embodied presence comes through practice – developing new neural pathways that allow us to bring ourselves present without having to think about it. Centring is a powerful way to bring ourselves present to ourselves, each other and the space.

Somatic practice – centring

Standing or sitting, let your attention drop from your thinking self to your feeling self: pay attention to your sensations, your mood and your environment. Purposefully let your breath drop down to your centre, that place a few centimetres below your navel. Align yourself physically, your head, shoulders, hips, knees and ankles into a vertical line, so you are no longer fighting gravity, but are in harmony with it, lengthening while settling into yourself, feeling your dignity and recognising it in others.

Find balance at your feet or at your hips if you are sitting. Allow yourself to unfurl, inviting more space, letting your shoulder blades slide down your back, opening your chest. As you expand into your width, feel your connection with others and your environment.

Next, align yourself in your depth, so you are neither leaning forward nor pulling away, but balanced front to back. Become aware of what is at your back, your experience, your history, and bring that forward to the present, to the space in front of you and incorporate your vision for the future.

Lastly, remind yourself of what you care about; let that inform your nervous system and shape the self, the instrument you are.

Bring grounded compassion

Liz Hall (2013: 70) describes compassion as "the motivation to empathise with another, to feel what they're feeling, to care deeply about their well-being, happiness and suffering, and to act accordingly . . ." Through my own work I have come to understand that our capacity for compassion for another comes from how we have compassion for ourselves. That place where we may struggle with ourselves is the place where we can cultivate self-compassion, learning to shift the part of ourselves that shows up when we are triggered, maybe from a setback or an irritating situation. In those moments, our survival strategy kicks in and we close down, we feel less; less of ourselves and less of others. Bringing ourselves present allows us to feel open and connected. Only then are we able to access compassion for ourselves, which in turn allows us to extend it to others. For me container-ship, empathy and resilience are the three key elements in cultivating compassion.

Deepen your container

I recall a conversation with my supervisor about a super-visee who was repeatedly rescheduling our sessions and then arriving unprepared. I was increasingly frustrated with her and myself. I could feel the physical manifes-tation of this in my body; I felt my chest tighten, my shoulders tense, my breath was shallow and fast, and I sat forward in my chair. An old familiar narrative played out in my head reminding me that I was not a good enough coach. Then my supervisor simply asked me: "What if you held her with compassion and love?" That question stopped me in my tracks. In that moment I realised how I had become hooked by my frustration, which was in turn shaping my interpretations and potential actions. As I took a deep breath and centred myself I began to feel more spacious and I could tolerate my emotions with-out letting them drive me. I settled and immediately saw the possible moves I could make with my supervisee that would allow us to move forward – and for me to hold her with compassion.

The supervision session reminded me of how we can be gripped by our own moods and emotions: it knocks us off cen-tre. As supervisors, it is incumbent upon us to build a large container within ourselves to hold the strong sensations and emotions that occur when we are triggered by our supervisee. By paying attention to our internal landscape, we can learn to resource ourselves in the moment and can contain what is moving through us so we can stay present to whatever may be unfolding for them.

Embody empathy

Empathy – the ability to acknowledge and understand the feelings of others – is an obvious cornerstone of supervision. Neurobiology tells us that, as humans, we are wired for empathy. Over 20 years ago, a team of scientists led by Giacomo Rizzolatti (Rizzolatti et al., 1996) at the University of Parma, discovered special brain cells called mirror neurons in monkeys. Mirror neurons respond equally when we perform an action and when we witness someone else perform the same action, which helps explain how and why we can "read" other people's minds and feel empathy for them (Blake, 2018).

So, empathy is built in part through these mirror neurons; when someone takes action or expresses an emotion, we assign meaning to it based on our own experience and assessments. It is our capacity to feel ourselves, and to have access to a full range of our own emotions, that enables us to express empathy for our supervisee. We might say that our understanding of another is connected to who we are and what we embody. If we don't have access to particular emotions because we have dampened them down and cut them off by contracting our physical system, then it is much more difficult for us to have empathy for others because those neural networks have not been built. By going inside ourselves, by doing our own work, we can access and expand our own emotional repertoire, able to feel the other – in this case our supervisee – and connect with them in a deep way without losing ourselves.

Build resilience

Carole Pemberton's research with coaches identified that resilience is "the capacity to remain flexible in our thoughts, feelings and behaviours when faced by a life disruption, or extended periods of pressure, so that we emerge from difficulty stronger, wiser and more able" (Pemberton, 2015: 2). In the somatic way of working, it is our innate capacity to renew and to rebuild our sense of wholeness that allows us to access all of what Pemberton is talking about, producing more choice and more possibility in our work with others.

As practitioners, this means paying attention to how we regenerate safety and connection for ourselves in those moments when we feel triggered. When we are caught in our automatic or habitual response, our capacity to access compassion for ourselves and for others is limited. Building our own resilience allows us to relax our system, which enables us to feel more, to feel our aliveness, increasing our capacity to feel more in others. Our in-the-moment ability to centre clears and cleans the supervision space, allowing the work with our supervisee to continue and deepen unhindered. By learning to resource ourselves we are inviting in more ease, more spaciousness, connecting to what is important to us.

Building our ability to access our innate capacity to renew requires us to engage in practices where we feel more open and connected and where we fundamentally feel more whole. Becoming mindful of the experiences that bring us resilience, be it a walk in nature or engaging in a creative activity (Lieberman and Van Horn, 2008), opens up our capacity to hold our clients with compassion and to be a strong container for those we work with.

Case study – Rebecca's question

What is too much – what is not enough?

The supervisee, whom we will call Rebecca, describes how a coaching relationship triggered deeply held historical patterns, and shapes how she engaged with this particular client. As the supervisor, it meant holding the space in such a way that Rebecca felt able to recognise and confront her own conditioning. Here is Rebecca's story:

"I don't always find supervision easy. I'm sure I'm not alone in that. However, turning my attention inwards and working through the body moves me away from my thinking self and creates opportunities for me to experience myself in a way that I cannot otherwise. A constant question that I am in about my practice is 'How far do I step into the relationship? How do I support my client effectively?' I recognise that people have different needs and assessments of their own space requirements, but my own need is very much around 'how can I support you?

"I brought my concerns about a coaching client to group supervision in order to uncover what to do next. My client, George, came to coaching because his boss needs him to step up at work. George was not convinced about coaching but after our initial meeting he decided to go ahead. Once in the sessions George is engaged and works hard but we have met sporadically, and I had not heard from him in a number of months. My emails had gone unanswered. I noticed myself fall into a mood of anxiety and an old narrative of "you messed up the sessions, you are not a good enough coach" started to play in my head. Indecision reigned. What should I do – step in again and contact him or hold the space and see what emerges?

"Once I had told the group my story, Eunice invited me to pick up my Jo staff (a wooden staff made from Japanese oak) and invited my colleague Rob to join me with his Jo staff. Eunice asked us to engage together in a series of moves using our Jo staffs (Strozzi-Heckler, 2007). As I turned to face Rob with my Jo staff in hand, I centred and invited my whole system to relax. We moved together, connected and energised.

"After a while we stopped, and Eunice asked Rob what was going on for him. "I feel I need more space," was his reply "Rebecca is too close. I feel cramped and don't have enough room to move". I was puzzled. I thought we were moving well together and it felt comfortable to me. I felt my mood shift to one of mild irritation. I centred and as we began our sequence of moves again I stepped further back to provide more space as we coordinated together. Rob felt miles away from me and yet I knew, through our synchronised moves, I had not lost connection with him. Eunice repeated her question and to my amazement Rob insisted he still needed more space and that I was "swamping" him. I was amazed. How could that be – I had given him so much room?

"As we debriefed it was evident that what felt to me like stepping back and leaving lots of space was to Rob claustrophobic and "in his space". What he was feeling was my "excess" energy and it was more than he needed. I was energetically overpowering him. Working through my body, in ten minutes of a movement practice, I gained a felt sense of how my natural response to "step in" could overwhelm others and rather than drawing them in, which is my desired outcome, it pushes people away, effectively increasing the space between us. I was able to sense what is too much and what is not enough and intuitively understand when to contain and hold my ground, and when to move in. Although it is still a struggle to hold back, with practice it is starting to feel more natural.

"Interestingly, I emailed my client the next day to "check in" with him and got a fairly firm push back in response. My automatic narrative of "I have to do something here" was so strong I was not able to let it go even in the face of my experience the day before. This time though, I heard the push back. I was back in my Jo practice with Rob and I was able to hold my ground, waiting until my client felt ready to re-engage, which he did, and we resumed our coaching after a break of some four months. As I prepared myself for our session I centred and noticed my mood: curiosity and compassion. I shifted my narrative to "I've got this", reorganised myself and centred around my intention to simply hold a deep, safe and compassionate space for George to do the work he needed to. Holding George with compassion and containing my energy gave him the space to truly let go and begin the work he really wanted to do. At the end of our session it was George who was asking me to get my diary out, so we could schedule our next session. I now hold that question with all of my clients: what is too much, what is not enough?"

My role as supervisor

Holding the space for Rebecca to really get a felt sense of how she overextends called for me to feel my ground and be present. Working through the body can rapidly take us to the heart of the matter, so in my role as supervisor, I too am paying attention to what is too much and what is not enough. What is enough challenge to trigger Rebecca's habitual response to be revealed but not too much that she feels unsafe or overwhelmed?

I invited Rebecca to engage in a movement practice with another member of the group so she could experience how she is in relationship with them. Her pattern of overextending was revealed, and she could see how it produced overwhelm in Rob. Furthermore, Rebecca could practice in real time how she might reorganise herself in the moment to create a centred connection with her fellow group member, which in turn would help her with her client.

Throughout the session I was continually checking in with my inner self, noticing my breath, staying relaxed but alert and present. In those moments when Rebecca felt particularly vulnerable, I was literally being the strong ground for her to do the work she needed to do for herself, neither getting in the way of her own process nor disappearing. I was also paying attention to Rob and what might be stirred up in him as he partnered Rebecca in this practice. I was centring and re-centring throughout, tuning into my inner self and using my whole being as the instrument of my work.

Conclusion

By paying as much attention to our feeling self as we do to our thinking self, we become intimate with the moment to moment messages hidden in our sensations. As we recognise our moods and emotions, we can interrupt our automatic responses and shift our way of being. By tuning into this present moment awareness, we can not only observe how we are showing up in the relationship with another or with a group, but we can notice the patterns that are being co-created inside of the interactions, including what might be unspoken, and yet present, in the social space. By developing our innate ability to tune into our inner wisdom we can access a source of data that increases our capacity for skilful action with our clients.

My aim with this chapter has been to provide some insight into how we can hone our self as the instrument in our practice as supervisors by working with and through the body. I have also sought to offer some practices for you to engage in so you may access your own deeper wisdom in this way. The supervisor–supervisee relationship can be a sacred space, one in which we hold our supervisees with compassion through our presence, by tuning into our own bodies and using our self as instrument. Let's use ourselves well.

Practice points

1. Commit to a daily practice to refine the instrument you are by continuing to deepen your awareness of your own internal landscape.
2. Recognise and manage your mood.
3. Pay attention to what you are sensing and picking up from your supervisee and when something is self-generated, coming from your own history and conditioning.
4. Practice expanding your language, so you can pick up and describe the nuances of sensation and emotion.
5. Engage in your own personal work to ensure you are "fit to practice".
6. Hold yourself with compassion.

Discussion points

1. What am I practising and what might I choose to practise that will deepen my capacity to use myself as the instrument in my work?
2. What are the appropriate boundaries for me to hold that take care of those I work with and myself?
3. How do I routinely resource myself?
4. What standards do I hold for myself in my practice? Who and what can support me to hold those standards?

Suggested reading

Aquilina, E. (2016). *Embodying Authenticity: A Somatic Path to Transforming Self, Team and Organisation*. London: Live It Publishing.

Murdoch, E. and Arnold, J. (2013). *Full Spectrum Supervision: "Who You Are, Is How You Supervise"*. St Albans: Panoma Press.

Palmer, W. and Crawford, J. (2013). *Leadership Embodiment: How the Way We Sit and Stand Can Change the Way We Think and Speak*. San Rafael, CA: CreateSpace.

Strozzi-Heckler, R. (1984). *The Anatomy of Change: A Way to Move Through Life's Transitions*. Berkeley, CA: North Atlantic Books.

References

Alexander, F. (1932). *The Use of Self*. London: Methuen.

Aquilina, E. (2011). Tuned in. *Coaching at Work*, 6 (2), 27–30.

Aquilina, E. (2016). *Embodying Authenticity: A Somatic Path to Transforming Self, Team and Organisation*. London: Live It Publishing.

Batchelor, S. (2011). *Confession of a Buddhist Atheist*. New York: Random House.

Blake, A. (2018). *Your Body is Your Brain: Get Smarter About What Matters by Awakening Your Brain*. USA: Embright LLC.

Cheung-Judge, M. and Holbeche, L. (2011). *Organisational Development: A Practitioners Guide for OD and HR*. London: Kogan Page.

Craig, A. D. (2009). How do you feel — now? The anterior insula and human awareness. *Nature Reviews Neuroscience*, 10 (1): 59–70.

Ekman, P. and Freisen, W. (2003). *Unmasking the Face: A Guide to Recognising Emotions from Facial Expressions*. Los Altos, CA: Major Books.

Flores, F. (2012). *Conversations for Action and Collected Essays*. North Charleston, SC: CreateSpace.

Flores, G. (2016). *Learning to Learn and Navigation of Moods: The Meta Skills for the Acquisition of Skills*. Gt Britain: Pluralistic Networks Publishing.

Fogel, A. (2009). *The Psychophysiology of Self-awareness: Rediscovering the Lost Art of Body Sense*. New York: W.W. Norton.

Hadhazy, A. (2010). Think twice: How the gut's "second brain" influences mood and well-being. www.scientificamerican.com/article/gut-second-brain/ (Retrieved 1 August 2018).

Hall, L. (2013). *Mindful Coaching: How Mindfulness Can Transform Coaching Practice*. London: Kogan Page.

Hanna, T. (1970). *Bodies in Revolt: A Primer in Somatic Thinking*. New York: Rhinehart and Winston.

Jamieson, D. W., Auron, M. and Shechtman, D. (2010). Managing use of self for Masterful Professional Practice. *OD Practitioner*, 42 (3), 4–10.

Lieberman, A. F. and Van Horn, P. (2008). *Psychotherapy with Infants and Young Children: Repairing the Effects of Stress and Trauma on Early Attachment*. San Francisco, CA: Guilford Publications.

Marlock, G. W. (2015). *The Handbook of Body Psychotherapy and Somatic Psychology*. Berkeley, CA: North Atlantic Books.

Ostaseski, F. (2017). *The Five Invitations*. London: Bluebird.

Pemberton, C. (2015). *Resilience: A Practical Guide for Coaches*. Maidenhead, Berkshire, UK: Open University Press.

Pert, C. (1988). The wisdom of the receptors: Neuropeptides, the emotions, and bodymind. *Advances, Institute for the Advancement of Health*, 3 (3), 8–16.

Rizzolatti, G., Fadiga, L., Gallese, V. and Fogassi, L. (1996). Premotor cortex and the recognition of motor actions. *Cognitive Brain Research* 3(2), 131–141.

Strozzi-Heckler, R. (1984). *The Anatomy of Change: A Way to Move Through Life's Transitions*. Berkeley, CA: North Atlantic Books.

Strozzi-Heckler, R. (2007). *The Leadership Dojo: Build your Foundation as an Exemplary Leader*. Berkeley, CA: North Atlantic Books.

Strozzi-Heckler, R. (2011). *Clairsentience: A Somatic Approach to Intuition. Choice*, 9 (4), 27–29.

Strozzi-Heckler, R. (2014). *The Art of Somatic Coaching: Embodying Skilful Action, Wisdom and Compassion*. Berkeley, CA: North Atlantic Books.

7

Creative forms of reflective and expressive writing in coaching supervision

Jackee Holder

Introduction

The evidence-based research field documenting the benefits of reflective, therapeutic and expressive writing has grown significantly over the last 20 years. From the seminal and ongoing trauma-based research approach of expressive writing pioneered through the work of Pennebaker (2013) at the University of Texas to the work of King (2001), who went on to demonstrate the significant gains and benefits of writing about the good stuff, the research is plentiful. It offers access to a fertile space in which to engage with reflective writing that contains therapeutic benefits both for the coach supervisee and the coach supervisor.

This chapter explores the application of expressive and reflective writing and how this growing field can be creatively introduced into the process of supervision as a way of harvesting insights, connection, deepening learning and motivating meaningful action. The chapter makes links between reflective writing, the body and mindfulness, both of which are explored in further chapters in the book. The psychological and physiological benefits of reflective and expressive writing now have a strong evidence base that draws on neuroscience, providing approaches for a restorative (also referred to as resourcing in other chapters) methodology for supervisors and supervisees.

The development of the approach to supervision

I came to supervision in the early 1980s fresh out of university, when I joined the youth and community service in London aged 21. It was an exciting time of political and social change and unrest and my role as a full-time youth worker was where I was first introduced to reflective practice. Until then, life was really something that happened to me rather than being a life where I reflected. It was through early work with a supervisor that reflection took root in my professional and personal life.

Bassot believes that "the overall purpose of supervision is to encourage professionals to reflect on their practice in a deeper way in order to enhance their professional development" (2013: 84). The very nature and essence of supervision is an opportunity to reflect on the work you do as a supervisor or coach as well as explore who you are as a supervisor or coach. Supervision as a restorative practice can be greatly enhanced through engaging with expressive and reflective writing activities; this has been highlighted by research, which has demonstrated a range of therapeutic and physical benefits.

Smyth's (1998) meta-analytic review highlighted the benefits of the use of written emotional expression. These included improved health outcomes in healthy participants relating to physical health, physiological functioning, psychological well-being and general functioning. Research on the effect of positive events and reflection found that women who wrote down three positive events, career-related or otherwise, at the end of each workday, plus a brief reason why they thought each good thing had happened, experienced reductions in headaches, back pains and muscle tension (Bono et al., 2013).

According to Fain, a psychotherapist at Harvard Medical School, writing is not only a great way to ease emotional distress, but also a proven method for bolstering a positive outlook. An added bonus: Writing out your troubles may allow you to recognize and prepare for the situations that provoke your harshest inner critic.

(Fain, 2012: 212)

However, some researchers have challenged the benefits of expressive writing, especially when used with people who have experienced stressful or traumatic events (e.g. Mogk, Otte, Reinhold-Hurley and Kröner-Herwig, 2006).

Although many coaching and supervision tools are rooted in cognitive models and theories, reflective and expressive writing as a practice offers a "multi-dimensional" meta approach to supervision that is underutilised, both in formal one-to-one supervision and group supervision sessions. Applied in the same way as one might introduce the use of other coaching tools, reflective writing can be contracted into the work of supervision. An ideal positioning for the contracting piece is during both the chemistry call and first sessions. With new supervision clients the quality of the supervision experience can be deepened through opening up a conversation about reflection and its real value and benefits. With experienced coaches, engaging in reflective and expressive writing can bring to the surface a richer understanding of your work that can get missed when writing is not integral to the work of coaching and coach supervision.

The Reflection/Write approach originating from the work of Adams and Ross (2016) provides a framework to reflect on your writing. It suggests the importance and value of reflecting back on any writing crafted inside and outside of sessions. It is a valuable method of self-coaching and self-supervision.

What keeps this all together is the practice of reflecting on your writing and extending the scope of your learning. Thompson and Thompson (2017: 86) believe that "the therapeutic potential of expressive writing is deepened when we add a feedback write after each initial piece of writing." The feedback write is a way of recognising, deepening and integrating the insights of the initial write. It takes the form of a reflection in writing, just a few observations or thoughts on the process or content. This simple device allows people to come into contact with themselves in a new way – first by reading and witnessing their own words, then by writing about the experience (Thompson, 2011).

Adams and Ross (2016, quoting Adams, 2013) talk of the Reflection/Write as a way of developing observational muscle so that we notice what happens as we write.

> The reflection write harvests insight, codifies thinking, and brings detached mindfulness to the writing process. It comes at the end of each writing session in the form of one or two sentences about the writing just completed, in response to prompts such as, As I read this, I am aware of . . . or What did I notice in my body as I am writing? or What is an action step I could take to move my intention and attention in the direction of what I want?
>
> (Adams and Ross, 2016: 45)

"Tracking the embodied experience of writing helps you to stay grounded in the present moment," (Adams and Ross, 2016: 45).

Practice

It is important to introduce a range of reflective writing approaches with potential for the writing to offer different perspectives and creative insights into the supervision conversation rather than stay with a fixed approach.

As a practice of engaging with one's own thoughts, reflective writing can provide new and different ways of reflection, uncover and highlight blind spots, boost creativity and stimulate the quality of thinking and provide the foundations of a coaching and supervision narrative and pedagogy to support your work. Reflective writing can help to discover that which is so easily hidden from view. Suggesting time limits, using free writing, or writing prompts for reflective writing practice to try out inside a supervision session, often leads to more writing, not less.

From the seedbed of my own personal and professional practice, reflective writing is an exquisite form of internal listening. It can drown out the external voices, allowing words to emerge that often reveal themselves from a deeper place inside the self that writing connects with. Very often the writing reveals things that would not have been recognised or listened to through the medium of talking.

In the following section we will look at a range of exercises and consider the background to their use.

Digital distraction and the importance of writing by hand

The impact of digital distraction on so-called "Deep Work" (Newport, 2016) continues to be a real challenge to self-care and well-being, both personally and professionally. Digital overload reduces the quality of focus and attention you bring to your work. Intentionally engaging in writing by hand creates a different learning and thinking space that interrupts the often automatic and addicted digital overload that consumes the working day and drains sensory capacities and working memory. There are many benefits to an analogue approach that get overlooked. In research about writing by hand, Berginger (Berginger et al., 2006) found that elementary school students who wrote essays with a pen, not only wrote more than their keyboard-tapping peers, but they also wrote faster and in more complete sentences. James and Atwood (2009) found that when people write by hand, instead of on a keyboard, their ability to memorise data was significantly improved.

Reflective writing mindfulness practice

One way to come into relationship with writing, particularly when immersed in digital overload, is to switch to analogue mode and connect with the simple instruments of writing with a pen or pencil. This practice can be used as a warm-up mindfulness practice before you begin a reflective writing exercise. It can be completed in one minute.

Exercises

Hold a pen or pencil between your thumb and first finger in your dominant writing hand. Spend a few seconds exploring the pen/pencil, connecting to as many of the senses as you can. Continue for one minute, then turn to your notebook or journal and use the prompts below to write about the experience. Give yourself permission to go wherever the writing takes you:

- How did the pen feel against the indentures of your fingertips?
- As your arm moves, what does it move in your body, in your emotions, in your thoughts?
- What are you noticing about your thinking and your thoughts as you write?
- What stands out about this form of engagement when you think cognitively or discuss your thinking verbally? Is there a different quality and association?
- What themes emerged from the writing?

Free writing

Another warm-up exercise is to use spontaneous, automatic, stream of consciousness or free writing. Free writing is writing about whatever is in your mind and in your thoughts. It's important to remind yourself and others not to worry about spelling or grammar when using these techniques. The idea is to write as quickly as you can, capturing thoughts and feelings in the moment, using no prompts or scripts and no expected destination to arrive at. Hay (2008: 24) highlights that "it is important that you make no attempt to analyze or evaluate at this stage".

For many years free writing has been a choice approach in getting started with reflective and expressive writing. But one of the major challenges with this approach is feeling blocked and having nothing to say. What if you can't access the immediacy of your thoughts, feelings and emotions? The fast pace of working life can numb feelings and emotions. The rapid-response culture can place pressure on reaction as opposed to reflection and responding. Focused writing in supervision can promote reflection.

In the next section you will find examples where varied forms of reflective and expressive writing were applied to explore a challenge or dilemma:

Vignette one

Using free writing to explore a relationship challenge

Kay wanted to explore a challenging and difficult relationship with her line manager. I suggested Kay write about her feelings in the session as well as explore her feelings about a meeting to discuss the issue with her manager the following week. Kay appeared stuck, and expressed feeling hopeless about the situation changing. I wanted to offer a different approach from Kay's usual talking about the situation.

At the next session Kay arrived looking relaxed and lighter in her energy and eager to share what had happened since our last session. Kay had decided to try out a similar reflective writing practice at the start of her meeting with her line manager, which they'd agreed to. She suggested they both take fifteen minutes to write about their perspective of the challenges in their relationship, what feelings and emotions they were in touch with, what responsibility they owned for their part in the breakdown in communication and trust and finally what they wanted to be different. They both sat in the same room writing for 15 minutes in their own bubble as they processed what they were feeling, using the questions as prompts.

Kay explained how, by the time they had both emerged from the writing, there was a different atmosphere in the room. Kay described it as feeling as if something had energetically shifted between them both for the better. The writing intervention opened the door to a more honest and vulnerable conversation between the two and Kay described it as the most effective conversation they had both had for ages that shifted the dynamic of their relationship in a much more positive direction.

I was curious to hear what Kay thought the reasons were for the shift. She felt the writing had given them both distance and ownership of their contributions to the break-down in communication. The actual practice of writing reflexively had provided them with a shared perspective and ownership, and the space of writing together with a common purpose had kindled a form of compassion and more restora-tive empathy between them.

It's worth emphasising here that Kay decided to sug-gest the reflective writing to her manager inspired by the experience from her supervision session. By having less reli-ance on, and attachment to, tools and techniques, there's a chance to see first-hand how writing invokes the power to create a level playing field in the supervision dynamic. Writing puts the supervisee in charge. It is a unique oppor-tunity for both supervisee and supervisor to listen at deeper levels to what really matters and what might be so easily missed. This approach to reflective writing does not need to be perfect or polished.

Vignette two

Free writing and reflective writing

After a first chemistry call with a potential new supervision client I noticed that at different points during our conversa-tion I found myself triggered by the close resemblance of the material the new possible supervisee was presenting. I was experiencing some form of counter transference. Before our first session I decided I would spend some time reflecting in writing to see what I could unearth about the stimulation for those initial emotional responses.

After ten minutes I read over what I had written in a spirit of open curiosity and without preconceived expecta-tions. Sometimes unexpected and surprising things are revealed in the writing. In mine I noticed a pattern of themes connected with mid-life, transitions and changing identity and roles. There were hints of a parallel process. Our conversation had raised questions in me that urged further time enquiring into them for my own well-being and self-understanding.

I found taking this time not only hugely rewarding but it also cleared psychological space, allowing more of me to become present and available to my client in advance of our session. It was a way of taking care of my own business, freeing up the executive function of the mind, my "working memory", ensuring that my stuff was processed and less likely to get in the way of our work together.

I could identify the threads of "counter transference" through the reflective writing. This is not always easy to spot and to hold the self accountable to. So a challenge when writing reflectively might be to work with the questions:

"So what's missing?"

"What did I not write about?"

"What's absent?"

By placing my thoughts into writing I was able to make better sense of what had been moved in me and what further exploration I needed to embark on. This kind of reflecting on your original writing can yield a number of insights and increase levels of self-awareness.

Where To start? Writing to be present

So how might you begin working with reflective writing or introduce it into a coaching supervision session? Making time to write in sessions is often cited as a common barrier. But reflective writing can be one way of reducing the noise in the spaces and environments we find ourselves in, but also the digital noise that fills up most of the working day and the internal chatter going on in your head. Regular reflective writing is an easy and accessible way of making more of that working memory available. At the start of a supervision session, rather than launching straight in, top and tail the session with a short reflective writing exercise as a way of arriving into the session.

Exercise

- How am I arriving today?
- What is on my mind that it makes sense for us to be talking about?
- How am I feeling in my body? What sensations am I in touch with or not in touch with right now?
- What do I feel disconnected from right now?

Reflective writing by hand can be a subtle way of connecting with the body. Right now, as you read these words on the page, notice how you are sitting or standing? How open does your body feel right now? What position is your back in? How straight is your spine? A simple noticing, then writing about or drawing what you notice, can generate a more mindful and grounded self within a few minutes of focus and concentration. By writing about what you see and feel or sense of the experience in the here and now, there is the potential for you to become more embodied. To continue to write on a digital device has the challenge of you keeping in place that disconnection that is so often present within the body (see Chapter 6).

These reflective writing questions yield interesting responses and are a way of slowing right down and connecting with what's really present in the here and now. So often what emerges through the writing is not what you might expect. Bolton shares an account about a practitioner who, finding herself in a difficult place one day, decides to go outside and work in her garden. She finds taking that space and time grounding and centring, so that by the time she returns inside the house she's inspired to write a poem, and has this to say:

> "This was a surprise! It was if the writing wrote itself. I really had no idea where I was going when I started to write, and, because it was so novel, I know that it came from a very deep place. Clearly the writing had information for me. It had something to say to me, rather than being something I had to say . . ."

> (Bolton, 2010: 195)

The hypothesis presented here is that, so often, more gets revealed through the writing and there is real value in paying attention to your own responses to a client. Making time to reflect in writing can be a way of gaining greater understanding and insight into what's going on underneath the surface.

Writing to your internal supervisor

So how can reflective writing connect you with your own internal source of wisdom? One practitioner describes how:

> I worked in a drug and alcohol rehabilitation unit for a while and at the end of the session or shift would write formal notes to be read by colleagues and clients. These notes gave me the bones, but left me with all the flayed flesh, which I had to heal before I re-entered the world. I felt in need of supervision after nearly every shift – so I would write to my inner supervisor, telling her about what had happened and how I felt about it. She would write a letter back, commenting on how I handled the situations, suggesting other things I could have done. She was tremendously supportive and encouraging, though she often saw things that the conscious Caroline had missed.
>
> (Bolton, 2000: 119)

In supervision I have used the theme of writing a letter (using actual letter writing paper) to your inner supervisor and then having clients write a response back from their internal supervisor. This often reveals hidden strengths and blind spots. In our work as supervisors this offers a creative way of building the muscle of the internal supervisor (for ourselves and our supervisees) so necessary for the restorative aspects of our work.

Having permission to give voice to the shadow lands of what you might be feeling or experiencing is essential to resourcing yourself in your work as a supervisor. Alongside your own reflective notes based on your work and relationship with supervisees (which must be stored in a safe and secure space in your home or place of work), you might want to consider keeping a personal learning journal where you capture emerging themes for learning, topics and issues for further exploration in the context of continuous personal and professional development, topics of personal interest, course design and content for articles, academic papers and books. Intentional reflective writing that is reflected on can shape who you are as a supervisor and your practice. It can also speak to the restorative aspects of our work.

Using metaphors from nature in supervision

There are rich layers of insight to be tapped into through a regular practice of reflective writing. Working with metaphors, the senses and story are additional ways to use writing. I have found using metaphors helpful when it becomes clear that an experience is too fresh, raw or too painful to use the immediacy of everyday language. Ryan believes using metaphors:

> . . . enables us to stay with an experience without becoming engulfed by it – it contains a supervisory quality of looking – being in it and seeing ourselves in it. The distance is not an emotional coldness but rather a transcendence created by an artistic, metaphorical experience.
>
> (Ryan, 2008: 79)

Inner and outer nature

Nature holds so many metaphors and insights that can be explored and examined through reflective writing. Barton and Pretty (2010) investigated being with nature and undertaking green exercise for improving mental health. Their results highlighted how acute, short-term exposures to facilitated green exercise improved mood and self-esteem. They concluded that five minutes' exposure showed greatest changes in both mood and self-esteem. When you're faced with feeling overwhelmed, stressed or close to burnout, supervision can become a refuge from which you can refuel. Reflective writing can deepen and expand your experience by giving it meaning. Exploring connections with nature can come to life on the page. I often invite supervisees to write about a favourite place in nature that is restorative as an anchor point to return to. It's a deliberate approach to embedding restorative practices into the fabric of everyday life as a form of ongoing self-care.

Begin with imagining a place in nature you find restorative or satisfying to be in or think about. It's surprising how a simple request to write about a favourite place in nature prompts many meaningful responses. Feedback has included, "I didn't realise how much I missed being in nature", "That took me back to the loss of my father", "I had a tree that I would sit under as a child that was so peaceful and calming." The feedback from this exercise continues to surprise me. But I think it's important to recognise the connection between the outer nature the exercise explicitly speaks to and your own inner nature, which the writing has great potential to tap into. Interestingly, Macfarlane (2012: 26–27) asks, "What do I know when I'm in this place that I can know nowhere else? And then, vainly, what does this place know of me that I cannot know of myself?"

An integration of reflective writing in your work as a supervisor and in supervision can generate a reflexive, creative space. You can choose what and when to share your writing. With the pen in your hand or your fingertips on the keyboard you are in the driving seat. You are in a place described as being ". . . a way of re-authoring experience: It can be argued that writing provides one mechanism through which persons can be more active in determining the arrangement of information and experience, and in producing different accounts of events and experience" (White and Epston, 1990: 37).

Sometimes sharing the Macfarlane quote with clients before the exercise can be really helpful. I wonder what the quote brings up in you. How about spending a couple of minutes capturing down your thoughts in writing about the above quote. I then pose the following questions based on an original exercise from Thompson and Thompson (2017: 84).

Reflective activity

Think of a place in nature you know of or love.
Bring the place to life on the page by describing it, engaging as many of the senses or metaphors as you can.
Once you have described your place in nature follow up with three more questions:

- What about this place brings you alive?
- Who do you know yourself to be in this place?
- What does this place know about you?

I experience these three final questions as a natural invitation to take a closer look beyond what we know of ourselves and who we reveal ourselves to be. The questions can be experienced as provocative and deeply inquiring.

Discovering hidden connection through writing

I sometimes describe the pen in your hand as a telescope, seeping into your subconscious and unconscious territory. "Supervision does not accept what is presented at face value. It is looking with interest into all that is there and includes the discarded, the discounted and the disgraced" (Ryan, 2008: 79). I have found myself describing the writing becoming a form of listening, the pen the ear writing what is heard or felt.

Self-reflection for supervisors

In writing this chapter my desire is to encourage more supervisors to become more reflective through the medium of writing as opposed to an over-reliance on thinking. This means putting reflection into practice and to practise what you preach. Callan quotes this example from a doctor, Danielle Ofri, who understands the value of the practice, which offers further contemplation for reflective practice:

> Writing is a complement to medicine. My days in the hospital are a dizzying, rapid-fire mix of people, illness,

cultural confrontation, pathos, joy and confusion. (And that's just the mornings!) Writing is a chance to let those stories percolate through my soul, an opportunity to weigh and consider all that has swirled around in me. Editing and revising my writing provides another angle for analysis of those human interactions. At times, I feel like I haven't fully processed a situation until I've written about it.

(Callan, 2007: 11–12)

Like Ofri, I feel that my work with each supervisee is only complete when I have made the time and space afterwards to write up my reflective notes. My reflective writing practice is varied. Sometimes I free-write a stream of consciousness, often surprising myself at what emerges. Other times I use the letter format of writing to and writing from my internal supervisor. Other times I find it enriching to work with a structured template of reflective questions, which open me out like peeling an onion. I find having the freedom to access a range of different reflective approaches keeps the reflection fresh (see Bisson, 2017: 65, reflective questions).

Case study

I have been working with SH for two years in the role of coach supervisor. SH is an accredited coach and trained as an Integrative therapist. SH brings to supervision practice issues around her work as a coach, as a facilitator and personal reflections on who she is in the diversity of roles she inhabits. SH also focuses on exploring the whole self through reflective and expressive writing. I invited her to share reflections of her experience of engaging with reflective and therapeutic writing as part of our supervision work together. What follows is an excerpt of SH's reflections from the pages of her reflective learning journal, with her permission.

"There are many different kinds of writing: journaling, academic essays, reflective and reflexive musing, research, proposals, designs, exploration and explanation and stream of consciousness expunging. And more. I've been doing all of the above for a while now, but all rather reluctantly. Whenever I set to writing, I freeze. I feel the first dusting of permafrost as I contemplate the task, then I get distracted and engage fully in something. . .no, anything, other than the writing. I take flight from myself and the seeds of ideas and inspiration and creativity shrivel in the face of the enormity of the task.

"In one of our first sessions I was invited to write about the things I would like to write about on coloured luggage tags. Icicles formed inside. Me? Ideas? Write? With a witness? Jackee observed and reflected back my reaction compassionately but with focused intention and encouraged me to put everything I was thinking and feeling to one side and just write.

"So, I did . . . I settled into the worn, comfy armchair and I started to write . . . and I wrote . . . and I wrote . . . and I didn't want to stop. I wrote about the process of writing. I needed to do that to get through the ice. That metaphor gave way to brambles and thwarted pathways as I wrote my way through the undergrowth until I could see a whole field ahead of me, waiting to be planted with ideas. The field was daunting. So I wrote about that. Then a smaller patch appeared more focused in my line of sight and I could see that I didn't need to plant the whole field in one go. Instead I could plant, patch by patch. Start here with wildflowers and move forward as ideas emerge, as surely they will. The simplicity of the metaphor and the connection to writing was profound. I don't have to do it all at once. I can start with what is in front of me and go from there.

"This acknowledgement has served me both in my own practice and with clients. It has allowed me to stay with what is emerging before me, rather than force things or need to plan for everything. However, it's also made me realise how much rich material there is in every encounter, all of which gets richer and deeper through the experience of writing about it.

"So now I keep detailed reflexive notes on all of my coaching and supervision clients (these are notes for myself that are used for personal reflection and stored safely). I muse for a few moments beforehand and recall my client before me.

What do I remember of them?

What features are in the foreground?

What do I imagine about them?

Then we meet and live the encounter. New insights and experiences and dynamics emerge.

"In one session I talked about finding a way to stay connected to my clients between formal sessions. I was clear I didn't want to put out a written newsletter but not clear what I did want. I shared a drawing I had recently pencilled and this became a catalyst for our supervision session.

"Our next session took place in Kew Gardens to find fresh inspiration in nature. We met and talked first and identified the focus for the session. As part of the session I walked over to Kew's treetop walkway, then had an agreed period alone to reflect. During this time I drew and wrote whatever moved me and naturally came to an understanding about what I might offer my clients.

"Initially, this new and different way of working threw me into a spin and I could feel the creative space shrinking as I wandered in the direction of the treetops. I worried about not finding the walkway, about climbing high (I'm afraid of heights), about not being able to draw anything, about wasting my coaching session, etc, etc. Fear and anxiety were creeping into every pore. I noticed I became calmer climbing the walkway, the anxiety dropping away as my senses took over. It's hard to stay gripped with anxiety when you're up high, among beautiful ancient trees, with a light breeze in the air and a whole different sense of perspective on the world.

"Our process was one of unhurried conversation, shared reflection, individual reflection, movement, expression and more conversation. As I reflect on my own practice, I can see that in nature is where I'm at my best too and able to bring out the best in my clients. However, I don't always give myself the licence to, and time for, reflection or creativity. I now draw and write a regular newsletter where I am sharing more of who I am with my audience.

"The day at Kew Gardens was special and I am still riding the luscious wave of that creative session. Since then, I have drawn many things . . . mainly trees, really beautiful, inviting and inspirational trees, under which I now sit and write. They have become my physical and metaphorical space that I create for reflection. I have developed ritual around them to recreate the space where everything stops, and I can be with my muse, be that on a train, at my kitchen table or with a client. Reflective writing is now woven into my practice. I can't say it's ever easy but it's always rewarding."

Conclusion

Regular engagement with writing as a practice in the context of coaching and supervision creates a sound foundation for professional practice and that art of self-reflection. According to a recent study at Harvard (Di Stefano, Gino, Pisano and Staats, 2016), once significant experience has been accumulated, reflection is the most valuable approach to improving productivity and performance. The study highlights ways in which reflection increases self-efficacy and your ability to learn through the practice of reflection.

Drawing on a range of reflective and expressive writing practices is one way of modelling the resource bank of reflective writing techniques that can be adapted in supervision. Through practical application recipients can experience first-hand the impact of regular scheduling of reflective writing as part of the supervision process.

Through reflective writing, coaches can synthesise and integrate learning in meaningful and productive ways, working at levels that are both cognitive and psychological. Writing is a clarifying and processing tool whose benefits include making meaning of experiences, lowering stress and anxiety levels as a counter action to the interruption of digital and information overloads.

The practices and case study presented here reveal that writing and what emerges from writing and reflection can often differ widely from the thinking mind. Therefore writing becomes a meaningful and self-authorised approach, generating natural pathways and connections with alternative perspectives and new solutions. Reflective writing is an act of self-care and restorative well-being.

Practice points

1. Switch from digital to analogue writing. Disrupt digital overload by writing by hand and practice reflective writing in the moment.
2. Use reflecting and expressive writing exercises to explore challenging and difficult situations as a way of connecting with different perspectives and new solutions that are self-authorised through reflective writing.
3. Develop your reflective writing practice through regular reflecting on your writing using the structure of Kathleen Adams' Reflection/Write approach.
4. Engage with your internal supervisor through letter writing and other creative practices.
5. Use metaphors to go deeper into reflective writing and self-enquiry that stimulates thinking and emotional intelligence skills.
6. Use nature as a restorative practice to explore both your inner and outer nature through reflective writing and self-care.

Discussion points

• What are the current challenges of maintaining an effective reflective practice in your work as a coach or coach supervisor? What are your greatest barriers to reflective writing?

- How might a reflective writing practice inform and add value to your work as a coach or coach supervisor?
- How would you evidence your reflective writing practice as part of your coaching and supervision CPD for professional accreditation and registration?
- How can a reflective writing practice contribute to more "deep work" as a coach and coach supervisor?

Suggested Reading

Adams, K. and Ross, D. (2016). *Your Brain on Ink: A Workbook on Neuroplasticity and the Journal Ladder*. London: Rowman & Littlefield.

Bisson, M. (2017). *Coach Yourself First: A Coach's Guide to Self-Reflection*. Kibworth Beauchamp: Matador.

Bolton, G., Howlett, S., Lago, C. and Wright, J. K. (2004). *Writing Cures: An Introductory Handbook of Writing in Counselling and Psychotherapy*. Hove: Routledge.

Bolton, G. (2014). *Reflective Practice: Writing and Professional Development*. London: Sage.

References

Adams, K. (2013). *Expressive Writing: Foundations of Practice*. Plymouth: Rowman & Littlefield.

Adams, K. and Ross, D. (2016). *Your Brain on Ink: A Workbook on Neuroplasticity and the Journal Ladder*. London: Rowman & Littlefield.

Barton, J. and Pretty, J. (2010). What is the best dose of nature and green exercise for improving mental health? A multi-study analysis. *Environmental Science and Technology*, 44, 3947–3955.

Bassott, B. (2013). *The Reflective Journal: Capturing Your Learning For Personal & Professional Development*. London: Palgrave Macmillan.

Berginger, V., Abbott, R. D., Jones, J., Wolf, B. J., Gould, L., Anderson-Youngstrom, M., Shimada, M. and Apel, K. (2006). Early development of language by hand: Composing, reading, listening, and speaking connections; three letter writing modes; and fast mapping in spelling. *Developmental Neuropsychology*, 29(1), 61–92.

Bisson, M. (2017). *Coach Yourself First: A Coach's Guide to Self-Reflection*. Kibworth Beauchamp: Matador.

Bolton, G. (2000). *The Therapeutic Potential of Creative Writing: Writing Myself*. London: Jessica Kingsley.

Bolton, G. (2010). *Writing Routes: A Resource Handbook of Therapeutic Writing and Writing for Therapy*. London: Jessica Kingsley.

Bono, J. Glomb, T. M., Shen, W., Kim, E. and Koch, A. J. (2013). Building positive resources: Effects of positive events and positive reflection on work, stress and health. *The Academy of Management Journal*, 56(6), 1601–1627.

Callan, J, C. (2007). *The Writer's Toolbox: Creative Games and Exercises for Inspiring the Write Side of Your Brain*. San Francisco, CA: Chronicle Books.

Fain, J. (2012). Writing can ease disease. *Oprah Magazine*, August.

Di Stefano, G., Gino, F., Pisano, G. P. and Staats, B. R. (2016). Making experience count: The role of reflection in individual learning. Harvard Business School, Working Paper No. 14-093.

James, K. H. and Atwood, T. P. (2009). The role of sensorimotor learning in the perception of letter-like forms: Tracking the causes of neural specialization for letters. *Cognitive Neuropsychology*, 26(1), 91–110.

King, L. A. (2001). The health benefits of writing about life goals. *Personality and Social Psychology Bulletin*, 27(7), 798–807.

Hay, J. (2007). *Reflective Practice and Supervision for Coaches*. Maidenhead: Open University Press.

Macfarlane, R. (2012). *The Old Ways: A Journey on Foot*. London: Hamish Hamilton.

Mogk, C., Otte, S., Reinhold-Hurley, B. and Kröner-Herwig, B. (2006). Health effects of expressive writing on stressful or traumatic experiences – a meta-analysis. *GMS Psycho-Social Medicine*, 3, Doc06.

Newport, C. (2016). *Deep Work: Rules for Focused Success in a Distracted World*. London: Piatkus.

Pennebaker, J. W. (2013). *Writing to Heal: A Guided Journal for Recovering from Trauma and Emotional Upheaval*, 2nd edition. Wheat Ridge, CO: Center for Journal Therapy Inc.

Ryan, S. (2008). Mindful supervision. In R. Shohet, (Ed), *Passionate Supervision*. London: Jessica Kingsley.

Smyth, J. M. (1998). Written emotional expression: Effect sizes, outcome types, and moderating variables. *Journal of Consulting and Clinical Psychology*, 66(1), 174–184.

Thompson, K. (2011). *Therapeutic Journal Writing: A Guide for Professionals*. London: Jessica Kingsley.

Thompson, M, R. and Thompson, K. (2017). Inner and outer landscapes: Bringing environment into the therapeutic relationship through expressive writing. In A. Kopytin and M. Rugh (Eds), *Environmental Expressive Therapies: Nature-Assisted Theory and Practice*. New York: Routledge.

White, M. and Epston, D. (1990). *Narrative Means to Therapeutic Ends*. New York: W.W. Norton.

8

Supervision in the Thinking Environment®

Jane Adshead-Grant, Anne Hathaway, Linda Aspey and Eve Turner

Introduction

The Thinking Environment® was originally developed by Nancy Kline in response to the question: If action is only as good as the thinking behind it, how do we create the conditions for the highest quality thinking? What emerged from her investigation of this question, and her close observation of the conditions under which people seemed to think as clearly, creatively and independently as possible, was a set of behaviours that Kline called The Ten Components of a Thinking Environment. Applied individually, each component will make a difference, but applied as a system, they can be transformational, and together they create a culture of deep respect for the Other. It is this deep respect that we believe gets to the heart of supervision.

By independent thinking, we mean the capacity to think for oneself, rather than relying on others' guidance or opinions so that you draw on your own experiences, feelings and creativity. It also means being able to think *as* yourself, rather than complying or conforming to what you think others want to hear. Paradoxically, it seems that most people do their best independent thinking when others are present, showing interest, being encouraging and listening without judgement or interruption. Thinking for yourself includes your feelings, and all the forms of intelligence we have access to as human beings. This lies at the heart of resourcing ourselves as coaches, mentors or supervisors; and it makes our Thinking Environment practice a way of *being* rather than a way of *doing*.

The development of supervision in a Thinking Environment

Supervision in a Thinking Environment is an easeful, rigorous, non-judgmental place for the supervisee to think for themselves on a topic they bring to the session. The Thinking Environment theory and practice was discovered through observation and systematic practice over many years and resonates with the work of, for example, Carl Rogers, George Fox, Peter Kline, Alice Miller, Humberto Maturana, Nassim Taleb and Margaret Heffernan.

We can see this resonance in Carl Rogers' person-centred approach and his practice of Unconditional Positive Regard. Cooke (2011: 133) suggested "the fundamental assumption . . . is that people are intrinsically motivated to grow and develop into optimally functioning human beings". However this self-actualising tendency "can only occur in an environment where the individual feels understood, valued and accepted for who they are, and without conditions."

Rogers believed that how we are is at the centre of how we practise and our skills would be determined to a large extent by our attitudes:

> How do we look upon others? Do we see each person as having worth and dignity in his own right? If we do hold this point of view at the verbal level, to what extent is it operationally evident at the behavioural level? Do we tend to treat individuals as persons of worth, or do we subtly devaluate them by our attitudes and behaviour? Is our philosophy one in which respect for the individual is uppermost?
>
> (Rogers, 1951: 20)

Rogers (1980:115) believed providing the right environment was essential. "Individuals have within themselves vast resources for self-understanding and for altering their self-concepts, basic attitudes, and self-directed behaviour; these resources can be tapped if a definable climate of facilitative psychological attitudes can be provided."

Biologist and neurophysiologist Humberto Maturana wrote "The Student's Prayer" when his son became unhappy because "he felt his teachers were making it impossible for him to learn. They wanted to teach him what they knew, rather than drawing out what he needed to learn" (Zohar & Marshall, 2001: 290). The prayer expresses the hope: "don't instruct me; let's walk together. Let my richness begin where yours ends".

Here are the Ten Components of a Thinking Environment, based on Kline's work (2015: 31–32):

Giving your **Attention** with deep interest in what the person is saying and where they will go next will help them think better around you than if you interrupt them or listen simply to reply.

Regarding the person thinking as your thinking **Equal**, regardless of hierarchy, will mean they think better around you.

Being at **Ease** yourself, regardless of the urgency or the rush outside of you, will help others think better than if you are in a rush yourself.

If you genuinely **Appreciate** people five times more than you criticise them, they will think more imaginatively around you than if you focus on their faults.

When you **Encourage** people, build with them their courage to go to the edge of their thinking by eliminating competition; they will think better around you than if you compete with them.

If you offer accurate **Information** that is in service of their thinking and respect what they may be facing, they will think better than if you withhold information.

When you allow for them to express their **Feelings** – their sadness, their anger, their frustration – they will think better around you than if you step over or seek to avoid their feelings.

If you are interested in the **Diversity** between you and others, the differences between you, they will think better around you than if you prefer others to think and be just like you.

If you can ask people an **Incisive Question** to cut through what is a limiting assumption and replace it with one that is more liberating, they will tap into their natural creative, resourceful self where breakthroughs and fresh ideas are born.

When you prepare the **Place** for thinking together that says "you matter" they will think better around you than if you allow the place to feel intimidating and peppered with interruptions.

Underpinning the Ten Components is a chosen philosophy called The Positive Philosophical Choice. It is based on the observation that if, when listening to someone, we focus on that person's capacity for "good" (fine thinking, connection, choice, creativity and joy), they will think better than if we focus on their capacity for "bad" (specious thinking, alienation, victimisation, repetition and misery) (Kline, 2016).

In 2017 Kline commented that

the Ten Components and all of their applications emerged, and continue to emerge, from practice, observation, scrutiny and fresh analysis, not from theories. In fact I mark the "beginning" of the Thinking Environment as circa 1985 when I consciously stepped back, as much as one can (which is challenging), from those theories and perspectives and attempted to see as objectively as possible what actually was happening when people moved from compliant or derivative thinking to independent thinking.

(Kline: 2017, personal communication)

Kline originally conceived the Thinking Environment as the basis for a one-to-one partnership between two people helping each other reciprocally to create the conditions for the highest quality thinking. However, over time further applications emerged, as practitioners of these Thinking Partnerships took the Ten Components and applied them in other contexts: meetings, interviews, presentations, facilitation, coaching, performance review, mentoring, mediation and, ultimately, coach supervision (Time to Think online, 2018). Applications were developed (and continue to be so) all around the world where the Thinking Environment has taken root.

The use of the Thinking Environment in supervision was first developed in response to the need to mentor and assess individual students in practicum seeking to qualify in the Thinking Environment approach to coaching. From there it extended to include post-qualification supervision for both Thinking Environment coaches and others, individually and in groups.

Organisational psychologist and neuroscientist Professor Paul Brown believes that Kline's approach is an intensely powerful way of reaching into the limbic system to create change. Brown says: "Her methods are one of the most interesting, disciplined, quiet approaches to letting the brain function at its best that it is possible to imagine" (Hall, 2013: 27). In our experience, it is the comfortable silence held by the supervisor that appears to calm any fight, flight or freeze response and supports the client's brain to work to maximum effect. The attention, and the curiosity in where the supervisee will go next, listening without interruption, and the fact (not the hope) that the supervisee knows they will not be interrupted, allows their brain to relax and new neurons begin to connect, generating more creative and insightful thoughts (Brown, P., 2011: personal communication).

The practice of individual supervision

Kline believes that "The distinguishing characteristic of supervision in a Thinking Environment, and therefore what it is like to supervise and be supervised, is the expectation that the supervisee is in charge of the session and that can take many forms" (Kline, 2017: personal communication). The supervisor's role is to be a generative force for the supervisee to come to insights and understanding as well as consolidate and crystallise their thoughts and questions.

The positive philosophical choice

As supervisors we enter a supervision session choosing the philosophical belief that our supervisee has the capacity for "good" and expecting them to think well for themselves, which frees us from any pressure to "know" what might be best for them. It is the quality of our attention, our listening, our interest, rather than the wisdom of our words, that seems to enable the most resourcefulness in our supervisees and gets to the heart of supervision. Rogers (Dryden, 2007: 165) echoes this view when he says "there is trust in the innate resource-fulness of human beings, given the right conditions, to find their own way through life". Remen (2006: 219) describes the impact of giving our attention, our wholeness, to another and accepting them for who they are, and says that it is one of the greatest gifts we can give to one another.

We believe that supervision in the Thinking Environment is a resourceful experience for both parties. The moment the supervisee starts thinking independently, trusts their own intelligence and capacity to think for themselves as well as *being trusted* to think for themselves, they become more resourceful. Being a Thinking Environment, embody-ing the Ten Components, seems to generate a safe space, an interconnection between us, free from competition and hierarchy; a true partnership based on equality is created. We experience the giving of generative Attention as having a dimension of compassionate mindfulness. From this place our questions may then emerge to further the thinking of the supervisee.

Contracting

One of the essential ingredients, as in other approaches to supervision, is the contracting. We explore the expectation in a Thinking Environment that there will not be much – if any – input from the listener (the supervisor). The framework for supervision in a Thinking Environment creates the opportunity for the supervisee to seek input when they want it, rather than when we as the supervisor think they need it. It would be perfectly possible for the supervisor to be totally silent – albeit utterly attentive – if nothing needed to be said, for the first part of the supervision session (Part I).

When asked for input, as the supervisor we may offer observations with the intention of encouraging fresh thinking, rather than imposing our own. We may ask a question because we are interested in where the supervisee will go next with their thinking, rather than to make a point. Most of all, as the supervisor we will give palpable attention, with an unspoken incisive question: "How much further can you go in your own thinking, before you need my thoughts?", which generates further ideas, exploration and new insights in the supervisee. Yalom (2015: 158) acknowledges this deep connection when he says *the most valuable thing I have to offer is my sheer presence*" (original emphasis).

Feelings

As part of the contracting conversation for supervision in a Thinking Environment, we discuss the component of Feelings as referred to above, recognising that thoughts and emotions are inextricably linked and that to overlook the impact of emotions would be irresponsible. We recognise that unacknowledged feelings may block us from thinking well.

As supervisors, we seek only to communicate that which is in service of our supervisee's increased self-awareness and fresh thinking, rather than commenting or asking a question merely for our own sake. It is the release of emotion and being one's whole and true self that is both resourceful and liberating for the supervisee. In response to the supervisee asking for observations, questions or input from the supervisor, we have permission to reflect what we notice in relation to the nonverbal communication and emotional states of our supervisee, in order to support them to express feelings and integrate them effectively with their ideas.

In our experience, this has an impact on both the supervisor and supervisee. Due to the deep trust and inter-connectedness created, often the supervisor feels equally resourced after the supervision conversation.

The emergence of trust

As Thinking Environment supervisors we observe how quickly a high level of trust emerges in the relationship. Glaser (2014: 24–25) describes this level of trust as formed when we engage the prefrontal cortex of our brain, which enables us to build societies, have good judgement, be strategic, handle difficult conversations and build and sustain trust. It is difficult to sustain when we are afraid to share our inner world. One of Anne's supervisees – a highly experienced coach working with senior executives – reported that, although they had regular group supervision, they came to Anne for one-to-one sessions in addition precisely because they felt safe enough in the relationship to think widely and honestly about client issues that had caused them difficulties and provoked feelings of shame.

The development of trust in our experience is an outcome of embodying the Ten Components of the Thinking Environment for ourselves as well as for our supervisees. Furthermore the component of Encouragement provides a resourceful antidote for our supervisee, enabling them to go beyond any internal competition they may be wrestling with to discover new insights.

Another distinguishing feature of supervision in the Thinking Environment is the component of Appreciation. The session concludes with an appreciation of the qualities and skills both supervisee and supervisor recognise in each other. This provides an opportunity to identify the skills and gifts that the supervisor or supervisee may or may not know they possess, and may be unaware of how valued those qualities are by others. Appreciation has a nurturing impact on the supervision relationship. In fact, research (Gottman and Silver, 1994; Zenger and Folkman, 2013), has uncovered the effect of a five to one ratio of appreciation to criticism: it deepens and strengthens relationships.

Getting to the core

Additional Thinking Environment expertise may be required of the supervisor when the supervisee finds themselves blocked in their thinking. Getting to the core of what is creating a block, a discomfort, a "not knowing" may be released by working with the supervisee at the level of assumptions, for we observe that it is often an untrue limiting assumption, lived as if it is true, that creates the impasse. Helping our supervisee to uncover their possible untrue assumptions, challenge them and then create a new liberating assumption forges the way for new insights, clear decisions and higher performance. A sequence of questions provides the framework for the supervisor to ask an Incisive Question, as referred to above, which liberates the impasse and resources the supervisee afresh. In very simplified form (which does not account for how trained practitioners deal with a limiting assumption which *is* true), these questions are:

What might you be assuming that is most stopping you from going forward?

Do you think that assumption is true?

What is true and liberating instead?

And the Incisive Question:

If you knew (insert liberating assumption) how would you go forward?

(Kline, 2015: 91)

The individual supervision framework

Our role as supervisors requires us to hold the belief that the supervisee *can* think for themselves. We then model that way of being, which in turn provides for the supervisee's development in how they are for their clients.

The supervision session begins with an invitation to the supervisee to choose a topic and then share their thoughts. Only when the supervisee has completed their wave of thinking will we ask (on request) a follow-up question with the sole purpose of generating more thoughts, feelings and expression from the supervisee.

Supervision in a Thinking Environment lies on a spectrum from more independent thinking by the supervisee at one end to more direction by us as the supervisor at the other, at the request – and only at the request – of the supervisee. To generate the finest independent thinking in the supervisee, the supervisor begins every session at the non-directive end of the spectrum, which we call Part I.

When the supervisee seeks input from the supervisor, we flex along the spectrum moving into a Dialogue (Kline, 2015: 199–201) by asking the supervisee what questions they have for us (Part II). The distinguishing element is that we, as the supervisor, will respond to the question asked from our experience and knowledge, rather than offering guidance or advice, and with the sole intention of generating further thinking in our supervisee.

There is then an opportunity for the supervisor to contribute our own thoughts and ideas in relation to what we have heard or witnessed by request of the supervisee (Part III).

The session concludes with an appreciation (Part IV).

In summary:

Part I Supervisor:

With regard to your (insert focus) practice, what would you like to think about and what are your thoughts?

What *more* do you think, or feel, or want to say?

This question may be repeated several times after each wave of thinking, until the supervisee has no response to the question, before moving to Part II. (We may also, if required, use the assumptions questions noted above.)

Part II Supervisor:

What question(s) do you have for me?

Part III Supervisee:

What observation, question or input do you have for me that we have not covered?

Part IV Supervisor and Supervisee:

What quality do we appreciate or admire in the other?

Duty of care

In an article, (Aspey, 2016) one of us, Linda, raises the question "What about duty of care?" She suggests that if the supervisor truly believes the supervisee or their client is in genuine danger, they naturally have a duty to ensure their safety and wellbeing. However, she suggests that initially they must provide the time and space for the supervisee to discover that for themselves. It is rarely a red-flag issue; it is more that the supervisor may assume that it is their role to "set them straight". In the rare event a red-flag issue does present itself, and we suspect our supervisee is endangering themselves, or there is potential evidence of malpractice, we would interject at an appropriate time and say, for example: "I have a concern I would like to share with you. When you said (insert area of focus) I found myself wondering (insert a question that the concern provoked). What are your thoughts on that?"

Equally, when there are times, as supervisors, we have specific information that it would be helpful for us to provide, in relation to topics such as accreditation, ethics or legality, then we would do so. In those circumstances, ideally at the supervisee's request, we then offer the information succinctly with the intention of generating more thinking, questions or reflections from our supervisee. As in many approaches to supervision, we are aiming to avoid creating a relationship where the supervisor could appear as an "expert"; instead we hold the expectation that the supervisee will draw on their own resources and decision-making capacity.

As an example, Anne worked with a supervisee who had been contracted by a corporate client to coach, via Skype, a dozen managers who were based worldwide. The coachees had been repeatedly cancelling at the last minute, or simply not turning up to their sessions, which had led to considerable extra administrative workload for the supervisee in reorganising appointments across multiple time zones. It was clear that the supervisee was both frustrated and exhausted by the client's demands, and wanted to think about how they could handle them better.

Anne reported:

> "For the first part of the session they examined what had been happening, and eventually identified some tasks that they could do differently to be more efficient and make things work more smoothly. As I listened, I noticed that everything seemed to involve working even harder than they obviously already were, and I became concerned for their wellbeing and the possibility of burnout. I didn't interrupt, but when they reached the point where they asked for my input, I simply said "I'm wondering where *your* needs are in all of this?" This led them to pause, notice they were putting themselves last, and revisit some of their thinking, whereupon they decided to put in place some boundaries with the client."

Our internal supervisor

One of the key aims for us as supervisors in the Thinking Environment is to help supervisees to build their own "internal supervisor". This was a term coined by Casement (1985) to describe the idea of a "friendly super-ego that can be consulted at times when formal supervision is unavailable" (Rickard, 2011: 26).

Rickard (2011: 26) asks: "Is our internal supervisor the combined voice of the best teacher and supervisor we have ever had, internalised in our head, that we can tune in to when need arises?" She cites Casement's (1985) observation that trainees

> often relied too much on the advice and comments of their supervisor and needed to develop a sense of their own internal supervisor that they could call upon during a therapeutic session, to guide them in their work with the client.
>
> (2011: 26)

The theme of developing one's own internal supervisor is underscored by Hawkins and Smith (2013: 280) as they suggest hard work in supervision helped us to gain access to a "fearlessly compassionate internal supervisor". This capacity is developed by consistently turning inward and moving away from being reactive. It moves us towards a new understanding, and then requires us to respond with fearless compassion.

Our experience is that the Thinking Environment approach supports this.

A fellow Time to Think Coach and Facilitator, Rachel Day, underlines the point that we are at our best when we have the chance to learn for ourselves and hold ourselves accountable.

> Recently I discovered that when we are in a shaky position with our thinking, and feeling lost around what we are trying to do, deep down we don't want to be rescued. We want to be given the space to rescue ourselves. We want to feel safe to share our most vulnerable thoughts without someone trying to make us feel better, we want to challenge ourselves to come through and succeed without a feeling that we only did it because of others, we want complete freedom to think without judgement or opinion and we want to hold ourselves to account.
>
> (Day: 2017)

The practice of Group Supervision

There are two approaches to Group Supervision in a Thinking Environment. In the first, over the past few years senior practitioners have been drawing upon the Thinking Environment to create a culture that brings greater levels of independent thinking into the supervision of groups. Practitioners draw on the Ten Components extensively and use some of the recognised Time To Think group applications, like Rounds, Thinking Pairs, Dialogue, Open Discussion and the Time To Think Council (Kline, 2015: 216–239), for mutual sharing of thoughts, experiences and ideas, in a way that honours the diversity of the group's needs.

The contracting encompasses three key elements: first, to set the expectation that everyone can think for themselves; second, to adopt the Ten Components of the Thinking Environment among the group itself; and third, to give the group choice about what they work on and how – they may wish to bring in other exercises, tools and approaches that can complement the Thinking Environment and the way that the supervisor facilitates discussion. However, the underlying components of generative Attention and Equality permeate throughout.

During our Group Supervision, we invite everyone to contribute, in turn, without being interrupted. The supervisor holds dual roles of a facilitator and a contributor (in this it is similar to Proctor's Type 3 Co-operative Group (Proctor, 2008: 32)). They are included in the Rounds, Dialogue and Open Discussions, allowing everyone to benefit from the component of Equality.

Supervisors will always hold a Round to gather what topics members of the group would like to bring to the supervision session. We will invite the group to negotiate how to use the time allocated for the session with the topics contributed. Then a volunteer will start with their topic. A range of applications can be employed to best suit the nature of the topic for supervision.

During an Open Discussion, for example, as the supervisor we will be listening to ignite the thinking of the initial contributor as well as the group. This may take the form of encouraging the group to think some more, it may be to challenge an assumption. There is the opportunity to share our insight and experience as a supervisor when the group asks for it. Our purpose, though, is to add value through our attention, encouragement and expectation that the supervisees can think for themselves, rather than imposing our thoughts and ideas.

As supervisors, we build in time during the session for reflection and note taking. Once everyone who contributed a topic has had the opportunity to address it, we may invite the group to consider any themes that have arisen from the session and what, if anything, they would like to do with these themes. This is particularly relevant when working with a group of internal organisational coaches.

When working with others to generate their best thinking, whether as a coach, supervisor, facilitator or teacher, Kline learned from her first employer, a Quaker head teacher, Thornton Brown, that "students are learning *you*" (Kline, 1999: 68–69). In this way we are role modeling embodying the Ten Components of a Thinking Environment in service of the participants building their own resourcefulness.

The second approach, a more formal practice of Group Supervision in a Thinking Environment (Kline, 2017: personal communication) derives from the individual supervision framework. It is in development (2018); the thinking so far is described below.

The Group Supervision framework

In this process there is a supervisor and several supervisees (colleagues), each of whom, ideally, has a turn with the Supervisor. It uses the Thinking Environment applications of Rounds and Dialogue, and ends, as in the individual supervision process, with the practice of Appreciation. Once an order has been agreed by the group it proceeds as follows:

Part I

Supervisor (to supervisee with colleagues observing):

With regard to your (insert focus) practice, what would you like to think about and what are your thoughts?

What more do you think, or feel, or want to say? Etc.

Part II

Supervisor (to supervisee with colleagues observing):

Conducted as Dialogue in a Thinking Environment

What question(s) do you have of me?

Colleagues in a Round (with supervisor observing):

Conducted as Dialogue

What question(s) do you have of us?

Part III

Supervisee (to supervisor with colleagues observing):

Conducted in a Round and as Dialogue

What additional observation or input, or questions of me, do you have?

Supervisee (to Colleagues in Round with supervisor observing):

Conducted in a Round and as Dialogue

What additional observation or input, or questions of me, do you have?

Part IV

Supervisee's final comments

Supervisor and Supervisee:

What quality do we respect in the other?

Case studies

A case study of one-to-one supervision

The supervisee is an experienced Time to Think coach working regularly with an international business school's clients, and attending regular supervision. Below they share their experience of a Thinking Environment Supervision with Anne.

"I was feeling uneasy about two encounters. Working with Anne as my supervisor I first voiced my disappointment about not challenging a client during a coaching call to Australia. I asked myself: why had I backed away, where had I been stuck, what could I do next time? Knowing that I would have the safe space to think with Anne's generative attention, I did it all in the blink of an eye. And then when I had gone as far as I could and I was ready – and because I was still unsure if I had the best words for next time – I asked her "What are your thoughts and what have you said in a similar situation?" And I was offered a brilliant piece of thinking and experience that I could integrate into mine.

"My second encounter takes longer to unravel. It was an exploratory meeting with an eminent figure as a potential coachee. I have a host of unexplored thoughts, feelings and assumptions that underpin a sense of "not convinced". In the supervision space I unfold my messy, ephemeral inner responses during and after the meeting. I feel no fear, no embarrassment, only relief that I can do so and make sense of this tumult of information. In the space where there are no interruptions and silence is generous I can look through and into the layers and questions coming up in my mind. I am struck that I have said "not convinced". Who was not convinced, about whom, of what? I realise: it was me unconvinced about me.

"With this thought and continuing generative attention, I then see how much the Thinking Environment components of Equality and Diversity were so absent from how I was with my potential client on that day. How did I not see that?! I ask myself: how in future can I feel truly equal with another eminent potential coachee? And there is a wave of new thoughts that are restoring and hopeful and an action. And then I reflect generally how much I am going through a period in my work that calls for resilience rather than joy. It is OK but it is a relatively tough time.

"I pause. I feel clearer. I have learnt and am encouraged to do better next time. And then because I can, and just in case, I ask Anne: "Listening to all of this, do you have a question or thought for me that won't go away?" And I am offered three thoughts that take nothing away from my thinking and instead affirm it, where I am and invite me to build on it practically.

"And then we close with an appreciation of each other. I acknowledge and recognise in a few words what I have valued so much: the outstanding generative attention with all that implies, the few powerful questions and the deep insight and wisdom when called on. Then I am appreciated in return. And I feel stronger – and my practice better – for this safe, honest, uniquely encouraging and enabling space."

A case study of Group Supervision

The group is formed of in-house executive coaches from PwC, an international professional services firm, who have monthly supervision drawing upon the Thinking Environment. The group worked for two years with Linda and this was one member's reflection:

"We all learnt a great deal during that time. For me the key elements that struck me most and have stayed with me are the emphasis on equality. The sessions had a spaciousness where everyone was given a chance to speak, and be listened to, without interruption or judgement. Even though most of us are already steeped in the Rogerian stance of unconditional positive regard, this approach took it to a new level. It was amazing for example, when discussing a tricky issue where I felt unresourceful and stuck, how, given a couple of questions, quality attention and space, I could access what I already had in my head, or generate completely new thoughts. So many new insights and deeper reflections emerged from those periods of time.

"The approach reinforced the importance of allowing others' innate knowledge and capacity to emerge. Working in this way fostered a new level of shared understanding, empathy and equality amongst us.

"Sometimes in group supervision, the default mode is to defer to the supervisor for their expertise. Linda worked with us in a way that held her authority with a light touch, very much an embodiment of this way of working. We never felt judged, rather encouraged and treated as equal thinking partners.

"As a result of working in this way, I am mindful of how I am operating as a coach, and the environment I'm creating. On a practical level in my own group supervision practice, I use a number of the principles, such as having everyone's voice in the room. At certain points where for example we want to explore a theme, I suggest a Round where everyone has uninterrupted air time allowing them to say what's in their mind. This is more productive than a general discussion.

"Or when we want to explore a dilemma that one of the group has, I run a Time to Think Council [Kline, 2015: 228] where the person with the issue decides on a question, then in the Round everyone has uninterrupted time speaking succinctly to the question, drawing on their experience but without giving direct advice. This results in new learning for all, yet done in a way that generates new thinking in the person presenting the dilemma."

Conclusion

The essence of supervision in a Thinking Environment is to create a partnership for thinking well and to support getting to the core of what is most important for the supervisee. It is for the supervisee to develop expertise in thinking for themselves about their work – and all its facets – with their clients. It is about the supervisor generating new insights in the supervisee through giving Attention and Encouragement – and giving input when asked for, rather than imposing it. Furthermore, it is about helping the supervisee develop expertise in helping their clients to think for themselves.

Supervision in a Thinking Environment has the potential to turn a supervision session on its head. What has to be achieved and prepared for by both parties is the idea that for much of the session the supervisor will only speak when asked to. They speak, yes, but their effectiveness is in being the generative force for the supervisee to come to insights and understanding as well as consolidate and crystallise their own thoughts and questions. Some might argue that supervision in a Thinking Environment is an "easy option" given the supervisor has seemingly less input than in other supervision approaches; whereas, in fact, it will challenge, encourage and take the supervisee to the edge of their thinking and provide opportunities for deep learning and development. For the supervisor, it is, as Nancy Kline puts it, "a step by step process towards humility" (Kline, 2017: personal communication).

In the Thinking Environment approach to supervision, both the supervisor and supervisee develop their skills, capability, experience and confidence. The supervision framework creates a structure that serves to develop further the relationship and the resourcefulness for both the supervisor and supervisee.

Supervisees benefiting from supervision in a Thinking Environment report that once they have experienced this approach, they know what changes they want to make for themselves to grow their capability, skills and confidence to do good work with their clients.

Practice points

1. As the supervisor, ensure that the supervisee is in charge of the session, and that *their* thinking is paramount.
2. Contract with the supervisee that they have uninterrupted thinking and reflection, without judgement, asking a question only when the supervisee requests one.
3. Observe and practise so that as the supervisor, you and your supervisee are equal in your thinking and relationship in the Thinking Environment.
4. When running group supervision, consider working in pairs on topics raised to increase each member's engagement and learning.
5. When issues such as ethics or aspects of credentialing/accreditation require our interventions, or when the supervisee does not appear to be aware of the impact of something that is going on with their client or other stakeholder, encourage their thinking and awareness first, before adding yours.
6. End supervision sessions with appreciation, offered equally for supervisor and supervisee.

Discussion points

- What do you think are the implications of putting the supervisee in the driving seat for their thinking in such a defined way?
- As supervisor, how comfortable would you be remaining silent until asked for your contribution?
- How might the Thinking Environment approach link to the three "pillars" of supervision: qualitative/normative, developmental/formative and resourcing/restorative?
- How might this way of working benefit the supervisor, the coach and the stakeholders? What might be any

drawbacks or missing elements? What might we need to pay attention to?

Suggested Reading

Brown, P. and Brown, V. (2012). *Neuropsychology for Coaches: Understanding the Basics*. Maidenhead: Open University Press.

Kline, N. (2015). *More Time To Think: The Power of Independent Thinking* (2nd ed.). London: Cassell Illustrated.

Maturana, M. and Verden-Zöller, G. (edited by Bunnell, P.) (2008). *The Origin of Humanness in the Biology of Love*. Exeter: Imprint Academic.

Remen, R. N. (2006). *Kitchen Table Wisdom*. New York: Penguin.

References

Aspey, L. (2016). Coaching supervision – Who is the expert in the room? Retrieved on 1 August 2018 from www.linkedin.com/pulse/coaching-supervision-who-expert-room-linda-aspey

Casement P. (1985). *On Learning from the Patient*. London: Tavistock.

Cooke, B. (2011). The person-centred approach in coaching supervision. In T. Bachkirova, P. Jackson and D. Clutterbuck (eds.). *Coaching & Mentoring Supervision Theory and Practice*. Maidenhead: Oxford University Press.

Day, R. (n.d.). Retrieved on 1 August 2018 from: www.thinking stream.co.uk/blog/4592108103

Dryden, W. (2007). *Dryden's Handbook of Individual Therapy* (5th ed.). London: Sage.

Glaser, J. E. (2014). *Conversational Intelligence*. New York: Bibliomotion, Inc.

Gottman, J. and Silver, N. (1994). What makes marriage work?' *Psychology Today*, 1 March. Retrieved on 1 August 2018 from: www.psychologytoday.com/articles/199403/what-makes-marriage-work

Hall, L. (2013). The limbic leader. *Coaching at Work*, 8(2), 24–28.

Hawkins, P. and Smith, N. (2013). *Coaching, Mentoring and Organizational Consultancy: Supervision and Development* (2nd ed.). Maidenhead: Open University Press.

Kline, N. (1999). *Time to Think: Listening to Ignite the Human Mind*. London: Cassell Illustrated.

Kline, N. (2015). *More Time To Think: The Power of Independent Thinking* (2nd ed.). London: Cassell Illustrated.

Kline, N. (2016). Fine point: The positive philosophical choice revisited. Retrieved on 1 Augusts 2018 from www.timetothink. com/uploaded/Fine%20Point%20Positive%20Philosophical%20 Choice%20Revisited.pdf

Proctor, B. (2008). *Group Supervision* (2nd ed.). London: Sage.

Rickard, A. (2011). The internal supervisor. *Therapy Today*, 22(1), 26–29: Retrieved on 1 August 2018 from www.bacp.co.uk/docs/ pdf/15282_therapy%20today%20february%202011.pdf

Remen, R. N. (2006). *Kitchen Table Wisdom*. New York: Penguin.

Rogers, C. (1951). *Client-Centred Therapy*. Trowbridge: Constable and Constable.

Rogers, C. (1980). *A Way of Being*. Boston, MA: Houghton Mifflin.

Time To Think online (2018). Supervision in a Thinking Environment. Retrieved on 1 August 2018 from www.timetothink. com/supervision

Yalom, I. (2015). Creatures of a Day and Other Tales of Psychotherapy. London: Piatkus.

Zenger, J. and Folkman, J. (2013). The ideal praise-to-criticism ratio. *Harvard Business Review*, 15 March. Retrieved on 1 August 2018 from https://hbr.org/2013/03/the-ideal-praise-to-criticism

Zohar, D. and Marshall, I. (2001). *Spiritual Intelligence*. London: Bloomsbury.

9

Resourcing through a peer supervision chain

Lesley Matile, Sarah Gilbert and Eve Turner

Introduction

Peer supervision is one approach to enable practitioners to resource themselves to be at their best. Through this and other reflective activities, practitioners can be stretched, stimulated and challenged, and facilitate deep personal and professional development.

Presented largely as a case study, this chapter draws on the experience of a group of peers, known as the Evolve Supervision Chain, and is a "how to" guide for running such a chain. Evolve was established in 2010 to support and resource each member (peer) holistically in order to secure enduring benefits for clients and other stakeholders. To May 2018 there has been an exchange of 606 hours as both supervisor and supervisee.

This chapter, written by three Evolve members with contributions from other members, shares what has been learned to date from the various challenges encountered on its route to increased maturity. Each Evolve member had the opportunity to be involved in the chapter and it is written with members' support, although it does not necessarily reflect everyone's views.

By its conclusion, readers, whether supervisors, coaches, mentors or, indeed, leaders, will have ideas on how to establish their own peer supervision chain, adding to how they resource themselves. Through sharing our growing pains, we hope that readers can move more quickly to enjoying the rich benefits that Evolve members continue to appreciate.

The development of professional peer approaches

Historically there has been significant use of peer support in many contexts, and over the past decade there has been increasing interest in professional peer arrangements. Peer coaching and co-coaching, often undertaken by coaches in training and in coaching circles, usually involves an equal, reciprocal relationship alternating the role of coach and coachee, sometimes including an observer. Lane, Watts and Corrie (2016: 63) comment: "The peer mentoring model reflects a belief that even inexperienced peers can facilitate one another's learning and development – albeit within certain boundaries." In the Netherlands, for example, some coaches have established Intervision Groups to bring together peers who are trained in having solutions focussed conversations to "practice, reflect and learn from one another" (Solutions Centre, 2017).

Defining peer supervision

There is no single, universally agreed definition of peer supervision by the professional bodies or writers in the field. Heiker (2016: 31) references Kassan (2010) who defines peer supervision as "two or more practitioners who meet regularly to supervise each other". Lane and colleagues (2016: 19) refer to McNicoll's (2008) description of how "neither party may hold content or process expertise and will often work to a protocol to guide them."

Hawkins and Shohet (2012: 65–66) distinguish "horizontal supervision" (peers at the same level support the development of their proficiency) from "vertical supervision" (a more experienced supervisor evaluates and monitors a less experienced supervisee). They see supervision as a joint endeavour with shared responsibility for holding process and content in the supervision roles.

The authors of this chapter see peer supervision as a purposeful, contracted-for, planned, "professional" and committed relationship; it is not a peer conversation or just-in-time support for practice issues. Our definition of a peer is of a person with similar depth and breadth of experience who works collaboratively. They may share similar status, education and ability, as in more standard definitions, but in our chain this will not necessarily be the case.

Emerging forms of peer supervision

Proctor (2008: 38) describes four forms of supervision groups: authoritative, participative, co-operative and peer. In a peer group, there is no "permanent" supervisor; members share the responsibility for supervising and being supervised. In an effective peer group, to an observer, no identifiable member would always lead or be the most authoritative. Everyone would appear expert at different times and, she argues, accountability must be specified at the start and refined over time.

With no one type of peer group suitable for all, Clutterbuck, Whitaker and Lucas (2016) suggest choices will be based on individual requirements. These include regularity, session location or platform for connection, open-ended or time-limited contract, flexible or static group composition, organisational setting, supervision format and approach, coaching developmental stage, learning styles, budgets and recognition for professional accreditation.

There is little research on the operation of peer supervision groups from the point of view of participants. One exception is Homer (2017), who studied a peer supervision group of six experienced coaches, none a qualified supervisor. The coaches saw the group's value as contributing to their broader development and improvement of their coaching practice.

Other forms of one-to-one peer supervision can be found, including among qualified supervisors. For example, circles exist by invitation, but with no collective decision-making, interaction or wider voice. Operationally simple, the peer rotations can be randomly drawn and the supervision pairings self-organising.

Research into the mix of supervision undertaken by coaches (Hawkins & Turner, 2017) indicates that many practitioners interpreted "peer" to include a range of colleagues and other coaching contacts. A third of respondents used peer arrangements so that there was no cost, and cited "peer networks where I can get support when I need it". Some respondents mentioned seeking a mix of individual, group and peer supervision.

The challenges and dilemmas for peer supervision

Two broad themes further set the context for the Evolve case study that follows.

The nature of relationships

Bachkirova and Jackson (2011) note the importance of peer supervisors being honest and open about the limits of their competence and regularly discussing their development as supervisors. Many peer relationships are set up with people already known and this could limit the curiosity, creativity and courage required to work in depth and uncover new insights. In overall contracting, it is worth exploring the potential for collusion in pre-existing relationships, familiarity of backgrounds and approaches to practice. There may be assumptions, and behavioural and cultural habits that are not initially identified. If members all share the same background and coaching model, there is a danger they can get stuck in their own blind spots (Carroll, 2014) and "group think".

On the other hand, where a peer supervision relationship is chosen through existing connection, mutual trust and respect can be established quickly. There will be sufficient shared understanding for mutual support and challenge and an agreed purpose for supervision. De Haan's (2017) research on safety, trust and satisfaction in supervision highlighted the generative potential of peer relationships, freer from judgement of competence. Henderson, Holloway and Millar (2014) argue the importance of members having similar needs, approaches and levels of experience. They note that a feeling of equality is a crucial aspect where peers work together without an identified "expert" supervisor. Without a group leader, they believe there is even more need for a rigorously negotiated working agreement to counteract a "danger of poor boundary maintenance, sloppy professional ethics and tricky personal dynamics" (2014: 131).

St John-Brooks (2014) discusses the challenges of internal peer/co-supervision, including competition, hidden agendas and confidentiality issues. She suggests that to work well, a given structure needs to be followed, and coaches need to be experienced, properly trained in how to use a specific model of supervision and comfortable with having their practice discussed by others. Homer (2017) refers to a broad consensus of how the peer supervision group sessions were structured, and unwritten but commonly accepted operating ground rules for the coaches.

The nature of power

The role of fear and shame is discussed by Carroll (2014) who notes their potential impact on the ability to learn, remain open and move forwards. Potential power imbalance in peer supervision groups can be a risk, as in more "traditional" models.

Wilkinson (2015) explores the tensions between power, responsibility and control within peer groups in person-centred counselling where there is no overall leader. Noting there are likely to be people who are more proactive, more confident, more committed, more knowledgeable and experienced in aspects of practice, the emphasis is on clarity of roles and expectations. She argues the need for each member to contribute, as evenly as possible, to avoid resentments.

Five pre-conditions for making peer supervision work are described by Heiker (2016). These include ensuring that: there is a similar level of experience of peer supervision; the emotional maturity of peer supervisors is similar; and the supervisors can self-reflect around their own handling of power or potential competition. Based on Heiker, Wilkinson (2015) suggests that power used well is important to hold the energy, trigger change and contain the supervision space. She believes there may be an implicit power differential if there is any sense that the supervisee is the person with problems and needs, not the supervisor.

Hawkins and Shohet (2012: 192) cite potential "traps and games" for supervision groups (quoting Houston 1985). Peer groups may also contain hierarchies, cliques, rivalries, peer pressures and distinct patterns of collective behaviour that may not be helpful to the supervision relationships and developmental experiences sought by members. The peer group framework described by Homer (2017: 103) includes individual and collective operation and notes "the unwritten conventions or protocols including both the expected behaviours and contributions".

The emphasis of several authors on peer capabilities suggests that peer supervision approaches are particularly beneficial when participants are trained and experienced supervisors. Carroll (2014) argues that the extent of their ethical maturity is also key to the quality of the supervision. Bachkirova and Jackson (2011: 232) note that the value of peer supervision among coaches at the beginning of their career will be limited and can have serious downsides, particularly if this form of supervision is the only one practised. They hold the view that there is a much better chance for success of a peer supervision chain if all members are experienced and knowledgeable as supervisors as well as coaches.

Practice

Evolve supervision chain's positioning

Since 2016, Evolve has recognised the need to have a clear statement of its position regarding supervision when talking with each other and those external to the chain. These points summarise Evolve's current position:

1. Supervision is an essential developmental and resourcing activity.
2. All coaches and mentors should work with a qualified supervisor wherever possible. Qualifying as a supervisor underpins both theoretical study and scrutiny of practice to maintain supervisory standards.

3. Peer supervision is a valuable part of a practitioner's portfolio of reflective practice activities, and groups or chains without qualified supervisors are encouraged, supporting deeper exploration and additional perspectives. However, ideally some supervision will be delivered by a qualified supervisor.

Development of Evolve

Eight graduates who completed their supervision course with the same provider in 2010 formed a peer supervision chain to continue their learning in a relatively safe yet stimulating way. The chain, named Evolve in 2015, consists entirely of qualified supervisors who are practicing as external providers in different settings.

Implicit in Evolve's core purpose and contracting approach is the concept: "Who we are is how we supervise", aligned with developmental models of supervision (Hodge 2016; Murdoch 2013).

Clear guiding principles have been established, reviewed and developed over time:

- equality between members (no leader/chair);
- a simple system of non-reciprocal pairing; A supervises B who supervises C, e.g. with paired members not meeting in the next one or two rotations where possible;
- based on the exchange of time, not fees (three 60-minute sessions as a minimum, four preferred, per four-month rotation);
- three rotations per year to bring variety and freshness;
- option to opt out of a rotation(s);
- a minimum of eight participants in the chain at any time for effective pairing;
- act as if the sessions are "paid for" supervision, including rescheduling, preparation, feedback and contracting;
- equal importance given to the role of supervisee and supervisor;
- focus on developmental opportunities as supervisor and supervisee to bring value to clients;
- freedom to bring personal and professional selves in both roles (supervisor and supervisee);

- freedom to bring coaching, mentoring or supervision topics for supervision;
- feedback between each pair (confidential) and from all members on the chain itself;
- chain administrative roles to be shared equally;
- regular whole chain reviews, some using an external facilitator.

The third International Supervision Conference at Oxford Brookes University in 2013 was pivotal for the chain's development. Several founding members presented, demonstrating the potential of the chain as a way to grow and support development as both supervisor and supervisee. Amidst all the genuine interest and affirmation of intention, the word "cosy" was offered from the audience and, "I wouldn't want to be in your group". Both comments landed rather uncomfortably. However, the chain is very grateful for the heartfelt feedback, which marked a watershed.

There had been two web-based, more informal chain reviews, but with the experience of several supervision rotations and the recent feedback, members felt that they wanted to take a more critical look. The first review day facilitated by an invited, external facilitator was held in December 2013. Some differences around possible future directions emerged through thinking about expectations, responsibilities, developing purpose and profile of the chain. Tensions were surfacing between fulfilling primarily individual purposes and the developing of a collective voice on peer supervision. Some tensions were spoken while some were unspoken, and perhaps unconscious, at that stage.

Data collection began with dates of sessions logged to monitor the level of supervision activity in each rotation. The content of the supervision sessions has always remained confidential to each pair. Evolve also conducted its first structured survey of members to explore their views on how the chain was resourcing them. (All quotes from members included below are taken from the annual surveys.)

A recruitment strategy was introduced as a first step to address the "cosiness" challenge. Candidates nominated by existing members were invited to join once the proposal was agreed by everyone in the chain. In 2013 three new members were brought in who had qualified as supervisors with other providers. The chain began to address the gender imbalance in 2015 with two new male members. Three members from the international community joined in 2016. Another international member joined in 2017, and a fifth person in 2018 and this diversifying will continue as members leave. The criterion for joining Evolve remains certified supervisor status following a substantial period of training in theory and practice.

The introduction of new members has been helpful. A founding member commented: "It was good to embrace additional perspectives via new members who kept us fresh and enthusiastic. It was like another new start, and a challenge to offer my very best to newcomers."

Evolve has continued to clarify its purposes, policies and processes through bi-annual group reviews and surveys of members. Additional activities, such as delivering presentations and writing articles, proactively invited comments that challenged every aspect of Evolve. By 2015 some external to the chain were suggesting that Evolve was contributing to developing thinking about the role of peer supervision. For some but not all, that positioning of Evolve by other professionals generated an increased sense of responsibility to spread wider the potential of supervision chains.

To increase the discipline and rigour of supervision, it was agreed that, when contracting, each new pair would set clear objectives for both supervisor and supervisee, against which they would receive feedback throughout that rotation. Members also encouraged each other to set specific objectives each year for their overall development through participating in Evolve. A member commented: "I have truly valued the feedback, which has been affirming and challenging. The added value is that it's from people I respect who are qualified supervisors and experienced coaches offering feedback underpinned by a wealth of knowledge."

Over a number of years, Evolve has consulted with key representatives of standards and accreditation (including the AC, EMCC, ICF, AOCS, APECS, BACP and BPS) to highlight the lack of clarity and/or consistency in their supervision guidelines around the acceptance of peer supervision. This dialogue, which informed the subsequent publication of two features by the chain (Gilbert, Lucas and Turner, 2015; Toolbox, 2015) raised awareness of the potential contribution of peer arrangements to practitioner development. The situation is now clearer; the following year the first Association for Coaching/European Mentoring and Coaching Council Joint Global Code of Ethics highlighted the role that peer supervision played in the supervision mix (2016: paras 4.3–4.6). The second version of the Global Code has retained these references (2018, paras 4.3 and 4.5) and further professional bodies have signed up to the Code.

Key learnings for Evolve

The practicalities

The current makeup of Evolve is 13 members, five of whom are living and practising abroad with English as a first language. Five of the original eight members remain and there are eight women and five men. Four members have left the group in seven years for a mixture of personal, professional prioritising and life/career stage reasons. Most members have taken up the option to "pause" as and when required.

The basic operation of Evolve works well. The regular rotations are very successful and sessions are long enough for depth work. Subsequently returning to the same supervisor has brought a deepening of the pair relationship, accelerated also by learning brought from other rotations. The data shows that active members consistently deliver the minimum expectations of three sessions per rotation as both supervisor and supervisee.

On occasions when the chain has had only six active members for more than a couple of rotations, mixing the pairs has obviously been more difficult. Ideally, a minimum of eight active members is needed. The opting in and out has generally worked, with most only missing up to two consecutive rotations. Longer absences can make the group feel a little disjointed, particularly if the absence coincides with new members joining.

Essential chain operational roles, which are rotated over time to balance members' participation and meet changing priorities, are filled as required. The reality is that some have volunteered and held those roles for a long period, while others have taken on fewer commitments. Sometimes, to make progress, it has also been helpful for a member to offer to step in, albeit without role "permission", to facilitate consensus on changes, clarify chain process and check on agreed actions.

Having explicit policies was important, particularly as Evolve looked outward and presented. The process of writing each policy helped Evolve think more strategically and practically about where it currently was and what it aspired to do. The clarity achieved was generally unifying. The data has also added to the authority with which members can speak when presenting.

Diverse supervisor perspectives

From the start, members describe Evolve as empowering, inspiring and hugely developmental. Members brought an eclectic mix of experience and expertise to the chain, from cognitive behavioural techniques to positive psychology, from gestalt to psychodynamic approaches, offering the potential of multiple perspectives over time. Each rotation offered a new opportunity to receive challenging and thought-provoking supervision. There were also many opportunities to learn how to use supervision even more effectively as a supervisee, always taking responsibility to gain as much as possible from each session.

Recognising that there is no "one right way" to achieve effective supervision, many models have been drawn on and there is no insistence on adopting a specific approach; members recognise that "fitness for purpose" depends on several factors, including the supervisee's learning style, values, theory and practice (Hodge, 2016; Lane et al., 2016).

One member reflected: "The variety of one-to-one relationships has helped deepen my reflection. I would not have had such breadth so quickly without the chain. The changing roles and styles of supervisor and supervisee also add to the richness of my experience." Another added: "Through members' diverse approaches, I am constantly learning different tools I can use for supervision. I have space and permission to try out what I'm learning in subsequent rotations. I now feel much more confident in my practice."

When relevant, members have also offered insights from their other professional roles. One member shared: "It feels like a double benefit; it's a fascinating and effective resourcing approach that is dynamic, fun, rewarding and constantly stimulating. When I need specialist knowledge, I can usually find that in another member."

Indications from the reviews and surveys

The external facilitator at bi-annual reviews helps Evolve attend to group process, and clarify and codify its purpose, ways of working and aims. The recent insights about culture alone (see below) are sufficient to underline the importance of a skilled external facilitator. So far, Evolve has chosen to have continuity of facilitator for her supervisory and systems expertise, and her knowledge of the chain. In the future, it may be part of Evolve's development to choose a different facilitator for fresh exploration.

Member surveys, using an online tool, have become an intrinsic way that Evolve evaluates the contribution of the chain to practice, and gives each member another voice in the chain. These show that the chain is now seen as the most effective type of reflective practice in relation to ongoing improvement of members' work; the 2017 survey shows it also forms 37 per cent of members' total reflective practice so is a major factor in resourcing. A newer member adds: "The resourcing aspect is so important to me. I feel supported and understood. I experience great care, even when challenged, and I know that everything offered is for my development as a person and professional." Some findings have also been published in the chain's presentations and articles. The aim will be to ensure that the chain remains useful through learning, evolving and staying at the cutting edge.

Summarising Evolve's member surveys, the main benefits of the supervision undertaken through the peer chain are:

- the high quality and variety of good-value supervision;
- voluntary participation and relative absence of role power;
- collaboration, commitment and reciprocity of the peer climate;
- shared group learning and meta-reflection on practice, and the opportunities for quality feedback with both challenge and support;
- experience of different supervision styles and coaching approaches;
- deepening connection over time as members are paired together again;
- sharper focus of practice, developmental stretch, growth in confidence.

Potential limitations are seen as:

- reaching clarity and consensus on guiding principles and expectations: this includes minimum core commitment to the supervision sessions and to operational roles/tasks and optional input to additional activities;
- managing boundaries and relationships, addressing group dynamics, ensuring parity among members;
- four-monthly rotations may not fit ongoing work with a client brought to supervision;
- integration of joiners to an evolving chain takes longer than induction to a static peer group;
- connecting remotely in pairs and rarely as an entire group can limit chain cohesion;
- some forms of peer/unpaid supervision may not be accepted by all accreditation schemes for coach, mentor or /supervisor.

Thoughts on the culture of Evolve

Any group that has existed for several years will have created a culture, although in Evolve this has not been specifically named and its nature has only recently been aired. In a learning community of individually practicing, independent supervisors there are likely to be differences in interpretation of what is experienced. There may also be differences between those joining Evolve at different times and mini-cultures within the evolving group. It would have been fascinating if Evolve had tapped into each new member's initial experience before those vital first impressions are potentially lost. It seems that new members noticed things, but didn't comment. That too may give a clue to the culture that existed. What is now clear is that in the first three years before the founding members were joined by others, implicit behavioural norms and ways of engaging were established and strengths were harnessed.

With Evolve's collaborative approach, members' mature life and career stages and their professional supervision training, the risk of power imbalance was thought to be minimal. That may have changed over time, with more recent members talking of: the "implied" leaders; most long-standing members; the event organisers; the meeting chairs; the writers; the holders of data and rotas; the completer-finishers; those that initiated or nudged others to fulfill their role commitments; or the ones who dealt with the chain challenges quietly behind the scenes. A new member commented:

> I was quite nervous at first wanting to demonstrate competence and fit in . . . That feeling began to disappear as the relationships developed. I have found that I can hold my own with people I consider to be more experienced as supervisors and in fact, my different approach was exactly what was most appreciated.

Recognising competing interests, Evolve has considered creating a rotating coordinator role to drive action and hold to account the agreements reached. However, the need for, or usefulness of, a "leading member" has not been agreed.

The tensions about primary chain purpose, individual priorities and Evolve's collective voice emerged at the first more formal review and continue to be present. Promoting supervision and peer chains more widely, and influencing professional bodies in particular, would be deemed a priority for some and not for others.

Not all members can attend the annual reviews; so how, and on what basis, does the chain make decisions about developments? Those attending the reviews have more of a voice. This challenge remains unsolved but demands attention. The review with the external facilitator was held entirely virtually in 2018, to make it easier for members, wherever based, to be present.

Joining by invitation has had much more power attached to it than was foreseen. New recruits have expressed a range of responses: honour, surprise, privilege, self-doubt and curiosity, on being invited to join. A member joining in 2015 said: "Coming into an established group was both flattering and slightly intimidating. Why me? Would I fit? Was I good enough? What was my role in shaping the future of Evolve?" Clearly new members each had their own, usually unspoken, assumptions and uncertainties about the running of the chain and about existing members. These included when newer members might have secured the right to offer to help, question the status quo, challenge the effectiveness of the chain or even the competence of more established members. Members continue to debate how else they might recruit while keeping to the guiding principles.

A challenge from the 2017 review, at least partly acknowledged by the group, was that Evolve was becoming more formal as an organisation, with a name, roles, policies, data collection and even a logo for presentations! The recurring question of whether to introduce membership fees to pay chain expenses was aired and decided against, at least for now. There remains discomfort and frustration by some about these developments and unresolved decisions.

Pair case study

Core principles for the chain have been to provide development and resourcing, both as supervisor and supervisee. As described above, Evolve members pro-actively exchange feedback, now using a simple template that provides structure and focus. The purpose of this is mutual learning in a spirit of give and gain, based on trust and confidentiality, and there are no set evaluation criteria. It underlines the

strong attention each pair pays to contracting, as emphasised by Bachkirova and Jackson (2011), to minimise the
risk of collusion and maximise quality.

During the initial contracting for each new rotation,
both supervisor and supervisee use the feedback template
to answer the simple question – What would I like to receive
feedback on from this rotation? Once these specific areas
have been noted, feedback is exchanged regularly; this can
be verbally and/or in writing, while ideas about impact are
very much "fresh in the moment". The person who sought
the feedback responds with their further reflections.

The case study is the written feedback exchange from a
recent pair. It starts with the areas for feedback requested
by the supervisor.

Supervisor:
   What's my balance between support and challenge?
   Am I using my own intuitive responses appropriately to
aid your reflections?

Supervisee's feedback:
   You honoured the things I mentioned about allowing
me space to think.
   You gave some useful summaries
   You joined me in my metaphorical world and helped
develop those, which was very useful
   You did share your reaction to my descriptions – and I
felt supported. I can take more challenge if there is more
going on for you!
   You are patient before you share your reactions, which
I appreciate. I like the way you deliver your thoughts with
conviction but let them go when they are not proving to be
helpful and the way you push again if you believe I should
look more closely at what you are saying. I still think I maybe
got away with a few things!
   I liked the way you express your thoughts. They didn't
come with lots of back up stories or lengthy explanations,
which meant I had to do more thinking myself!

In session two, I felt that you got a bit caught up in my story and shared my frustration quite quickly. On reflection, I think I needed a question about the impact that my client was having on me and the appropriateness of my response. I think that would have helped me make the shift I needed and take more responsibility for my emotions and less for my client's achievements.

Supervisor's response:
I feel like I am picking up on my own internal reactions and putting them out there as "offerings" that you can accept to work with or not. I am not attached to these offerings and so I am happy for you to decide if you want to use them or not. I agree that I could push back and challenge more. I need to think through what's getting in my way.

I have become much more aware of my own "inner discomfort" or personal alarm bells and I need to notice and use them more, and with greater confidence. I have noticed that I stop and reflect much more and enjoy doing so.

The case study now turns to the feedback requested by the supervisee. This is then followed by the supervisor's feedback and the supervisee's response to that feedback.

Supervisee:
When I am challenged, what do you as supervisor notice about my energy levels?

How flexible am I being when you offer a new lens for me to look through?

Supervisor feedback:
You seem to react openly and honestly when I share what's going on for me. You reflect on them, explore them and you decide how you are going to use them. I don't see you losing energy when challenged nor do I see you resisting. Rather, you process the offer by reflecting then thinking out loud.

More recently, I questioned you about your energy levels as there were some nonverbal clues that these might be dipping. You offered a feasible enough explanation, which on reflection I might have accepted too easily. There is something for me to think about around pushing back appropriately.

I do notice that you often default to your cognitive lens searching for thinking errors or assumptions and sometimes you answer my alternative lens questions from a thinking place! When I pointed this out, I think you were able to look again and gain some valuable insights from doing so.

I really enjoyed and appreciated the way you created clarity for yourself in our last session together. I sensed that you were using your own ethics and values to create a zone where you would be comfortable working.

Supervisee's response:

That's good to hear. I am increasingly trusting my own intuition and respecting the intuitive responses from others. Understanding the subtleties of my impact on others is important to me.

I am increasingly appreciating the added value of different lenses and my next challenge is to interrupt that mainly thinking pattern for myself! Thank you.

This case study is typical of the experiences of the three chapter authors. The detail in the feedback is a key element to the increased development, confidence and resourcing that members report in the surveys. The two-way feedback helps maintain the principle of equality and of giving equal importance to the roles of supervisor and supervisee and puts the chain successfully at the heart of members' supervision.

Conclusion

Evolve will no doubt continue to do what its name implies. The chain has come a very long way, refining itself as it has gone along, facing and working with some challenges head on, and, in fairness, ducking and diving a few others. There are exciting and potentially demanding challenges ahead and members will continue to have different energies regarding these. Writing the chapter has in itself prompted considerable further reflection, which may help shape future debate within the chain.

This chapter contains a mixture of process and best-practice points. Some are relatively easy for others to adopt or adapt, some are more subtle and emergent. Evolve hopes that its experience assists and encourages others in their planning and delivery of a peer supervision chain.

Importantly, the exchange of peer supervision has contributed to what members describe as significant personal and professional developments as both supervisor and supervisee, with clients benefiting from the attention paid by members to resourcing themselves well. Returning to the original purpose of this evolving peer supervision chain, to support and resource each member (peer) holistically to secure enduring benefits for clients and other stakeholders, repeated comments from its members affirm that it is delivering that aspirational vision.

Practice points

- Thorough contracting is crucial. Practice is at the heart of the chain and contracting and operation need to ensure its integrity, for example the minimum number of supervision sessions held per pairing.
- Members need to treat peer work as if they were paying, for example, when it comes to preparation, bringing cases and cancellations.
- Openness to feedback from outside of, and within, the peer chain is key to it flourishing long-term and remaining developmental.
- Processes need to ensure that there is a shared responsibility for the running of the chain and that aspects such as entering and leaving the chain, and how pairings are set up, are covered.

- Evaluation and feedback between pairs needs to be incorporated routinely into peer work.
- Renewal and refreshing the membership needs to consider diversity (of approach, background, culture, geography, etc.) to maintain "stretch" and avoid the possibility of collusion.

Discussion points

- What are the benefits of peer supervision work and how might these be harnessed?
- What are the potential challenges of peer work and how might these be dealt with?
- How would you consider using peer supervision chains? In what contexts and with what, if any, support? Where could any support come from?
- How important is it to have supervision with a trained, qualified supervisor if you are having peer supervision? What are the pros and cons of a mix of supervision activity?

The authors want to acknowledge all other past and present members of Evolve for their explicit and implicit contributions to this chapter:

Jill Ashley-Jones, Amanda Cunningham, Gillian Curtis, Mike Hurley, Nick Kambitsis, Janis Kent, Michelle Lucas, Stephen Murphy, Gilly Rutherford, Louise Schubert, Lily Seto, Georgina Woudstra and Ian Wycherley.

Suggested reading

Bachkirova, T. and Jackson, P. (2011). Peer supervision. In T. Bachkirova, P. Jackson and D. Clutterbuck (eds), *Coaching and Mentoring Supervision*. Maidenhead: OUP.

Clutterbuck, D., Whitaker, C. and Lucas, M. (2016). Types of supervision. In *Coaching Supervision: A Practical Guide for Supervisees*. Abingdon: Routledge.

Gilbert, S., Lucas, M. and Turner, E. (2015). Chain reaction. *Coaching at Work*, 10(1), 45–49.

Toolbox: members of the peer supervision chain (2015). To give is to receive. *Coaching at Work*, 10(2), 47–49.

References

Association for Coaching/European Mentoring & Coaching Council (2016). *Joint Global Code of Ethics for Coaches & Mentors*. Retrieved on 13 February 2018 from www.globalcodeofethics. org/

Bachkirova, T. and Jackson, P. (2011). Peer supervision. In: T. Bachkirova, P. Jackson and D. Clutterbuck (eds), *Coaching and Mentoring Supervision*. Maidenhead: OUP.

Carroll, M. (2014). *Effective Supervision for the Helping Professions*, 2nd ed. London: Sage.

Clutterbuck, D., Whitaker, C. and Lucas, M. (2016). *Coaching Supervision: A Practical Guide for Supervisees*. Abingdon: Routledge.

Gilbert, S., Lucas, M. and Turner, E. (2015). Chain reaction. *Coaching at Work*, 10(1), 45–49.

Global Code of Ethics (2018). Retrieved 1 August 2018 https://app. box.com/s/8s3tsveqieq6vr6n2itb0p9mpsxgcncd

de Haan, E. (2017). Large-scale survey of trust and safety in coaching supervision: some evidence that we are doing it right. *International Coaching Psychology Review*, 12(1), 37–48.

Hawkins, P. and Shohet, R. (2012). *Supervision in the Helping Professions*. (4th ed.). Maidenhead: OUP.

Hawkins, P. and Turner, E. (2017). The rise of coaching supervision 2006–2014. *Coaching: An International Journal of Theory, Research and Practice*. Online, 1–13. www.tandfonline.com/eprint/AxfVpA6637y9DYX2jg42/full

Heiker, C. (2016). Peer and traditional supervision: The balance of power. *Coaching at Work*, 11(6), 31–33.

Henderson, P., Holloway, J. and Millar, A. (2014). Exploring group supervision. In *Practical Supervision*. London: Jessica Kingsley.

Hodge, A., (2016). The value of coaching supervision as a development process: contribution to continued professional and personal wellbeing for executive coaches. *International Journal of Evidence Based Coaching and Mentoring*, 14(2), 87–106.

Homer, A., (2017). How executive coaches see value arising from peer group supervision. *International Journal of Evidence Based Coaching and Mentoring Special Issue No 11*, June 2017, 101–110.

Houston, G. (1985). Group supervision of groupwork. *Self and Society: European Journal of Humanistic Psychology*, 13(2), 64–66.

Kassan, L. D., (2010). *Peer Supervision Groups*. New York: Jason Aronson.

Lane, D. A., Watts, M. and Corrie, S. (2016). *Supervision in the Psychological Professions: Building your Own Personalized Model*. London: OUP.

McNicoll, A. (2008). The power of peer coaching. http://nzli.co.nz/file/Conference/Presentations/the-power-of-peer-coaching-tools-for-effective-leadership-coaching-groups.pdf

Murdoch, E., (2013). Introduction – overview of coaching supervision. In: Murdoch, E. and Arnold, J., (Eds), *Full Spectrum Supervision*. St Albans: Panoma Press.

Proctor, B. (2000). *Group Supervision*. London: Sage.

St-John-Brooks, K. (2014). *Internal Coaching*, London: Karnac.

Solutions Centre (2017). About Intervision Groups. Retrieved on 1 August 2018 from http://solutions-centre.nl/en/about-intervision-groups

Toolbox: members of the peer supervision chain (2015). To give is to receive. *Coaching at Work*, 10(2), 47–49.

Wilkinson, E. (2015). Peer supervision and collaborative power. *Therapy Today*, 26(4), 33–35.

10

Case studies

Eve Turner and Stephen Palmer, et al.

Introduction

The ten case studies that follow provide a variety of examples covering different cultures, perspectives and styles, ranging as they do from New Zealand to India and Canada to China. They add to the richness of the vignettes and case studies in the previous chapters. As Passmore and associates state, "case studies or scenarios have a valuable role to play in learning as well as in continuous professional development" (Passmore et al., 2011: 309). McFarlane (2015) describes them as being a useful bridge in teaching and learning between theory and practice as they "encourage and enhance dialogue and reinforce understanding". However, he advocates ensuring they are relevant and short. We believe the case studies that follow are both.

Contributors were able to choose how to write them:

1. From a supervisor perspective
2. From a supervisee perspective (reflecting that we all, as supervisors, have supervision)
3. Or from a joint perspective.

In all cases supervisees have given explicit permission for their case studies to be included and in many cases are fully named.

The case studies reflect the variety of challenges and issues that can be brought to supervision, and underpin how important the resourcing side can be, both for supervisees and supervisors. The majority are examples of one-to-one supervision, but the first discusses peer supervision and the seventh is a case of group supervision. The contexts tend to be business-focused, including education (10), but the outcomes are often as relevant to the supervisee's personal context as to the coachees that they serve. There are repeating themes, like being good enough, even trying to be "perfect", being and doing, the impact of our culture, the importance of providing space and listening. The results most often are about continuing a learning journey with deeper understanding, but in one case (2) the supervisee sets up a new not-for-profit organisation.

Using case studies as part of practice

The case studies can only provide a fragment of what has happened in the supervisory relationship. They are a simplification of what may include complex organisational and personal relationships. Here they are offered as a trigger for our own thinking. As you read the case studies we would encourage you to consider as appropriate to the case:

- What do you see as the issue(s)?
- If there is more than one, how would you prioritise them?
- What do you see as the perspective(s) the supervisor(s) and supervisee(s) have taken?
- What interpretations do you have? What others might there be?
- How would you go about dealing with the challenges posed?
- What would be the impact of your choices on the different stakeholders in the case, including the supervisor and supervisee, but more widely too?
- Considering the three "planks" of supervision, qualitative, resourcing and developmental (Hawkins and Smith, 2013), are there any elements missing?
- What ideas are you taking away and how will you integrate them into your practice?

The case studies

The case studies are presented in alphabetical order by surname:

1. Christina Baird and Sam Farmer, New Zealand – The supervisor – aspiring to resource myself and my supervisee.
2. Laurie Hillis and Leona deVinne, Canada – Air mattresses, gardens and supervision.
3. Sarah Jaggers and Stephen Palmer, UK – "You don't have to fix everything".
4. Michel Moral, France – A case of supervision of group supervision.
5. Edna Murdoch, UK— Session three: Letting go, to let come.
6. Alanna O'Broin and Siobhain O'Riordan, UK – One-to-one peer supervision.
7. Karen Pratt and Alex van Oostveen, South Africa – Supervising within a relational paradigm.
8. Ram Ramanathan, India – Afraid to challenge client.
9. Eve Turner and James Marshall, UK – A journey towards self-acceptance.
10. Qing Wang, China – Supervision on educational coaching: being present through the cultural kaleidoscope.

The supervisor – aspiring to resource myself and my supervisee

Sam Farmer and Christina Baird (New Zealand)

Supervisees' coaching clients "often have at least as much emotional intelligence [and] social, economic and intellectual power as they do" (Farmer, 2011: 37). It is therefore important that I am able to co-create with supervisees a safe working environment, which supports their professional development and is structured, boundaried and mutually accountable. Whilst this can be challenging, maintaining physically and psychologically focused practices that are values-focused – including regular exercise, gardening, mindfulness and sleep hygiene – contribute to my balance.

Listening to and modelling the expectations I have of my supervisees, and noticing how they manage these for themselves, further resource my role. In the Māori worldview, the concept of reciprocity (*ako*) embodied in the mutually supportive relationship between an older (*tuakana*) and younger (*teina*) sibling is highly valued (e.g. Smith, 2007).

In our work together, Christina has referred to some of the self-doubt that she feels when leading presentations to peers and other professionals. In sharing my own similar experiences with her – whilst not taking the focus from her – Christina can inform both of our perspectives and normalise and affirm their validity. This spirit of reciprocity contributes to my self-reflection and revitalises my own supervision.

The supervisee – my need for and expectations of the support / resourcing function of supervision

My clients work primarily in Christian ministry in which their own being is the source and resource for their work. Being their coach and supervisor requires the combination of sound practice, theoretical knowledge, skill development and authentic, attentive presence. I initially came to coaching with a head full of theories. However, Hawkins and Shohet's assertion that "we need to be continually learning, not just new knowledge and skills, but developing our personal capacity, for our own being is the most important resource we all use in our work" (2012: 3) has been instrumental to how I conceptualise my coaching and supervision. Supervision needs to give me the insight and support I need to support me to move from *doing coaching*, using the theories, models and knowledge that I have, to *being a coach*.

Sam has supported this integrative process through noticing and speaking to both my professional and personal self in supervision; this approach is critical for transformational supervision as described by Weld (2012). This enables us to explore the congruence – and occasional dissonance – between my values, my professional self and knowledge and how I integrate and apply that in my client interactions. The ability to attend to my personal self and professional self in supervision creates a natural space for discussing my own self-resourcing, and the impact of that on my client work.

A co-created review

We resource ourselves through being authentic with and valuing each other in co-creating a safe mutual learning space. In this way, we apply a supportive process in which both supervisee and supervisor are active participants. Because the supportive/resourcing aspect of supervision is often intangible, and difficult to define, it has been important for Christina's learning to see this way of being modelled. Both of us come to supervision with a similar value of co-creation and use of self and some shared knowledge of the processes involved.

We acknowledge that the resourcing aspect of supervision could appear differently if we came from more diverse perspectives. However, in the process of building, sharing and continually developing this context for supervision, we support and resource one another in a way that allows us both to develop as professional- and human-beings, and has the ultimate outcome of improving our client work.

References

Farmer, S. (2011). What is the nature of supervision in coaching psychology? *Psychology Aotearoa*, 3(1), 37–40.

Hawkins, P. and Shohet, R. (2012). *Supervision in the Helping Professions* (4th ed.). Milton Keynes: OUP.

Smith, K. (2007). Supervision and Māori doctoral students: a discussion piece. *MAI Review*, 3(2). http://review.mai.ac.nz/MR/article/viewFile/80/80-182-1-PB.pdf (retrieved 1 August 2018).

Weld, N. (2012). *A Practical Guide to Transformative Supervision for the Helping Professions: Amplifying Insight*. London: Jessica Kingsley.

Air mattresses, gardens and supervision

Laurie Hillis and Leona deVinne (Canada)

Background / context

Leona has been a coach for seven and a half years, and is a facilitator and entrepreneur of three successful businesses. We have been working together since the summer of 2014 when Leona completed her Daring Way™ training through Dr Brené Brown's organization (Brown, 2012 and 2013). We started initially as Case Consultant/Candidate, which was a wholehearted match and which morphed into a supervision/ coaching relationship, as it continues today. The point in time that we write about was a low for Leona. She had been working with corporate and business leaders and, while outwardly successful, she felt like an imposter at times, not showing up as her authentic self.

Case study

Leona reflects:

> "Something was shifting for me around this time and Laurie helped me drop into a more spacious place, to be able to honour what was coming up internally, to transform my outer world. I am very intuitive, visual and drawn to meta-phor. When I invite these gifts into my work the impact is magical, engaging my clients with the wisdom of their hearts as well as their cognitive abilities. I was feeling stuck with my client roster and not authentically using my best self.
>
> "In one powerful session the picture of an air mattress popped to mind. I saw myself lying on a metaphorical air mattress, trusting the current of life that ran through me like the water I was visioning. Under stress I know I aban-don the flow of my life to do the "expected" thing which depletes my joy and purpose.
>
> "A particularly stressful time that summer occurred ten days after my son's brain surgery. In our supervision session that day my life changed. Laurie asked "What do you long for Leona". Play came to mind along with the picture of

working/playing in a garden. In exploring this metaphor the truth emerged – I wanted to give away socks, colourful, crazy, joyful socks.

"While I had been in the hospital I had worn goofy socks every day to stay grounded; socks I called Joy Socks. Patients and nurses started to comment on my socks, wishing they had a pair because they said they made them smile. My joy expanded and the future become clear. My not-for-profit organization Joy Socks was born and it has now spread joy to thousands of children and adults in the form of gift-wrapped socks."

Discussion

Leona was trapped in what she thought she "should be" as a coach, not her heart's desire. She was very successful with her business clients but she felt joyless. Her inner critic rose fiercely when she attempted to rationalise that she wanted to shift the focus of her practice. With the gift of non-judgmental, playful and caring space, Leona accessed her inner mentor and let go of the need to be perfect and please others.

My learning in this powerful time with Leona was a parallel process. I too love intuition, creativity and play. And yet, a part of me whispered, "What if you are not supporting Leona in a way that helps her long term? What if all these metaphors don't translate into her dream?" Like Leona, quietening my "not enough-ness" allowed me to invite my best supervisor into the conversations, and the magic continues.

Leona's practice thrives now as she describes herself having transformed from a "super serious leadership coach to a true self, a goofy, wise, smart and a wee bit sassy self". And yes, she has brought these unwrapped gifts to her many successful clients.

References

Brown, B. (2012). *Daring Greatly: How the Courage to Be Vulnerable Transforms the Way We Live, Love, Parent, and Lead.* New York: Gotham Press.
Brown, B. (2013). The Daring Way™ curriculum. San Antonio: The Daring Way™.

"You don't have to fix everything"

Sarah Jaggers and Stephen Palmer (UK)

Background

Stephen and I (SJ) have worked in a supervisee–supervisor relationship for several years. This continues to be an immensely valuable space for me in which to share my practice with another pair of eyes and ears, and to support my development. For me, the quality of the relationship – as with the coach–coachee relationship – is an essential feature. That includes being able to discuss any aspect of the work without feeling misjudged, stupid or defensive. In other words, communicating from a position of openness and trust, and in our particular case, doing so straightforwardly and clearly.

Case study

Several years ago we noticed, at first subtly and then more specifically, a theme developing in our supervision conversations. When discussing coachees' progress or situations, it was clear that I was very focused on ensuring that coachees resolved their matter or achieved their goals. I could sense within my coaching sessions that I was becoming less "light" and working harder than I wanted to be, and aware of developing a slight anxiety in my concern to reach a good outcome. The supervision process and the quality of the relationship was pivotal in both identifying this and in working it through. As an experienced coach I *know* that my role as coach is not to resolve matters or fix things for my clients but rather to support and facilitate them doing so. However, in our conversations I became aware that *emotionally* I felt somehow responsible. It took an experienced supervisor to notice and see through the story I was telling myself about what was happening: in my practice many of the coaching situations under discussion were highly complex and it became apparent that my concern to "get it right" and to serve the clients well was confounded with this complexity and the gravity of some of my coachees' dilemmas.

My own interpretation at the time was that the *difficulty I was experiencing was in the complexity* and it became increasingly easy to get caught further up into this. After a couple of sessions I recall Stephen, initially lightly, drawing my attention to what he was noticing about *where* I was placing the responsibility for coaching outcomes. Initially I responded with the "correct" answer (i.e. with the coachee) but I wasn't internalising that, as I was still focused elsewhere (e.g. in understanding better, going deeper, looking at approaches, models or tools that would help, etc.). When I continued to fail to hear him, he was able to draw my attention to that, and eventually to say to me more directly, "You don't have to fix everything". That was a clear penny-drop moment of clarity for me as I then recognised that, of course, that was exactly what I had been trying to do.

"You don't have to fix everything" is now still a part of my pre-session personal prep, and in case I forget, it is also on a Post-it note by my desk!

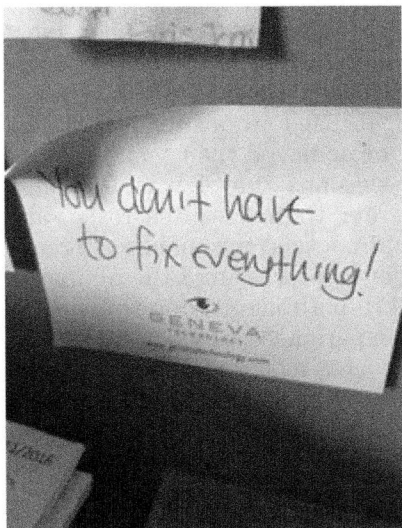

Photo 10.1   Post-it: You don't have to fix everything!

Discussion

Both in coaching and in coaching supervision, the under-lying themes that may be interfering with progress and goal achievement are not always obvious. In this particular example, when I (SP) identified the possible theme, at first I tentatively shared my hypothesis. As I collected more evidence to support this hypothesis, I finally provided feedback that was more concise and direct. Sarah's belief that "I have to fix everything" could be considered as a Coaching or Performance Interfering Thought (CIT or PIT; Neenan and Palmer, 2001) that could put pressure on a coaching relationship and on herself. Her Post-it strategy has proved successful.

References

Neenan, M. and Palmer, S. (2001). Cognitive behavioural coaching. *Stress News*, 13(3), 15–18.

202 EVE TURNER, STEPHEN PALMER, ET AL.

A case of supervision of group supervision

Michel Moral (France)

Background / context

Florence Lamy and I were selected to supervise a group of six supervisors who supervised coaches working in different, independent parts of the same organisation. In this industry segment the conditions are quite tough for the employees, due to extremely high competition. One of the supervisors is the coordinator of the group.

At the request of the coordinator we organised a four-hour group supervision in our office. Apart from the coordinator, the other participants had been trained as supervisors. Beyond the supervision of each supervisee, the request was to supervise the group as a team.

Our approach to coaching and supervision is psychodynamic, cognitive and systemic.

Case study

When we supervise groups Florence and I try to stimulate what we call the *collective intelligence* of the group for the benefit of each supervisee. In this case, in addition to the six supervisees, the group as a team was also a supervisee. Consequently, we designed a special process to address simultaneously the request of a given supervisee and the request of the group. We are used to creating new processes in group supervision when it is needed (Moral and Lamy, 2016).

On the day of this one-off session one supervisee was late and arrived with someone else, explaining that this person would be a supervisor in this group and that he thought that it was a good opportunity to include him in this session. The group coordinator was upset, but the other four members of the group said: "Why not?" This triggered a group discussion.

Florence and I prefer not to have stowaways. Consequently, we asked the additional person to leave. This triggered a second discussion because the additional person was here at the request of the late arriver, having spent four hours travelling to get here. A decision was made to start the supervision with the additional supervisee. We repeated the rules and the supervision began.

We proposed the process that we had designed. Half the group, led by the additional person, said that they wanted to co-create the supervision process instead. This initiated another discussion in which we asked everyone to share their expectations and emotions. This took some time and made clear several characteristics of the clients and of the supervision; for instance, the coaches were in need of more support (restorative/resourcing function). Finally, it ended in a form of open discussion focused on the functioning of the group and no case was explored in depth.

At the end of the session the supervisees (supervisors) were dissatisfied with us.

Discussion

After the session we did an in-depth systemic analysis, identifying all the actors involved, including those outside the room, their interactions, the subsystems, the unspoken, the secrets, the parallel processes, etc. Among the interactions were those that involved us, and we examined the nature of that subcategory: transference and countertransference, interconnected ego defences and active early maladaptive schemas, conflicts of values, conflicts of convictions, oedipal mechanisms, etc. To identify which mechanisms were active we examined what we felt during the session and established a chronology of our emotions.

Finally, based on the systemic principle of co-responsibility, we examined our share of responsibility in what had happened. We have finalised this analysis in a more generic representation of the potential sources of dysfunction in a group supervision, and more specifically in a group of supervisors (see Figure 10.1).

Our conclusion was that it was too ambitious to try to do a supervision of supervisors and address their team-functioning simultaneously. This had a negative effect on

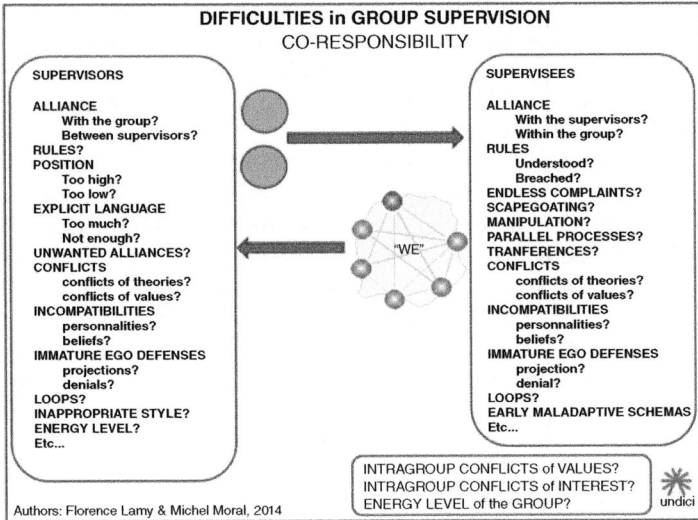

DIFFICULTIES in GROUP SUPERVISION
CO-RESPONSIBILITY

SUPERVISORS

ALLIANCE
  With the group?
  Between supervisors?
RULES?
POSITION
  Too high?
  Too low?
EXPLICIT LANGUAGE
  Too much?
  Not enough?
UNWANTED ALLIANCES?
CONFLICTS
  conflicts of theories?
  conflicts of values?
INCOMPATIBILITIES
  personnalities?
  beliefs?
IMMATURE EGO DEFENSES
  projections?
  denials?
LOOPS?
INAPPROPRIATE STYLE?
ENERGY LEVEL?
Etc...

"WE"

SUPERVISEES

ALLIANCE
  With the supervisors?
  Within the group?
RULES
  Understood?
  Breached?
ENDLESS COMPLAINTS?
SCAPEGOATING?
MANIPULATION?
PARALLEL PROCESSES?
TRANFERENCES?
CONFLICTS
  conflicts of theories?
  conflicts of values?
INCOMPATIBILITIES
  personnalities?
  beliefs?
IMMATURE EGO DEFENSES
  projection?
  denial?
LOOPS?
EARLY MALADAPTIVE SCHEMAS
Etc...

INTRAGROUP CONFLICTS of VALUES?
INTRAGROUP CONFLICTS of INTEREST?
ENERGY LEVEL of the GROUP?

undici

Authors: Florence Lamy & Michel Moral, 2014

Figure 10.1   Pitfalls in group supervision

our own functioning as supervisors of supervisors because we had difficulties managing the three unexpected events that triggered discussions. Also, the rule "no stowaway" was not shared prior to the meeting.

Another factor is that supervisors are more confident in who they are and maybe the group dynamics were impacted by that.

Reference

Moral, M. and Lamy, F. (2016). Selecting a supervision process in collective supervision. In Z. Csigás and I. Sobolewska (eds), *Papers from the Sixth EMCC Research Conference, 6th–7th July 2016*, EÖTVÖS LÓRÁND University, Budapest, 168–179.

Session three: Letting go, to let come

Edna Murdoch (UK)

Introduction

When John contacted me to resume our work, I was really pleased to hear from him and yet, in the pit of my stomach, there was slight discomfort. I did not dismiss that and it gave me courage to change tack in the third session after we had resumed.

John's background, including at board level, had given him an excellent basis for his coaching business. At 50, he had completed extensive coaching training and eventually led a successful global coaching partnership. Supervision had supported John to navigate his way through meetings, client work and complex contractual conversations within large organisations. Occasionally, he had doubted his competence, even amid great success.

Case study

Even the best coaches occasionally feel that maybe they are not quite up to the complex nature of high-level work. John was no different; as our third session proceeded, he said: "I seem to have lost my edge . . . I think that others in the team are doing better than I am".

These are common statements in supervision, especially when a threshold has been reached – usually unconsciously. This "Am-I-good-enough?" theme was recurring and the feeling in the pit of my stomach was reactivated. I had a sense of going round old stories with John without making much headway. So I offered him the choice of tracking to the source of his feelings or of stopping trying to think this through and let some air in. He chose the latter. We were silent for a minute or two, consciously breathing together. He agreed to play with a short visualisation on the theme of: "There's nothing to do and nowhere to go" (Nhat Hanh, 2007). This process allows what has been hidden, to surface. So we waited in the unknown, a deeper reflection now possible.

After a few minutes, John wondered if his discomfort was more than his familiar mutterings about not being good enough. As his energy brightened, he began to imagine that maybe he needed to trust himself more. I remained quiet. John said: "Maybe this is about how I stay fresh and motivated for the next ten years?"

His voice sounded stronger, as he began to touch the real track of his discovery. Not quite knowing why, I found myself asking: "So how do you see yourself in the next decade?"

This turned the session. Crucial awareness now flowed: John was at a turning point, personally and professionally. He would be 60 next year and had not considered if that had implications for him. As our dialogue found its true focus – and my stomach settled – many questions emerged for him:

Would keeping the same kind of work and the same level of responsibility keep him going? What really mattered to him?

The logjam had gone; feelings that had lain hidden, came to the surface. There was now greater energy in John's sessions; gradually, he made decisions about how he wanted to go forward.

Reflection

I notice that coaches' disenchantment with their work sometimes signals a new threshold and the need for change. It often begins with doubt about performance. Session three underlined how easy it is to overthink and how important it is to trust the unknown – "letting go, to let come" (Presencing Institute, 2017). We had let go of trying to think through John's issue and had opened up the imaginative space for something important to emerge. I trusted in my supervisee's resourcefulness and deeper knowing. The shift in the session had come from John, not me. He had been holding a deep discomfort that I had felt only mildly. The session had slowed down enough to let the real discomfort speak.

References

Nhat Hanh, Thich (2007). *Nothing to Do, Nowhere to Go: Waking Up to Who You Are.* Berkeley, CA: Parallax Press.
Presencing Institute (2017). Retrieved on 1 August 2018 from: www.presencing.org/#/aboutus/theory-u

Case study – one-to-one peer supervision

Alanna O'Broin and Siobhain O'Riordan (UK)

Background / context

This case study outlines a peer supervision relationship between two Chartered Psychologists, both of whom are Accredited Coaching Psychologists. Domains of work include coaching psychology practice, training, supervision (one-to-one and group, professional practice and academic), coaching psychology research and academic/professional body interests. The meetings are set up via a one-hour Skype format, scheduled approximately bi-monthly. Typical discussion topics cover themes arising from coaching assignments and work as coaching/coaching psychology supervisors.

Case study

These supervision conversations are primarily defined as a space for learning and reflection, drawing upon Carroll's observation that "At its simplest, supervision is a forum where supervisees think about their work in order to do it better" (2006: 4). Agendas are generally focused on areas that are front of mind at the time, including perspectives on boundary management, contracting, managing stakeholder relationships, ethical themes and self-care. Some discussions involve navigation around more complex coaching or supervision scenarios and contexts.

A key characteristic jointly identified and valued is the nature of the particular supervision alliance space, enabling any situation or topic to be addressed transparently and robustly. Examples of this include a desire to rescue clients when facing topics such as self-harm and redundancy. On these occasions the supervisory context offered opportunities for challenge, feedback, development and a climate in which to explore use of selves as coaches (Bachkirova, 2016). Hawkins and Schwenk's description of the *resourcing* function of the supervisory relationship – "providing a supportive space . . . to process what they have absorbed from their clients and their client's system" (2010: 211) – comes close to capturing this way of working.

Discussion

In underscoring this supportive space as an important constituent of this supervisory relationship, questions have emerged about

 i. the nature of the relationship in which such a space is able to occur

 ii. the impact of working in this space on supervision outcomes.

Ingredients supporting and contributing to this supervision bond include trust, transparency, honesty and objectivity. Having known each other prior to peer supervision, there was awareness of the need for an appropriate bond for achieving the goals and tasks of supervision, and for sufficient self-awareness to recognise the limits of supervisor bond and to avoid the potential for collusion.

As a function of peer supervision, this co-created supervisory relationship has emphasised *both* participants as supervisors *and* supervisees, at different points in the process. Without a "training" or "apprentice" model of supervision, and with an egalitarian and collaborative spirit adopted by the two individuals concerned, no power differential issues have occurred.

The greatest impacts of working in this space appear to be in permitting another level of self-examination and self-awareness. Each supervisee is able to share insights about their coaching practice and personal lens under the scrutiny of the other. Arguably this process has also contributed not just to *resourcing* the two coaching psychologists but has also enabled *qualitative* outcomes of helping keep the supervisee courageous and honest, as well as attending to what they were not seeing, hearing, feeling or saying. The example of navigating the topic of client self-harm is relevant here because the supervision has supported discussion without the need to "window dress" or "hide" areas of vulnerability as coaches. *Developmental* outcomes of this relationship include providing continuous professional development and assisting the confidence of the internal supervisor of the supervisee, all critical in supervision (Hawkins and Schwenk, 2010).

References

Bachkirova, T. (2016). The self of the coach: Conceptualization, issues, and opportunities for practitioner development. *Consulting Psychology Journal: Practice and Research*, 68(2), 143–156.

Carroll, M. (2006). Key issues in coaching psychology supervision. *The Coaching Psychologist*, 2(1), 4–8.

Hawkins, P. and Schwenk, G. (2010). The interpersonal relationship in the training and supervision of coaching. In S. Palmer and A. McDowall (eds), *The Coaching Relationship: Putting People First*. Hove: Routledge.

Supervising within a relational paradigm

Karen Pratt and Alex van Oostveen (South Africa)

Background

Alex has been in a supervisory relationship with me over the past seven years, both as a transactional analysis trainee and a coach.

Our work together is positioned within the cocreative transactional analysis philosophy (Tudor and Summers, 2014). The three principles are:

> We-ness – the co-created relationship is at the heart of the work and is bigger than the sum of each individual.

> Shared responsibility – even though as coach and supervisor we have different roles, the responsibility for the work is not weighted more heavily towards the supervisor.

> Present-centred development – both of us work in the here and now in our integrating Adult ego states.

The fundamental framework is Tudor's (2011) model of cocreative empathic relating in which both people remain grounded in their integrating Adult in the here and now, while simultaneously making new meaning in their respective Parent and Child ego states. It is within the quality of the empathic relating that the transformation occurs.

Case study

Alex reflects:

> "The overarching process that I experienced, has been the journey from dependence to gaining more confidence and stepping into autonomy and wholeness. At the beginning of our work, my preferred door of contact [Ware, 1983] was thinking – I had not yet given myself permission to explore my feelings, and my behaviour was quite guarded – I have a Be Perfect

working style [Hay, 1993] which leads to me putting a lot of effort into getting things right. As Karen and I worked within a growing empathic relationship, I began to be connected to my full complement of internal resources – cognitive, emotional and somatic. I was able to get deeper insight into my practice of coaching and work more fluidly with a diversity of clients. This has increased my presence and potency as a coach and invited my clients to access more of themselves as well. I have also experienced a growing ability to ongoing take a meta-perspective and self-supervise in the moment."

Discussion

We reflected on this journey using the metaphor of a dance. Alex was no longer just able to do one basic dance and attempt to use that with all his clients, he was now learning different dances and could partner with his clients in their dance. Through the supervision relationship he realised that coaching is more about the quality of connection and way of being than a mechanistic process. This attitude leads to ongoing transformational change.

We paid attention to the psychological level of our contracting – the unconscious, unsaid elements about how we worked together, and renegotiated this as Alex's sense of autonomy developed. By constantly believing in Alex's ability to explore, and asking provocative questions, he was able to be in touch with his natural, authentic Child ego state and become vulnerable, make new meaning, give himself new permissions and integrate the changes on a deep level. He has described his learning as a blend of cognitive and subconscious learning, which has enabled an ongoing expansion of his integrating Adult ego state.

At the same time, I as supervisor have learned and grown through my interaction with Alex. His honesty and courage in exploring his inner world has invited me to do the same. I have always felt inspired by his authentic work.

So, what has been at the heart of our work? An authentic and ever renegotiated relationship, a rigour of challenge held within an unwavering positive regard for Alex and his work, courage to work with the unseen level of his way of being, rather than just analysing his practice of coaching. What an exciting journey for both of us!

References

Hay, J. (1993). *Working it Out at Work*. Watford: Sherwood Publishing.

Tudor, K. (2011). Empathy: A cocreative perspective. *Transactional Analysis Journal*, 41, 322–335.

Tudor, K. and Summers, G. (2014). *Co-creative Transactional Analysis*. London: Karnac.

Ware, P. (1983). Personality adaptations (doors to therapy). *Transactional Analysis Journal*, 13, 11–19.

Afraid to challenge client

Ram Ramanathan (India)

Background

This case is from my supervisory perspective of a leadership coach, mentor and trainer, with a fellow executive coach. This case has some special features in respect of

- The coach (supervisee) is a young woman executive coach, uncommon in India
- The client is a successful alpha woman leader whose behaviour was seen by her team as aggressive, again uncommon
- Supervision itself is uncommon in India
- The supervisor had been a trainer, mentor and coach of the supervisee.

Case study

The supervisee described the client as an alpha manager, with a successful track record, aggressive to colleagues in her leadership team in a startup. The startup leadership team had provided feedback on the client's aggressive attitude and, unable to challenge the leader and make a change, had hired the coach.

The supervisee feels she has established trust with the client. However, she experiences the client as defensive, providing reasons why team feedback is not relevant, given her successful career thus far. She is also resistant to the coach's feedback. The client's limiting belief, as perceived by the coach, is that if she drops her aggressive defensive armour at work, it would indicate vulnerability, which she sees as a weakness unfit of a leader.

Within the startup system the leadership team was unwilling to challenge the client on her behaviour apart from hiring a coach. The reporting team seemed fearful. The client was provided with 360 feedback, pointing to aggressive behaviour, which she was defensive about.

The supervisee believes in unconditional positive regard dealing with clients. She is reluctant to challenge the client motto "I don't need feedback including from you". As coach she feels frustrated being unable to help the client open up, and feels helpless. Halfway through the journey the supervisee wonders if it is worthwhile continuing. She sought supervisory help at this point.

I have had several years of interaction as trainer, coach, mentor and supervisor to the supervisee. In this session both of us communicated directly with trust developed over time. I had coached aggressive men and women leaders unwilling to receive feedback. Though situations were parallel, process was not. I am by nature direct and challenging. I communicated my reflections on this situation and inquired if the supervisee's reluctance was a one-off response or part of a pattern.

Discussion

The supervisee admitted to a pattern of inability to confront and challenge clients. Direct communication is a challenge in the Eastern context (for example, see Ramanathan, 2017). Her background was in counselling. She agreed that she had two options – either to stop coaching this client or to challenge the client's beliefs, which may lead to termination of the relationship. She realised that the latter would help her break her pattern, and possibly benefit the client.

The interaction of supervisee with this client is ongoing. The supervisee accepted the need to challenge this client and future clients, which has been a problem area. Knowing the supervisee well, she is likely to act on this awareness. How the client changes is another question! At my supervision level the purpose is to enable learning and create awareness, which happened in this case.

My experience in supervising men and women coaches in India indicated that most of them were reluctant to engage with clients emotionally and communicate directly. They were reluctant to challenge the client even if they found that the client's words were not aligned to their emotions and the situation they described.

This is a generalised Asian style of elliptical rather than direct communication (for example, see Nangalia and Nangalia, 2010). This style has its advantages in a culture that believes in harmony and relationship. However, in coaching it has its limitations. In training coaches to mastery, I found this to be a serious issue that needs to be coached, to create awareness of cultural limiting beliefs.

NOTE

The supervisee permitted publication of the case, which has been presented with no names and references.

References

Nangalia L. and Nangalia, A. (2010). The Coach in Asian Society: Impact of social hierarchy on the coaching relationship. *International Journal of Evidence Based Coaching and Mentoring*, 8(1), 51–66.

Ramanathan, R. S. (2017), Coaching Across Cultural Boundaries – Corporate Executive Challenges. Belgium: European Mentoring & Coaching Council. Available from: www.emccbooks.org/book-contents/reflections-series/coaching-across-cultural-boundaries-corporate-executive-challenges

A journey towards self-acceptance

Eve Turner and James Marshall (UK)

Background / context

James is an experienced and highly successful facilitator and executive coach, who has been practising for ten years and has multinational clients. We have been working together since 2015. Initially James was unsure about supervision, and saw me as a potential judge, a voice for his inner critic (which was fuelled by some tough feedback whilst training); he lacked confidence in his coaching and unconsciously was seeking approval, wanting to be seen as an excellent coach. While he liked to think of himself as self-aware, James was wondering about the extent to which this was true in relation to his practice. He has a huge commitment to learning.

Case study

"As part of our work together Eve and I listened to a recording of a coaching session. Eve asked me some questions in advance to help my recording review:
   What were your aims and intentions in this session?
   What was the context?
   Select a ten-minute segment and do summary feedback

"As I listened I became increasingly aware that I could, at times, lead a client. For example, I realised that a desire to support my clients by offering potential solutions, albeit with their agreement could, overplayed, become a demonstration of a lack of trust for people to make decisions for themselves. I also heard that, at times, my questions were overly complicated. But I also began to accept that there were many things I was doing well, such as building strong rapport and trust, offering insights; I heard that when I am at my most simple I can be at my most powerful. I reflected that there is no need to worry about thinking of clever questions which brings a pressure to perform; space, silence, short open questions and just 'being' are as important as doing. One of my takeaways was to prepare more for sessions, to sit quietly and also think about the client's agenda, taking their perspective.

"I continue to worry about how I practise, and how I can ensure that I work both ethically and in a spiritual and purposeful way, enabling clients to find their own answers. I am reminded of a story I heard about the SAS taking on a group of Aborigines to see who could get to a waterhole first. The SAS took four days, but had a miserable journey, arriving exhausted. The aborigines thrived, taking four days, but arrived having enjoyed their journey, happy and full of energy.

"My journey continues. I still worry about what Eve thinks of my practice, but through reflection and acceptance, I've really noticed an increase in my self-awareness, confidence and skills and a change in results with my clients."

Discussion

James' desire to be an excellent coach is a huge strength; he demonstrates this in the care he shows, but he has the potential to be a harsh self-critic. Listening to tapes is part of James' journey to be more self-aware and self-accepting and develop his own "inner supervisor", better able to reflect-in-action, rather than just reflect-on-action (Schon, 1991).

As a supervisor I am reminded that while I firmly believe there are (at least) three functions of supervision – "Developmental, Resourcing and Qualitative" (Hawkins and Smith, 2013: 173) – James, like other supervisees, often worries that it is the qualitative lens that I will use. Supervisees may wait to hear the "judgements" of the "expert". I need to always ensure, through regular feedback and evaluation, that supervisees feel all these functions are being appropriately attended to and that at the heart of supervision there's a safe, trusting space where there may be challenge but there is also clearly support, acceptance and appreciation.

References

Hawkins, P. and Smith, N. (2013). *Coaching, Mentoring and Organizational Consultancy* (2nd ed.). Maidenhead: Open University Press.

Schon, D. (1991). *The Reflective Practitioner: How Professionals Think in Action*. Abingdon: Routledge.

Supervision on educational coaching: being present through the cultural kaleidoscope

Qing Wang (China)

Introduction

Educational coaching is an emerging field of coaching psychology research and applications (Wang, 2018). As an educational and coaching psychologist, I have attempted to explore different ways to use coaching psychology in various educational settings and integrate evidence-based coaching approaches and models for educational purposes. In a variety of learning contexts from secondary schools to higher education, teachers are coached by professional practitioners to become academic coaches or educational coaches and develop students' positive learning dispositions and self-determination in learning. The teachers coach alongside their teaching and definitely make an impact on students' learning, either cognitively, emotionally or socially. Coaching supervision for these teachers-as-educational-coaches has often been overlooked. In the following case study, I am writing from the joint perspective of my supervisee and myself, with the supervisee's permission.

Context

This case study is with a teacher from a well-known international school in Mainland China. The school's faculty consists of 20 per cent Chinese teachers and 80 per cent teachers coming from international backgrounds; all the students are Chinese and subsequently go abroad to university. My supervisee, Amanda (pseudonym), is a female Chemistry teacher, born in India, has a Master's degree in Chemistry from the UK and came to China two years ago. She has been using the Coaching for Learning Model (Wang, 2013) in her class. I invited Amanda to join in regular coaching supervision (monthly) and she has mainly focused on the challenges of implementing coaching in her class and her own problem of cultural adaptation.

The coaching supervision

Amanda and I co-designed a supervision approach that was mutually suitable and comfortable. At the beginning of each session, we practised three-minute mindful breathing together. With enhanced concentration and awareness, we explored the issues she brought. In the following extract, she explained what happened when applying coaching in teaching Chemistry:

Amanda:	Sometimes I feel that I am lost and struggling between what is really needed and what is to be assessed. I know I should cultivate students' higher learning capacities, but they need to pass the standardised exams. Time doesn't allow us to coach each student. In addition, the students need to have lessons on cultural adaptation, I mean, even I need this.
Qing:	So what is the real challenge here?
Amanda:	To balance coaching and teaching in my class, and this cross-cultural thing.
Qing:	To become more culturally competent, including your students and yourself?
Amanda:	Yes, and I may need to be more aware of the cultural differences when I coach these students.
Qing:	How would you like to work on that?

Discussion

Through our coaching supervision, Amanda has become more aware of the impact of her students' and her own cultural backgrounds on the coaching relationship. In addition, she is more engaged with reflective, in-depth conversations about her cultural identity, the mutual influence between her students and herself, and what she thinks of as "the positive characteristics and best practices' of education in India, China and the UK". She felt supported to integrate these reflective thoughts into the coaching with her students, and this approach was evidently effective. One of her students responded that he felt the classroom was "filled with warmth, care and wisdom" when Amanda was using her own experience of cross-cultural learning and working, and modelling how to develop adaptation strategies.

In the supervision of educational coaching, particularly in the context of international education, supervisees usually experience multifaceted challenges in coaching: 1) integrating coaching skills in everyday teaching; 2) balancing coaching feedback (formative) and exams (summative); 3) engaging students in coaching instead of allowing them to be passive learners; 4) adapting to the current culture themselves while helping students adapt to another culture; 5) having a sense of authenticity and self-determination, as the core of continuous self-coaching in education. The coaching supervisor may need to be equipped with cultural awareness and sensitivity in order to facilitate supervisees to work with people from different backgrounds in international education.

References

Wang, Q. (2013). Towards a systems model of coaching for learning: Empirical lessons from the UK secondary classroom context. *International Coaching Psychology Review*, 8(1), 35–51.

Wang, Q. (2018). *Coaching Psychology for Learning: Facilitating Growth in Education*. London: Routledge.

Conclusion

The richness of the case studies demonstrates the impact of culture on our practice. Reflecting on Chapters 2 and 3, understanding who we are and our diversity in its broadest sense, we can see the role that our backgrounds and values play, both in the cases that are brought to us and the way we may respond to them. We would encourage the joint writing-up of case studies as part of everyday supervision practice, as the discussion with a supervisee(s) can lead to insights on both sides and support the work that is being done together on behalf of all the stakeholders.

References

Hawkins, P. and Smith, N. (2013). *Coaching, Mentoring and Organizational Consultancy. Supervision, Skills & Development.* Maidenhead: Open University Press.

McFarlane, D. A. (2015). Guidelines for using case studies in the teaching-learning process. *College Quarterly Winter* 2015, 18(1) Retrieved on 1 August 2018 from: https://files.eric.ed.gov/fulltext/EJ1070008.pdf

Passmore, J., McMahon, G., Brenna, D., Lee, B. Christian, B. and Tenzyk, M. (2011). Using case studies for reflective practice. In J. Passmore (ed), *Supervision in Coaching: Supervision Ethics and Continuous Professional Development.* London: Kogan Page.

Personal and professional development

Eve Turner and Stephen Palmer

Introduction

In this concluding chapter we are drawing together some themes from previous chapters. We also touch on some important elements that contribute to reflection and self-care: from the role of contracting and ethics to professional support in the form of training and CPPD (continuous professional and personal development) and supervision of supervision. We also highlight the broader area of self-care, considering strategies that have been suggested throughout the book and highlighting a few more.

Over the course of the book the importance of looking after ourselves has been reinforced. As we have seen, there is a body of evidence that shows resourcing ourselves is crucial for us to do our best work, and support others, whether as coaches, mentors, leaders or supervisors. In an age when many people across the globe see time as a scarce resource, and therefore may believe they do not have the time for journaling, mindfulness, peer supervision or just sitting quietly for a few minutes, our role may be to challenge that. When Eve was discussing a supervisee in supervision, getting faster and faster as she described how he rushed everywhere and felt pulled in many directions personally and professionally, her supervisor, Peter Hawkins, said he found the question "What would you have to do for time to be your friend, not your enemy?" a useful one. Reframing time may be just one of the reframes we need to do for ourselves and others.

We may also have to consider how we frame our role as supervisor (and coach). Carroll argues that when supervising, and elsewhere in our lives, we need to be a "facilitator for learning". He adds, "Teach if you must" (2009: 215).

The development of the approach to supervision

Remen, a doctor, describes a visit to the Stanford medical faculty by Carl Rogers and how cynical the medical practitioners and psychologists were about his approach to therapy: "Unconditional Positive Regard seemed to me to be a deplorable lowering of standards" (Remen, 2006: 217–218). Remen's story describes the day-long masterclass that followed. Rogers tells his audience how he takes a moment before every session to remember his humanity, and that this allows the person he works with to share anything; he need not be afraid of disclosure as Rogers is also vulnerable, and because of this Rogers says: "I am enough" (Remen, 2006: 218). Remen continues: "The session that followed was profound. Rogers conducted it without saying a single word, conveying to his client, simply by the quality of his attention, a total acceptance of him exactly as he was" (2006: 218–219).

To provide that quality of attention is not easy. As we have seen in Chapter 8 (Supervision in a Thinking Environment) supervisees experience the benefits, and it seems being listened to can be crucial to our learning. Carroll (2009: 213) underpins the importance of working with others: "My work and experience have taught me that I cannot learn some things on my own. I need others. On my own I get stuck, I recycle the same issues and the same problems." He also talks with honesty about the need to keep himself out of supervision as the supervisor. Carroll asked supervisees how he might work better. One tells him: "I notice you are a fast thinker . . . You come to conclusions about 15 minutes before I do. I wonder if you could keep quiet and let me come to my own conclusion." Carroll writes: "What helpful feedback. I bite my tongue, I wait, and she comes to her own conclusions. Supervisees are so good at teaching us how to supervise them, if we let them" (2009: 214). Carroll describes his biggest change as moving "from supervisor-led supervision to supervisee-led supervision" (2009: 217).

As supervisors, we also need to attend to ourselves. When we listen with openness and concentration, we are impacted. As Hawkins, Phillips and indeed many authors in this book have written (see Chapters 4 and 5, for example), we need to connect with, and resource, our self, to connect with, and resource, others.

One way to resource all parties in supervision is through effective contracting. We can develop our way of working together collaboratively, with our supervisees, peers, colleagues, etc.; this is true in any role we are fulfilling, so not only as supervisor but as coach, facilitator or leader and so on. We can do this, paying attention to the needs of all stakeholders, including those not directly party to the agreement, paying attention to systemic elements. Ethical maturity (Carroll and Shaw, 2013) is another prerequisite for resourcing. By understanding ourselves better (see Jackson and Bachkirova, Chapter 2) and concentrating on our values, our morals and ethics we are going to the heart of how we practise and to the heart of those we supervise and coach. As O'Neill (2000: 13) puts it, we can develop a strong signature presence paying attention to both our backbone – "saying what your position is, whether it is popular or not" – and our heart – "staying in relationship and reaching out even when that relationship is in conflict". We do this in the knowledge of our hot buttons, our patterns, our social, educational and cultural background.

Supporting learning for ourselves and others seems to be an art. As we both seek and deliver training and CPD, as part of our resourcing, how much do we attend to our own, and others' learning styles? Carroll (2008: 17) believes that

> critical reflection allows us to become aware of how we come to our learning and knowledge, puts us in touch with our 'blind spots, deaf spots and dumb spots', brings to the fore the conversations we do not have with ourselves and helps us get in touch with our own integrity and authenticity.

How we learn, and how we provide learning for others, is key. Elsewhere Carroll describes how he spent many years, much of my life, being taught . . . Not once in those many years of being taught have I been asked how I learn. I want to ensure that those I supervise are supervised in a way that connects to their gender, their race and culture, their individual learning style, their ability and disability. Sensitivity to the uniqueness of how each of us learns ensures that the learning environment and relationship is adapted and geared in a personalized and individual way to specific human beings.

(Carroll, 2009: 215)

So, with learning, we are paying attention to factors described in Chapter 3 on diversity and inclusion. This will also impact on where we go for supervision as supervisors.

Practice

Ethics

Ethics and ethical practice is at the core of our work and it is part of our daily lives. It does not exist as an absolute; even in the case of killing someone, an extreme example, the context is everything. To protect someone that we love from being killed, what might we do? In contrast how do we respond when it is killing that is happening thousands of miles away, in a conflict? As Carroll and Shaw suggest:

We spend much of life at ethical crossroads as life and work decisions confront us and demand answers. Sometimes we are aware when these crossroads confront us with moral issues and sometimes we are not. Sometimes we don't realise there are crossroads.

(2013: 13)

In Chapters 2 and 3 we can see some of the influences on who we are and what we believe and therefore how we practice, from our upbringing culturally and socially to economically and philosophically. To some extent we could argue that we inherit our ethical decisions. As Carroll and Shaw suggest "Ethical decisions are not made on a blank page where there is no past. Who we are is determined initially by who we relate to and the contexts, environments and communities in which we are born and raised" (2013: 160). In countries like the USA and the UK many people lead comparatively privileged lives, where money buys us material comforts. How much might preserving this play a part too? In her book, entitled *Wilful Blindness*, Heffernan (2011: 262) argues that "we wouldn't be so blind if our blindness didn't deliver rewards: the benefit of comfort and ease".

As supervisors we are working with coaches who in turn are working with coachees, many of whom will be leaders. One of us (ET) attended a conference session in 2009 when Peter Hawkins asked this question of participants about the then global financial crisis: "What were the coaches doing when the banks were burning?" Someone in the audience said something along the lines of: "sending their invoices in quickly!" Even though it was a joke, I remember how disturbing I found that at the time. Since then there has been more literature considering ethical issues in leadership (such as Boaks and Levine, 2017; Heffernan, 2011). Boaks and Levine remind us of Plato's claim that "the only persons fit to rule are those who must be compelled to rule through fear of being ruled by those less worthy" (2017: 7). They outline some of the challenges facing leaders in operating ethically, question the ease of placing ethics, values and principle at the core of leadership and wonder why "leaders lie, and we don't care" (2017: 11).

This is all part of the backdrop to our, and our supervisees', work with leaders. Someone recently brought to supervision a situation where they were worried about their coachee: this person had observed some unsafe practices that they believed could have catastrophic consequences; at the same time their organisation had a reputation for getting rid of whistle-blowers and the coachee was the family breadwinner. Consider the complexity of ethical decision-making in the military. Heffernan talks to military leaders who both see the need for moral courage, "standing up for what is right", while balancing this with considering how much room there is for independent thinking when in conflict situations (2011: 158).

Iordanou et al, argue that in ethics "the focus . . . should be cast not on solving ethical issues but, rather on creating those conditions and conversations that will bring them to the surface" (2017: 186). While each of the professional bodies has a Code of Ethics (such as the AC/EMCC's Global Code, APECS, APS, ANSE, BPS, COMENSA, EASC, IAC, ICF, ISCP, WABC – see Appendix A) no code can cover the complexity of the situations that practitioners will face. So, ethics need to be part of our everyday thinking and of our ongoing work with supervisees. Iordanou et al. argue that "supervision is paramount for an ethical coaching practice, as it offers space for reflection and critical thinking" (2017: 42). The majority of professional bodies make supervision mandatory for membership and accreditation, although it is recommended and not required by the ICF (2018). The ICF differentiates supervision from its requirement for coach mentoring to become credentialed; coach mentoring is the development of the coach's coaching skills specifically to meet the ICF core competences and adherence to its Code of Ethics. It is also the case that not all coaches belong to a professional body, and not all supervisors have supervision of supervision.

To support ourselves we can put in place strategies, such as finding space for reflection, including writing as advocated by Holder, or by following an ethical decision-making model (Passmore and Turner, 2018). Passmore and Turner's Six Step *APPEAR* Model includes considerations such as:

1. Using coaching and accrediting bodies' codes of ethics and good practice.
2. Developing awareness and understanding of one's own values, beliefs and culture.
3. Looking at the different contracts and policies in place.
4. Using reflection – for example through writing and journaling.
5. Discussing the situation with your supervisor.
6. Drawing on professional insurers' resources such as legal helplines where available.
7. Paying attention to legal and statutory requirements.

In part, facilitating conversations can be through the use of dilemmas, discussed within the supervision session. Response to dilemmas are also a part of accreditation (credentialing) with some of the largest coaching professional bodies. Turner and Woods (2015) describe a situation when the police wanted to seize coaching notes. Others are offered by Hodge (2013: 9), including supervising a coach whose coachee wants the coach's help to prepare for an industrial tribunal; or misaligned outcomes, where the coachee believes the goals are about promotion while the manager believes the coachee's job is in jeopardy (also see contracting). Hodge lists several domains in coaching where issues may arise (2013: 5) that could provide insights, such as the coachee sharing with the coach personal reasons for poor performance but requiring the coach to maintain confidentiality; or the coach knowing organisational information that could lead to a coachee's redundancy of which the client is unaware.

It is also crucial to our work, to be clear when we are working outside our sphere of competence, training and capacity and therefore potentially unethically. Contracting and supervision of supervision are two elements that support the supervisor in creating boundaries for their work, which will ensure safe practice, and also in discussing situations that arise.

Contracting

Contracting and re-contracting is part of our role as supervisor, and as coach, mentor or leader. It begins when we first meet our potential supervisee, whether face-to-face or virtually, to consider whether we can work together. It then moves to our agreement on how we will work together and can be seen in Lee's differentiation of five types of contracting described as (2016: 40–41):

1. Pre-contracting, the decisions that precede the formal contracting efforts.
2. Change contracts, describing the ways the client (individual coachee) hopes to develop as an executive with the support of the coach and sponsoring organization.

3. Process contracts, which contain the methods and responsibilities of the coach, the client and others that combine to make coaching happen.
4. Business contracts, specifying the commercial and legal arrangements between the coach and the sponsor.
5. Psychological contracts, the tacit but potentially powerful expectations among the parties.

In each of these we can substitute supervisor for coach and supervisee for client, and the impact is the same. While the relationship between the supervisor and supervisee is core, in acknowledging that all change is relational, Lee is introducing the systemic aspects with the involvement of different parties. In his description it is organisational, but other systems may include, for example, the family, friendship groups, educational alliances and leisure memberships. O'Neill (2000: xv) argues that "coaches must tune in to how the client's force field impacts them, so they can maintain their equilibrium within it and help the leader do the same". This is true for the supervisor too. A key role for the supervisor is to acknowledge they are part of the system and ensure they stand back and provide perspective.

As in coaching, our experience is that too little time spent in contracting at the outset can lead to difficulties later, many of which could have been avoided or at least minimised; examples are supervisees who cancel at the last moment or who want to be told how to deal with something. This is highlighted by O'Neill (2000: 92) who writes: "in many ways, contracting is the most important phase". Drawing up an agreement for supervision is a collaboration, as in coaching, ensuring clarity on all sides. In contracting for supervision, Hawkins and Smith propose five key areas (2013: 175):

- Practicalities
- Boundaries
- Working alliance
- The session format
- The organisational and professional context.

Research by Turner and Hawkins (2016: 60–61) with 569 coaches has highlighted the key elements for effective stakeholder contracting in executive coaching, and elements of these are pertinent to supervision, so the supervisor understands the context:

1. The aims for the coaching – ensuring there is alignment between the coachee and the organisation
2. A shared understanding of what an effective outcome(s) for the coaching looks like and

   a) how this will be evaluated
   b) when it will be evaluated;
   c) and by whom.

3. A share understanding of confidentiality including what it means and the circumstances in which it could be breached. This considers: the law; health, safety and wellbeing; the use of supervision; any organisation requirements through procedures and working practices.

Each supervisor will contract according to the individual context, and we conclude this section with an example. This offers key elements from Eve's supervision contracts, which include discussion of:

1. What we have agreed in our work together (aims, outcomes, specifics to this relationship and the use of recordings as part of our work).
2. How we will work together – this may, for example, include a discussion about areas such as challenge and support (Daloz model in Blakey and Day, 2012: 19), listening and use of silence.
3. What supervision is – drawing on the three main functions – developmental, resourcing and qualitative (Hawkins and Smith, 2013: 173) – and the importance of paying attention to all three aspects.
4. Details of some of the approaches we may use with a discussion about them.

5. Professional practice such as

   a. confidentiality – what it means and limitations includ-
    ing my use of supervision of supervision;

   b. ethical codes to which I subscribe with links to how to
    raise concerns about my practice;

   c. data protection with my registration details;

   d. use of preparation and evaluation in our work;

   e. at what point in our relationship I will be happy to
    write a reference and how this will be done collabora-
    tively, including the role of recordings.

6. Process details such as duration, frequency, fees, cancellations, andavailability and contact details between
   sessions.

This draft supervision agreement, which is adapted for each
supervisee by Eve, is included as Appendix B.

Recordings

The draft agreement refers to the use of recordings of coaching sessions for supervision. Recordings allow both the
supervisor and supervisee to hear first hand what happened
in a session, rather than solely dealing with the supervisee's
recall, which can sometimes be inaccurate or unintention-
ally selective. There are important areas to consider (see
BPS, 2008) and these include ethics, confidentiality, relevant legislation such as around data protection, the time
needed to listen, the potential intrusiveness for the coachee,
and the supervisee's fear of being "found out". Each country will have different laws that may be relevant – but
good practice would encourage signed and informed con-
sent from the coachee to being recorded, and the transfer of
any recordings through a safe and encoded format. In our
experience it is important for the supervisee to listen back
themselves and lead any discussion, and examples of potential questions are given in Appendix B. The aim is for us, as
supervisors, to avoid coming across as "judges". Used effectively, recordings can be an invaluable means to work with
supervisees collaboratively.

Bird and Gornall (2016: 166) describe supervision as a "co-created learning relationship" and discuss different ways to use case studies in supervision to make meaning. They include "storytelling, re-enactment, written reflection, witness statements, audio and video recording". They describe how they will sometimes listen to recordings of coaching with their supervisees "so that we both hear the conversation simultaneously and can share reactions and ideas in the moment". Hay (2007: 25) believes that using recordings is part of continuing professional development and so "clients are well aware that any reputable professional will be engaged" in their use. She favours tapes over notes because she argues that "what we write down . . . consists of what we allow ourselves to be aware of" and we are unable to make notes of what is outside our awareness. Hay believes that using tapes, over time, will develop our understanding of how we function.

The development of supervisors through training and continuous professional development

There are increasing numbers of supervision training programmes available worldwide, the majority in Europe. Some are university-based or approved, some accredited by a professional body such as the EMCC or the ISCP, or by an umbrella organisation such as the UK's ILM (ILM, n.d.), or ANSE, the Association of National Organisations for Supervision in Europe. There are also independent providers (see Appendix A). The programmes vary widely in duration from two days to two and a half years where a postgraduate programme is followed. And some of these provide their own accreditation to their graduates, post qualification. There are also increasing numbers of accreditations and memberships available from coaching professional bodies. APECS, the AC, EMCC and the ISCP all offer individual supervisor accreditation. Requirements vary; for example, to gain ANSE's (2017b) membership their requirements include attending a programme of at least two years, with at least 300 training hours and at least 35 hours of supervision on supervision. The ISCP would expect that a coaching psychologist was already a fully qualified psychologist; it can take up to four to five years' full-time education and training (depending upon which country is being practised in) to become an accredited coaching psychologist. For supervisor accreditation additional experience would be required.

Alongside training programmes, there has been a sharp increase in the number of books and articles in the field of coaching supervision. However, as highlighted throughout this book, development is not just about competencies and capabilities, it is also about what Hawkins and Smith (2013: 151) term capacity, our human qualities: "It has more to do with how you are, rather than what you do." So, for wholeness, we also attend to our personal development, as demonstrated through the chapters in this book.

Contact with other supervisors is also helpful to professional and personal development. This can take the form of peer supervision (Chapter 9) or professional networks in supervision. One example is the GSN (Global Supervisors' Network, 2018), a participative network, free of charge to members, offering webinars in different time zones. It connects supervisors across the world working in coaching, mentoring and consultancy who provide each other with, and receive, Continuing Personal and Professional Development virtually, every month.

Supervision of supervision

Supervision is increasingly used by coaches, or at least those who receive and complete surveys who tend to belong to professional or training bodies. In 2006 it was reported that "only 44% of coaches receive continuous and regular supervision" (Hawkins and Schwenk, 2006: 4), but less than a decade later that figure had increased substantially, though with geographical differences. "By 2014 that figure was 92.3% in the UK and 83.2% globally . . . North America is significantly lagging behind other regions . . . at 47.6%; however, it is roughly where the UK was in 2006" (Hawkins and Turner, 2017: 106). This may, in part, reflect that the ICF (2018), which originated in the USA, has information about supervision on its website but does not specifically require members, including those with ACC, PCC or MCC credentials, to be supervised.

While there has been increased uptake in supervision and in writing on supervision, the area of supervision on supervision is still in its infancy. Hawkins and Smith advocate its use as a critical ingredient in supervisor training, in a ratio of one hour of supervision to five hours of practice, providing "the essential connectivity that links learning about supervision on courses with learning from the practice of supervising." (2013: 183). However, there is limited reference to its use for experienced supervisors: "It can also be beneficial . . . and here it can be incorporated into one's supervision on one's work as a practitioner, but it is important that it does get its fair share of time and attention" (2013: 184).

With increasing numbers of training courses for supervisors around the world, this is not yet matched by support for developing supervision of supervision as a field. Extensive work on supervision in Europe is supported by ANSE, with publications such as Van Kessel and Dinger (2016) and has looked at developments in relation to the helping professions including coaching (ANSE, 2017a). Moral, Turner and Goldvarg suggest

> The coachee needs a coach to get an external view of himself/herself, the coach needs a supervisor, and the supervisor in turns needs to collaborate with a supervisor to gain perspective too. So, having a reflective space is essential to the wellbeing and professionalism of supervisors. It is also a principle of accountability, and modelling good practice.
>
> (2017: 39)

A Global Supervisors' Network survey on supervision of supervision in 2017 with responses from 118 supervisors shows that while the majority, nearly 91 per cent, had received training in supervision, with 70 per cent having at least 80 hours of training, the figure was 47 per cent for those who had received training in supervision of supervision. And this training was more likely to be peer reflection or a discussion with an experienced supervisor of supervisors.

236 EVE TURNER AND STEPHEN PALMER

It also shows that nearly 62 per cent of supervisors received supervision of their supervision issues from the same supervisor to whom they took their coaching practice, two-thirds doing so at least every other month.

When supervisors were asked to describe the nature of the relationship between themselves and their supervisee when supervising supervisors, the top responses (Table 11.1) suggested that supervisors of other supervisors generally believed the relationship was much the same as when they supervised a coach. Occasionally supervisors suggested it was more challenging and was even more of a partnership, and felt they needed to show more vulnerability.

The similarities were borne out by another question comparing supervising to supervision of supervision in relation to the three elements of developmental, resourcing and qualitative, plus ethics and reflection. The most significant differences were in the areas of reflection and ethics where respondents thought there was significantly more discussion (23 per cent and 25.3 per cent respectively) in supervision of supervision.

For supervisors, the importance of having supervision of supervision is in part highlighted by the areas of resourcing, developmental and qualitative work, along with ethics and reflection, as described. But it is also about how we model ourselves as supervisors. Given the increasing numbers of highly experienced supervisors – and in the GSN survey half of the respondents had been practising for at least six years – and the potential to use peer supervision, there should be no barriers to finding effective supervision of supervision.

Table 11.1 The relationship in supervision of supervision

	Percentage selected	65 completions
1. Partnership	76.29%	50
2. Supportive	69.23%	45
3. Co-construction	66.15%	43
4. Challenge	55.38%	36

Self-care

This book has set out to provide support for all practitioners in self-care. Part of this is understanding our own lens on the world, coloured as it is by what we believe about the world and our personal circumstances and context. We learn self-compassion, as without it we may not be able to role-model compassion for others, and we learn choicefulness, the idea that the ultimate freedom is: "to choose one's attitude in a given set of circumstances" (Frankl, 2004: 9). Frankl writes with compassion, even in the extreme circumstances of being a prisoner in Nazi concentration camps. His words support the very concept of "choicefulness".

Authors in the book have advocated self-awareness, reflection, writing, mindfulness practice and self as instrument, to support us in our role as supervisors, which can be a demanding one. One area we may all encounter, for ourselves and others, is stress or trauma, sometimes reflecting what is going on elsewhere in our systems. However, with coachees, supervisees or ourselves, our ability to deal with that, or change, differs. Pemberton (2015: 42) argues "it is no longer possible . . . to claim that 'an old dog can't be taught new tricks'. Neuroscience has taken away that defence . . ." Instead, Kegan and Lahey demonstrate through years of research that our ability to change "does not unfold continuously; there are periods of stability and periods of change. . .and the intervals between transformations to new levels . . . get longer and longer" (2009: 15).

Carroll has described a continuum between competency and survival mode. He explored it

> in the context of how people learn and what blocks learning and in particular how stress, trauma and fear can propel us into survival mode which seriously curtails our ability to learn. I used it in supervision training to indicate how supervisors need to help supervisees stay in competency mode in order to be open to new learning.
>
> (Carroll, 2017, personal communication)

The phrase "amygdala hijack" (also see Hawkins, Chapter 4, p70), a reactive state, emerged from the work of Goleman (1996). Survival mode describes what happens to our bodies in stress where we are in fight or flight mode and the amygdala is activated and our normal reasoning partnership with the prefrontal cortex is disrupted. In fact, Lieberman and associates (Lieberman et al., 2007) found an inverse relationship between the activation of the amygdala and the prefrontal cortex. It can be summed up in Figure 11.1.

When parts of the brain increase in activity, then more blood flows to them. Thus when the amygdala is activated, more blood and therefore oxygen go to that area of the brain controlling our emotional response, whilst less is directed to our prefrontal cortex where our cognitive processing occurs. As a result, under stressful conditions, our thinking is likely to become more rigid and absolutist, so more liable to all-or-nothing, inflexible thinking and less able to see alternatives. Nadler (2011) describes estimates of our IQ falling up to 15 points under stress. So, when we freeze with a supervisee, or a supervisee freezes with a coachee, when we do not know what to do or feel stuck or are experiencing the trauma of the person we are working with, or get sucked into their "impossible" situation, which left them feeling they have no choices, the possibility is that our reasoning will diminish too. Therefore it is probable that we are less able to coach or supervise someone in survival mode, as the capacity for cognitive reasoning is reduced. So, we need to find ways back to competency mode.

Perry (2017) argues that there are only two ways back into competency mode: exercise or relaxation. Many people report that they find exercise helps to reduce their levels of stress; even a short walk has been shown to enhance well-being. However, mental exercise is as important as physical exercise. If we have developed our cognitive thinking skills (see Palmer and Cooper, 2013), for example during our coach and/or supervisor training, then we can challenge and modify our own unhelpful, coaching or supervision interfering thinking when we are becoming stressed (Palmer, 2017). Relaxation or mindfulness techniques or exercises may also be beneficial for some practitioners. Williams and Penman reflect that "mindfulness has been found to boost resilience – that is, the

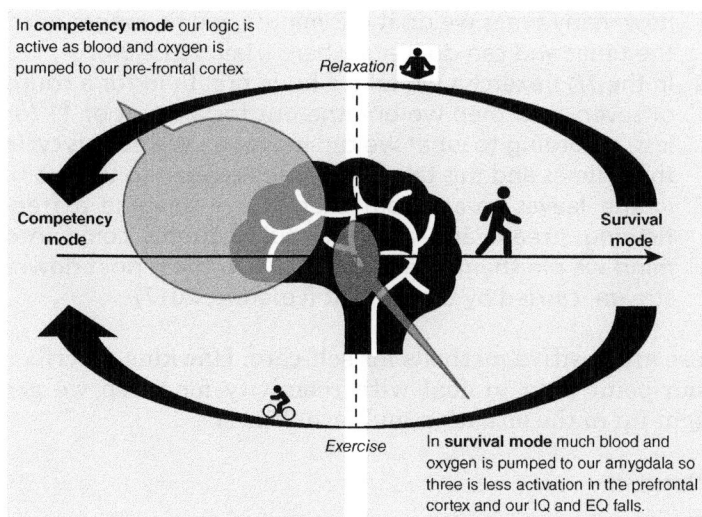

In **competency mode** our logic is active as blood and oxygen is pumped to our pre-frontal cortex

Relaxation

Competency mode

Survival mode

Exercise

In **survival mode** much blood and oxygen is pumped to our amygdala so three is less activation in the prefrontal cortex and our IQ and EQ falls.

Figure 11.1   The competency–survival continuum

ability to withstand life's knocks and setbacks – to quite a remarkable degree" (Williams and Penman, 2011: 53). They point out that mindfulness is a practice, to be done regularly for the most benefit. Pemberton (2015) describes mindfulness, and other approaches to boost resilience such as Acceptance and Commitment Therapy, Cognitive Behavioural Therapy, Solutions-Focus and Positive Psychology. The one-minute, 7/11 or leaves-on-a-stream exercises are a few examples of helpful exercises and, as they may take as little as a minute, it is hard for us, or anyone else, to say we have no time!

Exercises

We first sit comfortably with feet anchored on the ground.

1. With the one-minute exercise we time ourselves breathing in and out (one count) for one minute, concentrating on our breathing, our diaphragm expanding as we breathe in and contracting as we breathe out, and perhaps the air coming out of our nostrils. Once we know

how many times we do it per minute, we no longer need the timer and can do it anywhere (Hall, 2013: 94).

2. In the 7/11 exercise we take a huge breath in for a count of seven, and then we breathe out for a count of 11 (or less, according to what we can manage). We do this cycle three times and this takes blood and oxygen to the brain.

3. In the leaves-on-a-stream exercise we imagine a free-flowing stream and as unhelpful thoughts come into mind we pin them to a leaf and watch them float down-stream, carried by the current (LeJeune, 2017).

These are positive methods for self-care. Hawkins describes a four-point plan to deal with reactivity for when we get caught up in the situation and face "hijack":

Notice It

Catch it

Use it as Data

Act on It (see Hawkins, Chapter 4, p.71).

The noticing may be about patterns, understanding what our hot buttons are. Eve is triggered by bullying – when she hears about it, she knows that she can react without the wide-angled compassion Hawkins talks of (see Chapter 4, p74) and become stressed by hearing of someone's experience. So, it is important to listen to my intuitive reaction, catch it before I act in some way that would not be compassionate, understand what is going on (using it as data) and then act appropriately.

In her book that looks at the top five regrets of the dying, Bronnie Ware (2011: 214) reflects that the top regret was her patients "wishing they had been true to themselves". In our busy, complex, challenging and rewarding world, it is a thought worth remembering.

Conclusion

In this chapter we have touched on some of the elements that support our work as supervisors. Each of the topics covered – ethics, contracting, recordings, continuous professional development, supervision of supervision and self-care – are important and we would encourage further exploration. They are reflections of the way both the wider world and that of coaching and supervision is constantly changing and becoming more complex.

Practice points

- Notice how much you contribute and how much your supervisee speaks in sessions. Try varying this, for example by saying less, and only when the supervisee has exhausted their ideas.
- Consider the role of personal values and ethics in supervision and use cases, models and other means as appropriate so this becomes a greater part of your own and supervisees' everyday thinking and experience.
- Review your agreements with supervisees regularly as a model for their own attention to contracting and re-contracting.
- Encourage supervisees to record coaching sessions regularly and use them together in supervision.
- As neuroscience has shown us that we can constantly renew ourselves, reflect on the new learning each supervisee brings and changes you are making on a regular basis.
- Find ways to incorporate mental and physical exercise and relaxation as part of your practice and, as appropriate, encourage your supervisees to do the same.

Discussion points

- Should supervision be mandatory for all coaches?
- How easy and appropriate do you consider it is to allow our supervisees to teach us how to supervise them as described in this chapter?
- Consider how much attention you, and your supervisees, pay to contracting, and re-contracting. What are the challenges?
- How often, and in what circumstances, do you refer to the ethical code of your professional body? When is it likely to be most helpful and what might be any limits? What would you do if you thought your supervisee, or their

coachee, was behaving illegally and would the type of illegal act make a difference?

Suggested reading

Carroll, M. and Shaw, E. (2013). *Ethical Maturity in the Helping Professions*. London: Jessica Kingsley.
Iordanou, I., Hawley, R. and Iordanou, C. (2017). *Values and Ethics in Coaching*. London: Sage.
Remen, R.N. (2006). *Kitchen Table Wisdom*. New York: Riverhead Books.
Turner, E. and Hawkins, P. (2016b). Multi-stakeholder contracting in executive/business coaching: an analysis of practice and recommendations for getting maximum value. *International Journal for Evidence-Based Coaching and Mentoring*, 14(2), 48–65.

References

Association of National Organisations for Supervision in Europe (2017a). Homepage. Retrieved on 1 August 2018 from www.anse.eu
Association of National Organisations for Supervision in Europe (2017b). Standards. Retrieved on 1 August 2018 from www.anse.eu/about-anse/standards
Bird, J. and Gornall, S. (2016). *The Art of Coaching*. Abingdon: Routledge.
Blakey, J. and Day, I. (2012). *Challenging Coaching*. London: Nicholas Brealey.
Boaks, J. and Levine, M. P. (eds) (2017) *Leadership & Ethics*. London: Bloomsbury Academic.
BPS (2008). General professional practice guidelines. Leicester: British Psychological Society.
Carroll, M. (2008). Supervision and transformational learning. *Psychotherapy in Australia*, 14(3), 12–19.
Carroll, M. (2009). Supervision: Critical reflection for transformational learning, Part 1. *The Clinical Supervisor*, 28(2): 210–220. Retrieved on 1 August 2018 from https://www.tandfonline.com/doi/abs/10.1080/07325220903344015
Carroll, M. and Shaw, E. (2013). *Ethical Maturity in the Helping Professions*. London: Jessica Kingsley.
Carroll, M. (2017). Personal correspondence with Eve Turner, 3 December 2017.

Frankl, V. (2004). *Man's Search for Meaning*. London: Rider.

Goleman, D. (1996). *Emotional Intelligence: Why it Can Matter More Than IQ*. London: Bloomsbury.

GSN – Global Supervisors' Network (2018). Virtual professional network: CPD webinar schedule. Retrieved on 1 August 2018 from www.eve-turner.com/global-supervisors-network/

Hall, L. (2013). *Mindful Coaching: How Mindfulness Can Transform Coaching Practice*. London: Kogan Page.

Hawkins, P. and Schwenk, G. (2006). Coaching Supervision, a report for the CIPD. London: Chartered Institute for Personal and Development.

Hawkins, P. and Smith, N. (2013). *Coaching, Mentoring and Organizational Consultancy: Supervision and Development* (2nd ed.). Maidenhead: Open University Press.

Hawkins, P. and Turner, E. (2017). The rise of coaching supervision 2006–2014. *Coaching: An International Journal of Theory, Research and Practice*, 10(20), 102–114.

Hay, J. (2007). *Reflective Practice and Supervision for Coaches*. Maidenhead: Open University Press.

Heffernan, M. (2011). *Wilful Blindness*. London: Simon & Schuster.

Hodge. A. (2013) Coaching supervision – an ethical angle. In E. Murdoch and J. Arnold (eds), *Full Spectrum Supervision*. St Albans: Panoma.

ICF (2018). ICF Coaching Supervision. Retrieved on 1 August 2018 from www.coachfederation.org.uk/professional-development/coach-supervision/definition-of-coach-supervision/

Iordanou, I., Hawley, R. and Iordanou, C. (2017). *Values and Ethics in Coaching*. London: Sage.

ILM – Institute of Leadership and Management (nd). Level 7 Coaching Supervision. Retrieved on 1 August 2018 from: https://www.i-l-m.com/Learning-and-Development/management/coaching-and-mentoring/8582-level-7-coaching-supervision

Kegan, R. and Lahey, L. L. (2009). *Immunity to Change*. Boston: Harvard Business Press.

Lee, R. J. (2016). The role of contracting in coaching: Balancing individual client and organizational issues. In J. Passmore, D. Peterson and M. Freire (eds), *The Wiley-Blackwell Handbook of the Psychology of Coaching and Mentoring*. Chichester: John Wiley.

LeJeune, J. (2017). Leaves on a stream. Retrieved on 1 August 2018 from: http://portlandpsychotherapyclinic.com/mindfulness_and_acceptance_exercises/

Lieberman, M., Eisenberger, N., Crockett, M., Sabrina, T., Pfeifer, J. and Baldwin, W. (2007). Putting feelings into words. *Psychological Science*, 18(5), 421–428.

Moral, M., Turner, E. and Goldvarg, D. (2017). Supervision of supervision: Where are we? *Coaching Perspectives*, 15, 39–41. Retrieved on 1 August 2018 from www.associationforcoaching. com/page/CoachingPerspectives

Nadler, R. (2011). Where did my IQ points go? *Psychology Today*. Retrieved on 1 August 2018 from www.psychologytoday.com/blog/ leading-emotional-intelligence/201104/where-did-my-iq-points-go

O'Neill, M. B. (2000). *Executive Coaching with Backbone and Heart*. San Francisco, CA: Jossey-Bass.

Palmer, S. (2017). Beyond the coaching and therapeutic relationship: the supervisee-supervisor relationship. Keynote given on 15 September at the 7th International Congress of Coaching Psychology, 2017, Aalborg University, Aalborg, Denmark.

Palmer, S. and Cooper, C. (2013). *How to Deal with Stress* (3rd ed.). London: Kogan Page.

Passmore, J. and Turner, E. (2018). Reflections on integrity – the *APPEAR* model. *Coaching at Work*, 13(2), 42–46.

Pemberton, C. (2015). *Resilience: A Practical Guide for Coaches*. Maidenhead: Open University Press.

Perry, J. (2017). Stress management, wellbeing and resilience. Presentation to the University of Southampton internal coaching community supervision group, 23 November.

Remen, R.N. (2006). *Kitchen Table Wisdom*. New York: Riverhead Books.

Turner, E. and Hawkins, P. (2016). Multi-stakeholder contracting in executive/business coaching: an analysis of practice and recommendations for getting maximum value. *International Journal for Evidence-Based Coaching and Mentoring*, 14(2), 48–65.

Turner, E. and Woods, D. (2015). When the police come knocking. *Coaching at Work*, 10(6), 28–34.

Van Kessel, L. and Dinger, W. (2016). Lehrsupervision in Entwicklung. In E. Freitag-Becker (ed), *Lehrsupervision Im Fokus*. Göttingen, Germany: Vandenhoeck and Ruprecht. See: www.v-r.de/de/lehrsupervision_im_fokus/t-0/1039498/

Ware, B. (2011). *The Top Five Regrets of the Dying*. Bloomington, IN: Balboa Press.

Williams, M. and Penman, D. (2011). *Mindfulness: A Practical Guide to Finding Peace in a Frantic World*. London: Piatkus.

Afterword

Co-editing this book and working with the many chapter contributors has been an exciting journey, as we have learnt about how our colleagues think, feel and practise coaching supervision. As editors we formulated our ideas about this book in early 2016, signed contracts on 4 November 2016, and our voyage commenced. As we progressed, the book took shape and developed on from our original proposal. We thank our colleagues, not only for their chapters and case studies, but also their invaluable input and feedback. It has been a privilege to work with the team on this project. We hope that practitioners will find the *Heart of Coaching Supervision* informative and helpful for their supervision practice.

We would appreciate feedback and suggestions for new topics for later editions. We can be contacted by email:

Eve Turner: eve@eve-turner.com
Stephen Palmer: stephen.palmer@centreforcoaching.info

Appendix A[1]

Associations, codes of ethics and training organisations

Association for Coaching (AC)

The Association for Coaching is an independent, not-for-profit professional body whose purpose is to inspire and champion coaching excellence, to advance the coaching profession and make a sustainable difference to individuals, organisations and society. Established in 2002 in the UK, it has members in 60 countries and accredits coaches, supervisors and approves training programmes.
www.associationforcoaching.com

Association of Integrative Coach-Therapist Professionals (AICTP)

The aim of the AICTP is to remain relevant and reflect the voice of integrative coach-therapy practitioners both in the UK and internationally.
www.aictp.org.uk

Associazione Italiana Coach Professionisti (AICP)

The Italian Association for Profession Coaches serves coaches and promotes coaching in Italy, supporting research and training. It recommends training programmes.
www.associazionecoach.com/

Association of National Organisations for Supervision in Europe (ANSE)

ANSE was established in 1997 by the national professional organisations for supervision of Austria (ÖVS), Germany (DGSv), Hungary (MSZT), the Netherlands (LVSB) and Switzerland (BSO). It is a European umbrella association that promotes co-operation and discussion among professionals in supervision and coaching. It represents more than 8,000 qualified supervisors and coaches in 22 European countries and more than 80 training institutions.
www.anse.eu

Australian Psychological Society (APS)

The Australian Branch of the British Psychological Society was formed in 1944 and was later incorporated as The Australian Psychological Society Limited in 1966. It now represents more than 22,000 members and applicants must be qualified in, or studying, university courses accredited by the Australian Psychology Accreditation Council (APAC).
www.psychology.org.au

Association of Coaching Supervisors (AOCS)

The Association of Coaching Supervisors was set up to raise the profile of coaching supervision, to generate media attention, and support coach supervisors and coaches with both practical and personal benefits.
www.associationofcoachingsupervisors.com

Association for Professional Executive Coaching and Supervision (APECS)

The Association for Professional Executive Coaching and Supervision is a professional membership body for executive

coaching, supervision and advisory services to corporate organisations. Founded in 2004 it accredits executive coaches, team coaches and supervisors.
www.apecs.org

American Psychological Association (APA)

The American Psychological Association (APA) is a scientific and professional organisation that represents psychologists in the United States. It has 115,700 researchers, educators, clinicians, consultants and students as its members.
www.apa.org

British Psychological Society (BPS)

The British Psychological Society is a registered charity, which acts as the representative body for psychology and psychologists in the UK, and is responsible for the promotion of excellence and ethical practice in the science, education and application of the discipline.
www.bps.org.uk

Coaches and Mentors of South Africa (COMENSA)

Coaches and Mentors of South Africa was launched in 2006 as an inclusive, umbrella professional association for individual and corporate providers, buyers and trainers of coaching and mentoring services.
www.comensa.org.za

European Association for Supervision and Coaching (EASC)

The European Association for Supervision was founded in 1994 by a group of experienced supervisors and supervision trainers to develop quality in coaching and supervision as a supra-regional, European trade association. As members increasingly offered coaching the association developed quality standards for coaching and training in coaching

based on the existing quality standards for supervision and added coaching to its name in 2010.
www.easc-online.eu

European Mentoring and Coaching Council (EMCC)

The European Mentoring and Coaching Council exists to develop, promote and set the expectation of best practice in mentoring and coaching across Europe and beyond, for the benefit of society. It has 26 affiliated countries throughout Europe and individual members around the world and accredits coaches and supervisors, and approves coach and supervision training courses.
www.emccouncil.org

Fédération Des Superviseurs Professionnels (PSF)

The Professional Supervisors Federation is an organisation promoting high ethical and professional standards of supervision in France, focussed on client satisfaction.
www.professional-supervisors.org

Global Supervisors' Network (GSN)

The Global Supervisors' Network is a participative network, free of charge, for supervisors working in coaching, mentoring and consultancy to provide each other with, and receive, Continuing Personal and Professional Development virtually. There are more than 130 members around the world and members have access to recordings and papers from the virtual, monthly sessions.
www.eve-turner.com/global-supervisors-network

International Association of Coaching (IAC)

The IAC® is an independent, non-profit, global professional association of coaches dedicated to the ongoing pursuit of coaching mastery. Founded in 2003 it credentials coaches.
www.certifiedcoach.org

International Coach Federation (ICF)

The International Coach Federation is a US-based international professional membership body with members around the world. Established in 1995, and with approximately 30,000 members in more than 140 countries, it is the largest coaching body and campaigns worldwide for professional standards within the coaching profession. The ICF credentials coaches and coach training.
www.coachfederation.org

International Society for Coaching Psychology (ISCP)

International Society for Coaching Psychology is an international professional membership body established to further the discipline and profession of coaching psychology. It publishes a journal, recognises courses, approves centres, and accredits psychologists and supervisors.
www.isfcp.net

La Société Française de Coaching (SF Coach)

SF Coach was set up in 1996 in France to develop and promote coaching. It supports research and development and professionalisation of its members, who all go through accreditation before joining.
www.sfcoach.org

Worldwide Association of Business Coaches (WABC)

The Worldwide Association of Business Coaches was set up in 1997 and was the first global professional association to exclusively represent the business coaching industry. It aims to raise the profile of business coaching and differentiate it from coaching in general.
www.wabccoaches.com

Codes of Ethics

AICTP Code of Ethics:
www.aictp.org.uk/code-of-ethics

APA Code of Ethics and Multicultural Guidelines: An Ecological Approach to Context, Identity, and Intersectionality, 2017:
www.apa.org/ethics/code/index.aspx and www.apa.org/about/policy/multicultural-guidelines.pdf

ANSE Code of Ethics:
www.anse.eu/wp-content/uploads/doc/Code_of_Ethics_2012.pdf

APECS Code of Ethics:
www.apecs.org/ethical-guidelines

APS Code of Ethics:
www.psychology.org.au/about/ethics/#s1

BPS Codes of Practice:
www.bps.org.uk/news-and-policy/bps-code-ethics-and-conduct

COMENSA Code of Ethics:
www.comensa.org.za/Information/EthicsRead

Global Code of Ethics (AC and EMCC with APECS, AICP and Mentoring Institute, UNM):
http://www.globalcodeofethics.org/

ICF Code of Ethics:
www.coachfederation.org/about/ethics.aspx?ItemNumber=854

ISCP Code of Ethics:
www.isfcp.net/ethics.htm

PSF Code of Ethics:
www.professional-supervisors.org/lassociation/charte-deontologique

SF Coach Code of Ethics:
www.sfcoach.org/deontologie

WABC Code of Ethics:
www.wabccoaches.com/includes/popups/code_of_ethics_2nd_
edition_december_17_2007.html

Training Organisations

In listing some of the supervision training available we are not intending to endorse any particular programmes. Our encouragement would be to find out more, get an overview of the training, and speak to past and present students. While we have indicated the country base, some of the programmes are offered in other countries, through local representatives and on demand.

A number of professional bodies approve supervision training programmes, such as the EMCC which awards the European Supervision Quality Award (ESQA). The up-to-date list can be obtained here: http://accreditation.emc-council.org/esqa/?url=eu/en/accreditation/esqa/esqa_holders.

In the UK, there are also providers recognised by the Institute of Leadership and Management (ILM) to deliver the Level 7 Coaching Supervision programme: https://www.i-l-m.com/Learning-and-Development/management/coaching-and-mentoring/8582-level-7-coaching-supervision.

The ISCP recognises courses and approves training centres. This includes supervision courses for coaches and coaching psychologists: www.isfcp.net/iscpcentrescourses.htm

In Europe programmes may be found through member organisations of ANSE: http://www.anse.eu

Training providers

Ashridge Executive Education, PG Certificate in Advanced Coaching & OD Supervision UK
www.hult.edu/en/executive-education/coaching-programs/quals-in-coaching

Associatie voor coaching, The Netherlands, but virtual globally
www.associatievoorcoaching.com/coachopleiding/training/supervisie-voor-coaches

Blue Sky International, Certificate in coaching supervision UK
www.blueskyinternational.com/coaching-mentoring

Centre for Coaching, London, UK, Primary certificate in supervision UK
Coaching supervision: www.centreforcoaching.com/coaching-supervision
Coaching psychology supervision: www.centreforcoaching.com/coaching-psychology-supervision

Coaching Supervision Academy, Diploma in coaching supervision UK
www.coachingsupervisionacademy.com

Goldvarg Consulting Group, Coaching Supervision Certification USA-based, but virtual globally
https://goldvargconsulting.com/executive-coaching/coaching-supervision/

Henley Centre for Coaching, Certificate in Coaching Supervision
www.henley.fi/en/executive-education/coaching-programmes/

Human Technics UK
www.humantechnics.com/coach-supervision-certificate/

Novum PG Certificate in Coaching Supervision UK
www.novum-uk.com/service/pg-dip-coaching-supervision

OCM, Advanced Certificate in Coaching and Mentoring Supervision UK but virtual globally
www.theocm.co.uk/products-and-services/supervision

Oxford Brookes University, Professional Certificate UK
www.brookes.ac.uk/iccams/opportunities-for-study/
professional-certificate-of-advanced-study-in-coaching-
supervision

Results Driven Group, ILM Certificate or Diploma UK
http://www.resultsdrivengroup.co.uk/course.aspx?Course
ID=1402

UNDICI International, Formation de superviseurs de coachs
France
www.undici.fr

Note

1. All information has been obtained from the websites of the
   organisations referred to.

One example of a draft supervision agreement – bespoke to each supervisee

September 2018

Agreement between xxx xxx and Eve Turner

The Agreement

This agreement puts in writing what we have both agreed to ensure that our expectations are met and to reduce the likelihood of misunderstandings. In entering supervision there is an expectation that we are committed to an ongoing relationship. So, we will meet/speak for at least six hours a year and these sessions will normally take place at least once every two months. If you decide to apply for accreditation we may need to increase that. Should frequency fall below every two months we will need to discuss whether I can remain as your supervisor as I only work with a fixed number of supervisees at a time.

It is also agreed that termination of our supervision relationship will be addressed in a session prior to the final one, and we will have a planned, final closing session.

What we have agreed

- To talk approximately every six weeks by Skype with a minimum of six conversations a year, with a caveat that we may talk in-between at short notice if you want to at any time. We will work together for a year and then review this.

- We will do an initial review of how things are going after the first session.
- I will send a preparation form for you to use if you would like to.
- Your main objectives are to have:

  o Exposure to new ideas, models and approaches
  o Challenge to your thinking
  o Someone who is supportive in a crisis.

- To bring live cases to supervision to explore as part of your commitment to your continuing development as a coach.
- To do a recording of a coaching session at least once over the year of this agreement and bring this to supervision. The first will happen before a reference is written. The choice will be to select a c.10-minute section which we listen to in the session together, or to send me an hour recording which I will listen to in advance and make notes, for which a nominal one-hour charge at your usual rate will be made. In either case please prepare the following in advance:

  o Provide a side of A4 explaining what your aims and intentions were in the session
  o Provide a short context for the session (e.g. brief information about the client context, number of the session etc.)
  o Do a summary of your own feedback on the chosen section/hour.

- To do regular evaluation together to ensure that supervision is supporting your work appropriately and to support my learning.

What supervision is

There is considerable literature around supervision, sometimes written as super-vision. Through our time together we will hope to take a meta-perspective of your work with you in the lead. Hawkins and Smith (2013: 173–174) place the functions into these three broad areas:

i.   Developmental – of us as coaches, our craft and our business. Developing skills, understanding and abilities of supervisees; understanding the client better, being aware of our own reactions and responses; looking at interventions and exploring other ways of working; growing the capacity of the business (e.g. where it is now, where you want it to be, who you want to work with, what income you hope to earn, how can that happen?).

ii. Resourcing – responding to the effect of the client's emotions; listening, supporting and challenging.

iii. Qualitative – providing the quality control function; this could include looking at gaps in training, blind spots, vulnerabilities; ensuring work is professional and ethical.

(Bridget Proctor called these respectively: Formative, Restorative and Normative). I currently use several approaches or none! Included are: first, the seven-eyed model, developed by Peter Hawkins with Robin Shohet and then Nick Smith; second, one I have adapted from Petruska Clarkson; third, the CLEAR model, again from Peter Hawkins and Nick Smith; and fourth, one in interventions, developed by John Heron. But these are not exhaustive as approaches we may use.

Professional practice

The relationship is one of mutual respect and I will treat what you say in confidence and you will do the same with me so that our discussions stay "in the room". This would only be breached in very rare circumstances where required by law (Terrorism, Money Laundering, Treason) or ethical practice (Child Protection), or for the safety or well-being of the supervisee, coachee or another person. In such cases (except where proscribed by law), as the supervisor it would be my intention to talk to you first. Professional coaches and supervisors are also expected to have supervision to ensure high standards of professional practice and this may mean discussing some details of current client/supervisee work (anonymously).

I subscribe to the ethical codes of three leading coaching professional bodies the AC (Association for Coaching, membership number xxxxxx), EMCC (European and Mentoring Coaching Council) and APECS (Association for Professional Executive Coaches and Supervisors) which accredit me as a Master Executive Coach and Coach Supervisor. Links to these codes are provided below. They require me to have professional liability insurance, continuing professional development and coach supervision. All the bodies operate a complaints procedure, and should you have serious concerns about my practice, please contact them:

AC/EMCC: www.globalcodeofethics.org/download-the-code/ and https://app.box.com/s/8s3tsveqieq6vr6n2itb 0p9mpsxgcncd

Complaints:

www.associationforcoaching.com/general/custom. asp?page=ACComplaintsProc

www.e-russell.com/images/EMCC_Complaints_ Procedure.pdf

www.apecs.org/ethical-guidelines

I am also a member of, and follow the ethical code of, the ICF (International Coach Federation) Member ID xxx:

www.coachfederation.org/code-of-ethics

I conform to current best practice in data protection and am registered with the Information Commissioner's Office, Registration Number xxxxxxx. Emails will be held in a sub-folder on a stand-alone PC which is password protected in my office. Brief notes are handwritten and retained for a period of up to 3 years from programme completion before being destroyed by secure shredding. A copy of my privacy policy is available on request.

Eve Turner Associates also operates an Equal Opportunities Policy, a copy of which is also available on request.

Our work together (supervisee and supervisor)

I will send you a preparation and evaluation form for our sessions, which you are welcome to complete and return. Written or verbal evaluation and feedback is crucial to my development.

References

It is common for supervisors to be asked to write references when supervisees are applying for work in organisations or for accreditation. My normal practice would be to work with someone for around a year or have done at least six supervision sessions before providing anything beyond a confirmation that I am their supervisor, how many sessions we have had and of what duration. However, contributing factors will include how frequently we have been meeting or speaking. I will also ask to listen to, and work with you on, a recording of at least one of your coaching sessions before writing a reference. The time taken to do this will be charged at our normal hourly rate. My aim would be to write the reference in collaboration with you as an agreed reflection of our work together.

Fees, cancellation and contact

The fees for supervision are based on the agreed rate of £xxx + VAT plus agreed expenses. These fees will rise in line with your top client charge-out rate and we will discuss this at least annually.

It may be helpful for us to be in touch between our sessions and some contact between meetings is included within the supervision fee; for example, if we had one 15-minute conversation about a client or situation we would treat it as part of the ongoing support. But if it becomes apparent a longer period is needed we will check out how long and book a proper time to do so, which is chargeable pro rata.

With cancellations, there is no charge with ten working days' notice or longer. Less than ten days but up to six days I charge 50% and if five days' notice or less is given the full fee is charged. I will invoice you as agreed, and this is likely to be for three sessions at a time following the first of the three sessions unless we agree differently. BACS details will be provided for payment.

If you need to contact me between sessions the ideal way is by leaving a message on my mobile phone. I will then commit to get back to you within 48 hours provided I am in the UK. If you email I will respond within 24 hours of logging in, but please bear in mind that I sometimes work away from my base.

Any other questions

If you have any questions, please do contact me. Thank you very much.

Eve Turner
DATE and YEAR

CONTEXT

In addition, the supervision agreement has five Appendices covering:

1. Several possible supervision models explained.
2. Questions to support the development of the supervisee's coaching model: the PPP with questions (see Chapter 2).
3. Ethical, moral and legal questions to reflect on.
4. A preparation and evaluation form for supervision sessions.
5. Reading list for supervision and ethics, most with a coaching focus.

This Agreement is published for illustration purposes only. As it stands, it was only intended for use with adult clients. And there's no suggestion this is a perfect model! Please note, in the event of this Agreement being used as a template elsewhere, the authors do not accept any legal liability.

References

Hawkins, P. and Smith, N. (2013). *Coaching, Mentoring and Organizational Consultancy Supervision, Skills & Development.* 2nd ed. Maidenhead: Open University Press.

Index

Abrams, D. 64
AC *see* Association for Coaching
acceptance 15; *see also*
  self-acceptance
Adams, Kathleen 127, 128, 143
Adshead-Grant, Jane 12, 147–168
age 11, 41
AICP *see* Associazione Italiana
  Coach Professionisti
AICTP *see* Association of
  Integrative Coach-Therapist
  Professionals
Alexander, Frederick 105–106
ambivalence 95, 96
American Psychological
  Association (APA) 11, 248, 251
amorphousness 95
amygdala 70, 238
anger 88–89, 90
ANSE *see* Association of National
  Organisations for Supervision in
  Europe
"anti-fragile systems" 67
anxiety 67, 141, 143
AOCS *see* Association of Coaching
  Supervisors
APA *see* American Psychological
  Association
APPEAR Model 228

appreciation 149, 154, 156, 161,
  163, 166, 217
appreciative inquiry 69
APS *see* Australian Psychological
  Society
Aquilina, Eunice 12, 105–124
archetypes 94–95, 101
Aspey, Linda 12, 147–168
Association for Coaching (AC) 5,
  177, 178, 233, 246, 251, 258
Association for Professional
  Executive Coaching and
  Supervision (APECS) 177, 233,
  247–248, 251, 258
Association of Coaching
  Supervisors (AOCS) 177, 247
Association of Integrative Coach-
  Therapist Professionals (AICTP)
  246, 251
Association of National
  Organisations for Supervision
  in Europe (ANSE) 233, 235,
  247, 251
Associazione Italiana Coach
  Professionisti (AICP) 246, 251
assumptions: about oneself
  83–84; culture 41, 44, 45–46,
  47; intersubjective systems
  theory 50; PPP model 25, 26–27,